WOMEN IN TRANSNATIONAL HISTORY

Women in Transnational History offers a range of fresh perspectives on the field of women's history, exploring how cross-border connections and global developments since the nineteenth century have shaped diverse women's lives and the gendered social, cultural, political and economic histories of specific localities.

The book is divided into three thematically organised parts, covering gendered histories of transnational networks, women's agency in the intersecting histories of imperialisms and nationalisms and the concept of localizing the global and globalizing the local. Discussing a broad spectrum of topics, from the politics of dress in Philippine mission stations in the early twentieth century to the shifting food practices of British women during the Second World War, the chapters bring women to the centre of the writing of new transnational histories.

Illustrated with images and figures, this book throws new light on key global themes from the perspective of women's and gender history. Written by an international team of editors and contributors, it is a valuable and timely resource for students and researchers of both women's history and transnational and global history.

Clare Midgley is Research Professor in History at Sheffield Hallam University, UK, and was President of the International Federation for Research in Women's History (IFRWH) between 2010 and 2015. Her publications include *Feminism and Empire* (2007), *Gender and Imperialism* (1998) and *Women Against Slavery* (1992/1995). She is currently completing a new book titled *Liberal Religion and the Woman Question*, which explores collaboration among Indian, British and American reformers.

Alison Twells is a Reader in History at Sheffield Hallam University, UK. Her publications include *The Civilising Mission and the English Middle Class, 1792–1850* (2009). She has extensive experience working with public and community-based historians and has written resources for school history.

Julie Carlier is the Research Coordinator of the Ghent Centre for Global Studies, an interdisciplinary research network at Ghent University in Belgium, where she also teaches on the transnational history of feminism. Between 2010 and 2015 she was a board member of the IFRWH. Her publications include contributions to *Women's History Review* and the edited volume *Gender History in a Transnational Perspective: Biographies, Networks, Gender Orders* (2014).

Women's and Gender History
Edited by June Purvis

**Emmeline Pankhurst:
A Biography**
June Purvis

**Child Sexual Abuse in Victorian
England**
Louise A. Jackson

**Crimes of Outrage: Sex, Violence
and Victorian Working Women**
Shani D'Cruze

**The Romantic Fiction of Mills &
Boon, 1909–1995**
Jay Dixon

**Feminism, Femininity and the
Politics of Working Women:
The Women's Co-operative
Guild, 1880s to the Second
World War**
Gillian Scott

**Gender and Crime in
Modern Europe**
*Edited by Margaret L. Arnot and Cornelie
Usborne*

**Gender Relations in German
History: Power, Agency and
Experience from the Sixteenth to
the Twentieth Century**
*Edited by Lynn Abrams and Elizabeth
Harvey*

**Imaging Home: Gender 'Race'
and National Identity, 1945–64**
Wendy Webster

**Midwives of the Revolution:
Female Bolsheviks and Women
Workers in 1917**
Jane McDermid and Anna Hillyar

**No Distinction of Sex? Women in
British Universities 1870–1939**
Carol Dyhouse

**Policing Gender, Class and Family:
Britain, 1850–1945**
Linda Mahood

**Prostitution: Prevention and
Reform in England, 1860–1914**
Paula Bartley

Sylvia Pankhurst: Sexual Politics and Political Activism
Barbara Winslow

Votes for Women
Edited by Sandra Holton and June Purvis

Women's History: Britain 1850–1945: An Introduction
Edited by June Purvis

The Women's Suffrage Movement: A Reference Guide, 1866–1928
Elizabeth Crawford

Women in Teacher Training Colleges, 1900–1960: A Culture of Femininity
Elizabeth Edwards

Women, Work and Sexual Politics in Eighteenth-Century England
Bridget Hill

Women Workers and Gender Identities, 1835–1913: The Cotton and Metal Industries in England
Carol E. Morgan

Women and Work in Britain Since 1840
Gerry Holloway

Outspoken Women: An Anthology of Women's Writing on Sex, 1970–1969
Lesley A. Hall

Women's History, Britain 1700–1850: An Introduction
Hannah Barker and Elaine Chalus

The Women's Suffrage Movement in Britain and Ireland: A Regional Survey
Elizabeth Crawford

Students: A Gendered History
Carol Dyhouse

Women in the British Army: War and the Gentle Sex, 1907–1948
Lucy Noakes

Quaker Women: Personal Life, Memory and Radicalism in the Lives of Women Friends, 1780–1930
Sandra Stanley Holton

Her Husband was a Woman!: Women's Gender-Crossing in Modern British Popular Culture
Alison Oram

Women's Activism
Edited by Francisca de Haan, Margaret Allen, June Purvis and Krassimira Daskalova

Women, Diplomacy and International Politics since 1500
Edited by Glenda Sluga and Carolyn James

Women in Transnational History: Connecting the Local and the Global
Edited by Clare Midgley, Alison Twells and Julie Carlier

WOMEN IN TRANSNATIONAL HISTORY

Connecting the local and the global

Edited by Clare Midgley, Alison Twells and Julie Carlier

LONDON AND NEW YORK

First published 2016
by Routledge
2 Park Square, Milton Park, Abingdon, Oxon OX14 4RN

and by Routledge
711 Third Avenue, New York, NY 10017

Routledge is an imprint of the Taylor & Francis Group, an informa business

© 2016 Clare Midgley, Alison Twells and Julie Carlier

The right of the Clare Midgley, Alison Twells and Julie Carlier to be
identified as the authors of the editorial material, and of the authors for
their individual chapters, has been asserted in accordance with sections 77
and 78 of the Copyright, Designs and Patents Act 1988.

All rights reserved. No part of this book may be reprinted or reproduced or
utilised in any form or by any electronic, mechanical, or other means, now
known or hereafter invented, including photocopying and recording, or in
any information storage or retrieval system, without permission in writing
from the publishers.

Trademark notice: Product or corporate names may be trademarks or
registered trademarks, and are used only for identification and explanation
without intent to infringe.

British Library Cataloguing-in-Publication Data
A catalogue record for this book is available from the British Library

Library of Congress Cataloging-in-Publication Data
Names: Midgley, Clare, 1955– editor. | Twells, Alison, editor. | Carlier,
    Julie, editor.
Title: Women in transnational history : connecting the local and the global /
    edited by Clare Midgley, Alison Twells and Julie Carlier.
Description: Abingdon, Oxon ; New York, NY : Routledge, 2016. |
    Includes bibliographical references and index.
Identifiers: LCCN 2015042641 | ISBN 9781138905764
    (hardback : alk. paper) | ISBN 9781138905788 (pbk. : alk. paper) |
    ISBN 9781315626802 (ebook)
Subjects: LCSH: Feminism—Cross-cultural studies. | Feminism—History. |
    Feminist geography.
Classification: LCC HQ1150 .W656 2016 | DDC 305.42—dc23LC record
    available at http://lccn.loc.gov/2015042641

ISBN: 978-1-138-90576-4 (hbk)
ISBN: 978-1-138-90578-8 (pbk)
ISBN: 978-1-315-62680-2 (ebk)

Typeset in Bembo
by Apex CoVantage, LLC

CONTENTS

List of figures	*ix*
List of contributors	*x*
Introduction	1
Clare Midgley, Alison Twells and Julie Carlier	

PART I
Gendered histories of transnational networks and connections

11

1 Indian feminist Pandita Ramabai and transnational liberal
religious networks in the nineteenth-century world 13
Clare Midgley

2 The International Labour Organization, transnational
women's networks, and the question of unpaid work in the
interwar world 33
Susan Zimmermann

3 Reimagining Greenham, or the transnationality of the
nation in activist women's narratives in 1980s Japan 54
Ulrike Wöhr

viii Contents

PART II
Women's agency in the intersecting histories of imperialisms and nationalisms

75

4 'New women', American imperialism, and Filipina
   nationalism: The politics of dress in Philippine mission
   stations, 1898–1940   77
   Laura R. Prieto

5 The woman question and the national question in the
   Russian Empire: Interconnections between central and
   borderland women's suffrage organizations during the
   First Russian Revolution, 1905–1907   98
   Olga Shnyrova

6 The Italian Empire 'at home': Fascist girls, imperial
   propaganda and the racialized memory of Italy, 1937–2007   117
   Barbara Spadaro

PART III
Localizing the global/globalizing the local

145

7 Total war, global market and local impact: British women's
   shifting food practices during the Second World War   147
   Natacha Chevalier

8 The local and the global in women's organizing in the
   Pacific region, 1950s–1990s   163
   Patricia Grimshaw and Hannah Loney

9 Women at the intersection of the local and the global in
   schools and community history in Britain since the 1980s   180
   Alison Twells

Index   *201*

FIGURES

3.1	Hiro Sumpter	63
3.2	Cover of pamphlet documenting Hiro Sumpter's visit to Japan	65
4.1	Singer Manufacturing Company, 'Costumes of All Nations' series advertising card	82
4.2	'Under the Pines' at the Third Annual Woman's Conference at Baguio, December 27–31, 1920	86
4.3	Mary J. Johnson Methodist Hospital nurses' basketball team, 1910	89
4.4	Emilia Cavan with Miss Clyde Bartholomew	92
4.5	Florence L. Fox, Evelyn Fox, Isabel Maandig, 1925	93
6.1	Photos of a colonial training course for women in Trieste	122
6.2	Fascist colonial girls parading as Roman legionaries on the Via dei Trionfi in Rome	128
6.3	Illustrated article on the colonial camps, 'Bella e fiera gioventù femminile fascista in Africa'	129
6.4	Cruise advertisements	130
6.5	Fascist colonial girls disembarking to attend a training camp in Libya	131
6.6	Report and photo from a training camp for women in Libya	132
7.1	Map of prewar commodities' provenance	152
7.2	Imports of food into the United Kingdom (in thousands of tons)	153

CONTRIBUTORS

Julie Carlier is the Research Coordinator of the Ghent Centre for Global Studies, an interdisciplinary research network at Ghent University in Belgium, and a board member of the IFRWH (2010–2015). In 2010, she received her PhD in History from Ghent University with a dissertation entitled 'Moving Beyond Boundaries. An Entangled History of Feminism in Belgium, 1890–1914'. She is currently reworking this transnational history of Belgian feminism toward a book publication. As a postdoctoral fellow of the Research Foundation Flanders (2010–2013), she studied men and masculinities in European first-wave feminisms.

Natacha Chevalier is currently undertaking a PhD at the University of Sussex, UK. She previously completed a BA in History and Sociology at the University of Geneva, Switzerland, and an MA in Contemporary History at the University of Birmingham, UK. Her doctoral research is based on material in the Mass Observation Archive and focuses on the consequences of World War II on the food practices, behaviours and perspectives of those, predominantly women, who were in charge of food matters in the household.

Patricia Grimshaw is a Professorial Fellow in the School of Historical and Philosophical Studies at the University of Melbourne. She has sustained a research interest in women's history in Australia and the Pacific across several decades, with special attention to social movements, humanitarianism and settler colonialism. Her books include *Paths of Duty: American Missionary Wives in Nineteenth Century Hawaii* (1989); the co-edited *Women's Rights and Human Rights: International Perspectives* (2001); the cowritten *Equal Subjects, Unequal Rights: Indigenous Peoples in British Settler Societies* (2003); and *Missionaries, Indigenous Peoples and Cultural Exchanges* (2010). She is currently working with colleagues on an Australian Research Council funded project on women, democracy and leadership in Australia since 1900. She was president of the IFRWH from 1995 to 2000.

Contributors **xi**

Hannah Loney is completing a PhD in the School of Historical and Philosophical Studies at the University of Melbourne. Her research focuses on East Timorese women's experiences, memories and perceptions of life under Indonesian rule from 1975 to 1999. Currently she is exploring East Timor women's links with Pacific Island women's groups. She has presented papers at a number of national and international conferences and has published articles on oral history, violence, gender and memory.

Clare Midgley is Research Professor of History at Sheffield Hallam University, UK, and was President of the International Federation for Research in Women's History (IFRWH) between 2010 and 2015. Her research has explored the intersections between the history of women and the history of imperialism, and publications include *Feminism and Empire* (Routledge, 2007), the edited collection *Gender and Imperialism* (Manchester University Press, 1998) and *Women Against Slavery* (Routledge, 1992/1995). She is currently completing research for a new book titled *Liberal Religion and the Woman Question in the Nineteenth-Century World: A Transnational Network of Indian, British and American Reformers*.

Laura R. Prieto is Professor of History and of Women's and Gender Studies at Simmons College, Boston, USA. She is the author of *At Home in the Studio: The Professionalization of Women Artists in America* (Harvard University Press, 2001). She has also contributed essays to B. Reeves-Ellington, K.K. Sklar and C.A. Shemo, eds, *Competing Kingdoms: Women, Nation, Mission and American Empire* (Duke University Press, 2010), T. Padilla, ed., *Subjecting History: Building a Relationship between History and its Alternatives* (Ohio University Press, forthcoming) and the online resource *Women and Social Movements in the United States* (Alexander Street Press). Her current research focuses on American womanhood and imperialism in the Caribbean and Pacific during the era of the Spanish American War.

Olga Shnyrova is an Associate Professor of History at Ivanovo State University and the Director of its Center for Gender Studies. She researches women's history and women's movements in Russia and Great Britain. She was a contributor to *Aftermaths of War: Women's Movements and Female Activists, 1918–1923*, edited by Ingrid Sharp and Matthew Stibbe (Brill, 2011); *Suffrage, Gender and Citizenship – International Perspectives on Parliamentary Reforms*, edited by Irma Sulkunen, Seija-Leena Nevala-Nurmi and Pirjo Markkola (Cambridge Scholars Publishing, 2009); *The Women's Movement in Wartime: International Perspectives, 1914–19*, edited by Alison S. Fell and Ingrid Sharp (Palgrave Macmillan, 2007); and *Biographical Dictionary of Women's Movements and Feminisms in Central, Eastern, and Southeastern Europe, 19th and 20th Centuries*, edited by Fransiska de Haan and Krassimira Daskalova (Central European University Press, Budapest, 2006). She also was the editor of the Russian translation of Richard Stites's book, *Women's Liberation Movement in Russia: Feminism, Nihilism and Bolshevism 1860–1930* (ROSSPEN, 2004) and one of the translators into Russian of five volumes of *History of Women in the West* (Aletheia, 2007–).

xii Contributors

Barbara Spadaro received her PhD in history from the Istituto Italiano di Scienze Umane, SUM, in Italy, and is currently a postdoctoral fellow at the University of Bristol, UK. Her research on forms of memory, imagination and material culture among Italians in the Mediterranean (nineteenth–twentieth centuries) investigates the historical transformation of ideas of gender, citizenship and Eurocentrism. She is the author of a book on the memories, representations and social practices of the Italian bourgeoisie between Italy and Libya and has published a series of articles on the history of gender, Italian fascism and colonial relations. A parallel strand of her work examines memories of the Jewish diaspora from Libya across Europe and the Mediterranean. She is a member of the Editorial Board of the journal *Genre et colonisation/Gender and Colonization*.

Alison Twells is Principal Lecturer in history at Sheffield Hallam University, UK. She initially worked in secondary education, writing materials for the new national curriculum which explored the global context of local history. Her monograph, *The Civilising Mission and the English Middle Class, 1792–1850: The Heathen at Home and Overseas* (Palgrave, 2009), explored local and global contexts for the emergence of the nineteenth-century missionary movement and the Christian reform movement more broadly. More recently, she has published an article in *Journal of Women's History* on Swedish novelist Fredrika Bremer's transnational faith journeys in the mid-nineteenth century. She is currently director of a new public history digital archive which aims (among other things) to develop and make available teaching resources which explore the local and global in the South Yorkshire context.

Ulrike Wöhr is Professor of Japanese Studies and Gender Studies at Hiroshima City University, Japan, and the author of *Frauen zwischen Rollenerwartung and Selbstdeutung* [Women between Role-Expectations and Self-Representation] (Harrassowitz, 1997), a historical reading of Japanese feminist thought of the 1910s, and co-editor of *Gender, Nation and State in Modern Japan* (Routledge, 2014). Research interests include gender and feminism in modern Japan, from a transnational perspective.

Susan Zimmermann is University Professor at the Central European University in Budapest, Hungary, and also teaches at the University of Vienna. She has widely published on social policy and poor relief in local and transnational contexts, the history of women's organizations and movements internationally and in the Habsburg Monarchy and on internationalisms and the politics of global inequality. Currently she is working on a book manuscript titled *International Labour Standards, Women's Work, and Unequal Development. The ILO, Woman Internationalists, and Globalizing Gender Politics, 1919–1939*. She is co-editor with Eileen Boris and Dorothea Hoechtker of *Women's ILO. Transnational Networks, Global Labour Standards and Gender Equity, 1919 to Present* (Palgrave, forthcoming).

INTRODUCTION

Clare Midgley, Alison Twells and Julie Carlier

This collection of essays has a dual purpose. First, it offers a set of fresh transnational perspectives on the study of women's history by exploring how cross-border connections and global developments have shaped diverse women's lives and the gendered social, cultural, political and economic histories of specific localities. Simultaneously, it seeks to advance scholarship in transnational and global history, which has become increasingly central to the study of the past as scholars, activists and the general public wrestle to understand the contemporary globalized world. By placing women's lives and experiences at the centre of the writing of new transnational histories, and by paying attention to the interactive relationship between 'local' and 'global' developments which can be traced through these lives, we seek to create a corrective both to inward-looking nation-based studies of women's lives and to 'grand narratives' of globalisation which, in their focus on 'macro' levels of analysis, lose sight of the grounded 'micro' realities of everyday lives and of the role of human agency in affecting change.

Transnational history and feminist history

Transnational history – and its related manifestations as *histoire croisée* and *Transferschichte* – involves the application of a fresh perspective to the study of the past: it is the study of history across or beyond geopolitical borders.[1] It is anchored in a critique of methodological nationalism – the assumption that the nation-state is an adequate spatial framework for understanding the past – and it stresses intercultural connections, interactions and entanglements. Here it differs not only from national history but also from comparative history. The latter tends to take nation-states as discrete self-contained entities that can then be compared, an approach which can result in an underestimation both of internal variables within the nation and of the impact of cross-border connections on the nation.[2] This does not, however, mean that transnational history denies the importance of the nation-state: as Middell

2 Clare Midgley, Alison Twells and Julie Carlier

and Naumann point out, 'On the contrary, it emphasizes its capacity to control and channel border-transcending movements.'[3] Transnational perspectives can also enhance the writing of national histories: as Janz and Schönpflug argue, a transnational perspective 'makes possible an analysis of a national phenomenon by considering its connections, interactions and relations to other nations and supra-national institutions alike'.[4]

Transnational perspectives have become central to historical study over the past two decades, and feminist history has, as Curthoys and Lake observe, 'been a prime site for the development of more transnational approaches'.[5] However, feminist scholars have voiced their disappointment that this has not resulted in a profound gendering of transnational and global history at the levels of both research or teaching: women tend to still be treated simply as 'add ons'.[6] Nevertheless, there are grounds for optimism for the future. Transnational – and global – history had begun to move on from its original focus on political elites and macro-economic change to encompass the social and cultural dimensions of the past. Women and gender are gradually becoming central to the study of key topics in the field, including global migration and diasporic communities, shifting patterns of consumption, imperial and colonial cultures and intercultural exchanges. Methodologically, too, women's history and transnational history potentially have much in common: as Wiesner-Hanks notes, 'Both emphasise relationships and interactions, multiple perspectives and the crossing of disciplinary boundaries.'[7]

Feminist scholars' pioneering contributions to transnational history lay in their research into international women's organisations, and this has remained an important area of scholarship.[8] Such studies, however, have primarily been focused on the added value of transnational approaches to women's and gender history rather than on writing women into global history or integrating gender into transnational perspectives on the past. Similarly, in the arena of university teaching, works like Bonnie Smith's *Women's History in Global Perspective* are primarily concerned with ensuring breadth of global and chronological coverage in the teaching of women's history rather than with bringing women to the centre of the study of global history.[9]

Seeking to address this limitation in the existing literature head-on, *Women in Transnational History* aspires to advance research agendas in *both* women's/gender *and* transnational/global history. Placing women at the heart of its analysis, it seeks to move debates forward on a broader front by covering a wider range of themes and topics and opening up a broader dialogue between women's and gender history and transnational and global history. This includes offering new perspectives from 'below' – indigenous, subaltern, grassroots, local, community, everyday – that destabilize established categories and binaries in both fields, including the dichotomy between the global and the local and the binary of resistance to/complicity with imperialism. As such, our approach perhaps has more in common with essay collections edited by Tony Ballantyne and Antoinette Burton in *Bodies in Contact. Rethinking Colonial Encounters in World History* and in *Moving Subjects. Gender, Mobility and Intimacy in an Age of Global Empire*.[10] However, the essays in these two volumes concentrate exclusively on colonial and imperial contexts rather than on the range of global connections covered in this volume, while their focus on bodies and intimacies complements rather than overlaps with the topics covered in *Women in Transnational History*.

This collection does not aspire to be comprehensive in its chronological, geographical or thematic coverage. Rather, it offers a set of detailed case studies focused on the period between the late nineteenth century and the present. These studies present the results of new research into neglected aspects of transnational history, offering fresh perspectives and innovative conceptual approaches. They critically deploy and develop the analytical insights of subaltern studies, intersectionality studies and feminist postcolonial studies to illuminate how gendered inequalities of power – in their intersection with race, class, religion and nationality – shaped global interactions and exchanges. At the same time, rather than presenting women as simply the victims of powerful transnational forces for change, they throw new light on the variety of ways in which Indigenous, subaltern and non-western women carved out new spaces to assert agency in a globalising world. Taken together, the essays suggest a range of new sources and methodologies for developing and combining the fields of women/gender and transnational/global history in ways that can mutually enrich both.

In giving space to varied perspectives and approaches rather than seeking to provide a homogenising blueprint for writing women into transnational history, the collection seeks to respect the diverse global trajectories of research into women's history, in accord with the objective of the International Federation for Research in Women's History (IFRWH): the chapters develop from papers originally delivered at the IFRWH conference titled 'Women's Histories: the local and the global', convened by Clare Midgley at Sheffield Hallam University in the UK in 2013. This conference was held in conjunction with the annual conference of the (British) Women's History Network, and additional papers from the rich range presented will appear in a second, complementary publication.[11]

The historians who have contributed essays to this collection have deliberately been chosen from a range of different countries and comprise both well-known scholars and those at early stages in their careers. A number of the contributors themselves have transnational academic histories, perhaps suggestive of the interconnections between personal life histories and trajectories of scholarly research. Many also bring an interdisciplinary or cross-disciplinary sensibility to bear on their research, variously combining approaches from history with those from sociology, women's and gender studies, English, cultural studies and Japanese studies. The perspectives of the editors are similarly informed by their diverse career trajectories: Clare Midgley's first degree, in archaeology, marked the beginnings of a fascination with the long history of global cultural connections and cross-influences; Alison Twells's original training as a secondary school teacher informs her current collaborations as an academic historian with local schools and community history groups in bringing global perspectives to the fields of school and public history; Julie Carlier completed a PhD on the history of a national women's movement

4 Clare Midgley, Alison Twells and Julie Carlier

from a transnational perspective before taking on the role of research coordinator of an interdisciplinary research network in global studies.

Connecting the local and the global

Before proceeding to outline the individual chapters in this volume, we want to explore a little further the question of conceptual frameworks for the writing of gendered transnational history. In particular, we focus on how an understanding of the co-constitution of the 'local' and the 'global' can provide a productive conceptual framework. This leads into a consideration of how the process of writing women into transnational history entails the adoption of innovative and imaginative approaches in terms of the creation, identification and use of sources and the development of research methodologies.

The relationship between transnational and global history, and indeed the very terms themselves, constitute a definitional minefield. As Merry Wiesner-Hanks points out, the terms 'global' and 'transnational' are 'as contested and entangled as any other borders'.[12] However, we do not think it is productive to become over-preoccupied with identifying fine distinctions between global and transnational history, or indeed among *Transferschichte, histoire croisée*, and entangled history. Rather, following Naumann and Middell, we view all these approaches as a set of related 'poststructuralist reactions to the new global conditions that characterize the present'. They stem from the recognition that 'for the historicization of the globalized world, we need histories that describe the meshing and shifting of different spatial references, narratives in which historical agency is emphasized, and interpretations acknowledging that the changing patterns of spatialization are processes fraught with tension.'[13]

Developing a gendered understanding of these relationships between 'historical agency' and 'changing patterns of spatialization' lies at the heart of our project in this book. As suggested by our subtitle, we are particularly concerned in this volume with elucidating the relationship between the 'local' and the 'global'. We understand these as co-constituted: processes and actors at the local level shape the global, while at the same time global changes impact local lives. Thus, rather than defining the global as a straightforward level or scale of analysis, separate and distinct from the local, we focus on how globe-making or world-making projects were anchored in specific localities and on exploring the role of local agency in the construction of these multiple globalisations or worlds.

This reconceptualization of globalisation is rooted in the insights of feminist scholarship. It contests what Freeman has described as the 'implicit, but powerful, dichotomous model' that has emerged 'in which the gender of globalization is mapped in such a way that global : masculine as local : feminine'. This is a model which, she notes, 'has depicted women and femininity as rooted, traditional, and charged with maintaining domestic continuity in the face of flux and instability by global movements that, explicitly or not, embody a quality of masculinity'. Freeman's study of Caribbean higglers (women market traders) shows how the economic, social and cultural practices of these women are not just effects of globalization but active enactments of new modes of globalization. Women's agency thus crafts 'multiple modes of global capitalism'. Such a dialectical and gendered analysis of the relationship between the global and the local moves beyond dichotomous models to provide us with 'a feminist reconceptualization of globalization whereby local forms of globalization are understood not merely as effects of but also as constitutive ingredients in the changing shapes of these movements'.[14] In this reconceptualization, women are no longer confined to a secondary and passive role in global history, and the potential of local empirical studies to rethink the 'big picture' of globalisation is made clear.

Sources and methodologies

What kind of sources and methodologies does this feminist rethinking of transnational history require? The problem of sources in the writing of transnational history has been widely recognised. First, historians have highlighted the role of methodological nationalism in the creation and use of sources. Collected, preserved and organised according to national systems and practices, sources are housed in archives and museums that reflect the foundational relationship between the discipline of academic history and nineteenth-century nation building. It has been recognised that this national housing of material can obscure the acquisition of many supposedly 'national' artefacts through imperial plunder and that the ordering and cataloguing of materials often render invisible transboundary flows of goods, capital, people and ideas. Second, language has also been identified as a particular problem in researching transnational history. Scholars' language competences and limitations impact the scope and emphasis of their research, giving it a tendency to run within the linguistic zones created by empires and prioritise the use of official sources written in the language of governance over sources in local vernaculars, as well as exposing the difficulties and inadequacies of translation. In addition, specific issues arise in relation to the presence of women in the sources preserved in major nation-based archival, library and museum collections. Partly because these are easiest to access, many of the sources originally favoured by transnational historians related to the organisation of economic activity and political power by western governments and centres of imperial power and by commercial elites, to the exclusion of social networks, cultural practices and non-elite and subaltern groups, including women.[15]

Indeed, Deacon *et al.* argued that there exists in transnational history a 'gendered schism'[16] in which macro-level histories and analyses making use of sources about elite men's activities dominate the field and, in Sassen's words, often present 'technical and abstract economic dynamics' as if they are 'inevitably gender-neutral'.[17] One way forward is clearly to develop a critical gendered analysis of these political and economic elites, one that explores how masculine identities and subjectivities were shaped, masculinist agendas forged and patriarchal power deployed in the transnational arena. In tandem, however, we need to also question

6 Clare Midgley, Alison Twells and Julie Carlier

the value of broad-brush top-down grand narratives of globalisation. Here we can draw on cultural history's fundamental challenge to the privileging of economic and political history by asking pertinent questions about language and representation, and postcolonial scholarship's critique of the creation of master narratives and chronology as a western way of ordering history amidst different historicities and forms of historical consciousness.[18] Finally, we need to further develop a culturally informed transnational history by seeking out new sources that expose the transgressive, transformative spaces formed of contact zones, flows and entanglements, and by adopting methodologies informed by subaltern studies and feminism to bring to the fore the hitherto neglected historical agencies of 'ordinary' people who lived 'transboundary lives'.

Gayatri Chakravorty Spivak's classic discussion of the silencing of women within the imperial archive remains relevant here,[19] and historians of women are well acquainted both with the necessity of new gendered readings of extant sources, with the need to search for neglected archives, and with the importance of questioning a traditional hierarchy that prioritises the written and the official over the fragmented, the personal and the non-textual. The recent focus on emotion and intimacy and on the history of the body has drawn on such unconventional sources to produce a new understanding of transnational 'contact zones'.[20] Cohen and Frazier's feminist analysis of the student movements of 1968, for example, 'posits dynamics of sexuality, intimacy, and desire writ large as a thoroughly global phenomenon' to show that 'the category of "global scale" is emergent from the very case itself, here the racialized and sexualized ideologies of Cold War capitalist modernization.'[21] In the field of migration history, historians are moving beyond the abstractions of large-scale demographic studies to make detailed explorations of diverse and gendered migrant experiences using such sources as local newspapers and magazines, the archives of small community welfare organisations and oral histories.[22] Larger scale transnational organisations, including missionary societies, labour organisations and international agencies such as the World Health Organisation, have also been identified as having rich archives that are relatively neglected but can provide researchers with a much richer picture than available from a study of the publications of these organisations alone – and expose the hidden contributions of women. Herren *et al.*, for example, point to the opportunities for new readings of the activities of the League of Nations that focus on oral evidence given to the League rather than on the official protocols which erase individual participants.[23]

Transnational history has also seen a rehabilitation of biography, memoir and family archives. Biography is a form that has, in the past, often been 'pressed into the service of nation'. However, when it focuses on 'lives lived in motion', it can 'threaten the stability of national identity and unsettle the framework of national histories'.[24] Biographical approaches also do not have to follow the conventional focus on prominent public figures – they can be a way of writing vivid non-elite histories, as with the convict lives uncovered by Lucy Frost and Hamish Maxwell-Fraser in their groundbreaking *Chain Letters: Narrating Convict Lives*.[25] Clare Anderson, finding that the fragmentary nature and limits of archives made impossible a traditional biographical approach to convicts in the Indian Ocean, has nevertheless built up a rich picture of their lives through painstaking use of penal inventories, convict musters, petitions, court records and official correspondence in conjunction with personal diaries, letters and photographs and the genealogy websites developed for use by family historians.[26] Pamela Scully's research on Sara Baartman, the Khoisan woman from South Africa who was exhibited in the west as the 'Hottentot Venus', introduces the concept of 'heterography' to denote the practice she developed of identifying and presenting glimpses of transboundary lives as they emerge in scattered archives and diverse genres of sources.[27]

Such innovative feminist research should alleviate Yves Saunier's expressed fear that, in their focus on the reinterpretation of existing data, transnational historians are moving ever further from primary sources.[28] We hope here, too, to present transnational histories that are about flesh-and-blood people rather than abstract processes, and thus, in the words of Herren *et al.*, 'enliven[s] the as yet bloodless idea of globalisation with colours, smells, stories, beliefs, and concepts'.[29]

The contents of the book

The main body of the book is divided into three parts, each focusing on a key theme in transnational history. Part 1 presents a set of gendered histories of global and transnational networks. The study of cross-border and intercultural networks, webs, circulations, contacts and interactions is central to the agenda of transnational history, and the chapters in this section foreground women and gender analysis in the study of these transnational and global networks. They also move us beyond the usual focus within feminist transnational history on international women's organisations. The opening chapter by Clare Midgley presents a case study of Pandita Ramabai, a pioneering nineteenth-century Indian feminist who sought to position herself beyond the authority of formal western-dominated Christian missionary networks through her involvement in an informal transnational and cross-cultural network of liberal religious activists. This network involved intellectual exchange, spiritual connection and practical collaboration between Indian Hindu religious and social reformers and British and American Unitarian Christian activists. Midgley argues that this network opened up liberatory spaces for Ramabai, enabling her to assert spiritual and feminist agency and leadership as an Indian woman in the age of empire. Moving us forward into the interwar period, Susan Zimmermann's chapter shifts our attention from informal religious and cultural networks to those formal, international, non-governmental organisations that actively sought to intervene in politics and policy making on the world stage in the late nineteenth and early twentieth centuries. Her chapter examines how the formulation of international labour standards by the International Labour Organization in the interwar period pivoted around the question of the status of women's unpaid work for family and community, which was debated in the context of the intersections between culturally specific gender inequalities and globally racialized inequalities, and she explores the role played by women's organisations in these policy debates. The final chapter in this section, by Ulrike Wöhr, moves us into the era of rival nuclear powers, throwing fresh light on the non-hierarchical direct-action networks that

8 Clare Midgley, Alison Twells and Julie Carlier

developed in the 1980s through exploring the significance to women activists in Japan of Greenham Common women's peace camp, located outside at an American nuclear weapons' base in the UK. It suggests how new understandings of women's grassroots activism, and new gendered insights into debates on national identity, can develop when historians become alert to the transnational inspirations which may underpin and inform localised activism.

Part 2, 'Women's Agency in the Intersecting Histories of Imperialisms and Nationalisms', focuses on another key arena of research in transnational and global history: the study of empires and their metropoles and colonies. It brings together three essays that focus on the 'Age of Empire' between the late nineteenth century and the Second World War. Breaking with the more usual focus on the British, French and German empires, the chapters explore less well-studied aspects of nationalism, imperialism and anticolonial nationalism in relation to the histories of the US, Russian and Italian empires. All three chapters analyse the intersection of gender, race and/or national identities, thus building on the intersectional exploration of female agency and the engagement with feminist postcolonial theory already evident in Part 1. Laura R. Prieto's chapter on Philippina 'new women' who developed a form of national dress combining indigenous elements with aspects of western style introduced by American missionaries offers new insights into the gendered histories of anticolonial nationalisms. In paying attention to the material of everyday life, she reveals the presence in nationalism of cultural syncretism alongside the rejections of western culture often seen as characterising male discourse. In so doing, she provides an interesting counterpoint to the better-known history of debates around gender, westernisation and 'denationalisation' current among Indian nationalists during the same period. Her work also helps to globalise the literature on 'new women', which has tended until very recently to focus on western women. Olga Shnyrova's chapter presents new research into the relationship between women's movements and nationalist movements at the centre and on the borders of the Russian Empire. It shows how common feminist agendas could bring together women living under imperial domination who might otherwise have been divided by distinctive and conflicting regional nationalist agendas, and, like Prieto's chapter, suggests some of the reasons why women's engagements with nationalism could be distinct from those of men. Finally, Barbara Spadaro's exploration of imperial propaganda directed at girls in fascist Italy enhances our understanding of the gendered impact of 'the empire at home' – hitherto studied mainly in relationship to Britain. It offers fresh insights into the specific form that the construction of whiteness took in the Italian context through exploring the integration of fascist and imperialist ideology and reveals the active involvement of women in this process. In drawing on oral history interviews with former fascist women propagandists, Spadaro also suggests the continuing resonance of these ideologies into the twenty-first century.

Part 3, 'Localizing the Global / Globalizing the Local', encourages us to adopt a critical perspective on dominant analyses of globalisation through exploring the ways in which the global is also locally produced, with local processes and agency shaping multiple forms of globalisation. They encourage us to bring together 'micro' and 'macro' histories and to take seriously women's local agency in shaping globalisation. Natacha Chevalier, drawing on British women's diaries housed in the Mass Observation Archive, shows not only how global war's disruption of global trade patterns affected women's everyday lives but also how women's agency created new patterns of household consumption. In the process she offers a fresh intervention into the debate over the nature and extent of the impact of Britain's role as a global imperial power on 'ordinary' people in Britain. Patricia Grimshaw and Hannah Loney's chapter explores the intersections between the local and the global in the activism of women advocates for indigenous rights in different localities in the postcolonial Pacific, exploring how these women brought rights issues to the fore amidst the global scrutiny and varied internal national contestations that followed the postwar decolonisation of Asia. Highlighting the importance of rooted local studies to understanding broad regional and global developments, they show how these activists negotiated different paths within their countries' specific racialized contexts and in relation to regional women's movements dominated by non-indigenous women. Finally, Alison Twells encourages us to broaden our vision beyond the confines of academic history by considering the co-production of the local and the global as a focus for teaching history in schools and in the community. She discusses how a gendered and localized global history can challenge recent attempts to reassert top-down masculine imperial narratives in the national history curriculum in English schools and combat the marginalisation of women and minority ethnic groups in heritage discourse and community history projects.

Notes

1 For a useful introduction see P.-Y. Saunier, *Transnational History*, Basingstoke: Palgrave Macmillan, 2013. See also M. Werner and B. Zimmermann, 'Beyond comparison: Histoire croisée and the challenge of reflexivity', *History and Theory*, 45, 2006, 30–50.
2 M. Middell and K. Naumann, 'Global history and the spatial turn: From the impact of area studies to the study of critical junctures of globalization', *Journal of Global History*, 5:1, 2010, 161.
3 Middell and Naumann, 'Global history and the spatial turn', p. 160.
4 O. Janz and D. Schönpflug, eds., *Gender History in a Transnational Perspective: Networks, Biographies, Gender Orders*, Oxford: Berghahn Books, 2014, p. 2.
5 A. Curthoys and M. Lake, M., eds., *Connecting Worlds: History in Transnational Perspective*, Canberra: ANU E Press, 2005, p. 15.
6 M. E. Wiesner-Hanks, 'Crossing borders in transnational gender history', *Journal of Global History*, 6:3, 2011, p. 361; T. Ballantyne and A. Burton, eds., *Bodies in Contact. Rethinking Colonial Encounters in World History*, Durham: Duke University Press, 2005, p. 7.
7 Wiesner-Hanks, 'Crossing borders in transnational gender history', p. 378.
8 L. J. Rupp, *Worlds of Women. The Making of an International Women's Movement*, Princeton: Princeton University Press, 1997; E. Schöck-Quiteros, A. Schüler, A. Wilmers, *Politische Netzwekerinen: Internationale Zusammenarbeit von Frauen 1830–1960*, Berlin: Trafo Verlag, 2007; P. Johnson, S. Neumsinger and J. Sangster, eds., *Crossing Boundaries: Women's Organizing in Europe and the Americas, 1880s–1940s*, Uppsala: Uppsala Universitët, 2007; K. Jensen and E. Kuhlman, eds., *Women and Transnational Activism in Historical Perspective*, Dordrecht: Republic of Letters Publishing, 2010; F. Paisley, *Glamour in the Pacific: Cultural Internationalism and Race Politics in the Women's Pan-Pacific*, Honolulu: University of Hawaii

10 Clare Midgley, Alison Twells and Julie Carlier

Press, 2009; K. Offen, *Globalizing Feminisms, 1789–1945*, London: Routledge, 2010; F. de Haan, M. Allen, J. Purvis and K. Daskalova, eds., *Women's Activism. Global Perspectives from the 1890s to the Present,* London: Routledge, 2013; Janz and Schönpflug, *Gender History in Transnational Perspective.*

9   B. G. Smith, ed., *Women's History in Global Perspective,* 3 vols, Urbana: University of Illinois Press, 2004–6.

10 T. Ballantyne and A. Burton, eds., *Bodies in Contact*; T. Ballantyne and A. Burton, eds., *Moving Subjects: Gender, Mobility and Intimacy in an Age of Global Empire*, Urbana: University of Illinois Press, 2009.

11 B. Bush and J. Purvis, eds., 'Connecting Women's Histories: The Local and the Global', Special Issue of *Women's History Review*, 25:4, August 2016.

12 M. Wiesner-Hanks, 'Crossing borders in transnational gender history', *Journal of Global History*, 6:3, 2011, 362.

13 M. Middell, and K. Naumann, 'Global history and the spatial turn: from the impact of area studies to the study of critical junctures of globalization', *Journal of Global History*, 5:1, 2010, 149–170.

14 C. Freeman, 'Is local: Global as feminine: Masculine? Rethinking the gender of globalization', Special issue on globalization and gender, *Signs*, 26:4, 1991, 1007–1037; quotes from pp. 1008, 1017, 1030, 1031, 1013 respectively.

15 M. Herren, M. Rüesch and C. Sibille, *Transcultural History: Theories, Methods, Sources*, Heidelberg: Springer, 2014, pp. 8–9; D. Deacon, P. Russell and A. Woollacott, eds., *Transnational Ties: Australian Lives in the World*, Canberra: ANU ePress, 2008; A. Burton, 'Not even remotely global? Method and scale in world history', *History Workshop Journal*, 64, 2007, 323–328.

16 Deacon et al., *Transnational Ties*, p. 5

17 S. Sassen, 'Towards a Feminist Analytics of the Global Economy', in S. Sassen, ed., *Globalization and its Discontents*, London and New York: The New Press, 1998, p. 82.

18 Herren et al., *Transcultural History*, pp. v, vi; 41, 52–53, 57–59; A. Nandy, 'History's Forgotten Doubles', in P. Pomper, R. H. Elphick and R. T. Vann, eds., *World History: Ideologies, Structures and Identities*, Oxford: Blackwell, 1998, pp. 159–178; D. Chakrabarty, *Provincialising Europe: Reflections on Questions of Method and Strategy,* Princeton: Princeton University Press, 2000; G. G. Iggers, Q. E. Wang and S. Mukherjee, *A Global History of Modern Historiography*, Harlow: Pearson, 2008.

19 G. C. Spivak, 'The Rani of Sirmur: An essay in reading the archives', *History and Theory*, 24:3, 1985, 247–272.

20 Ballantyne and Burton, eds., *Bodies in Contact*; Ballantyne and Burton, eds., *Moving Subjects.*

21 D. Cohen and L. J. Frazier, 'Scale – Exploring the "Global '68"', in H. E. Kahn, ed., *Framing the Global: Entry Points for Research*, Bloomington: Indiana University Press, 2014, pp. 272–273.

22 I. Hofmeyr, *Gandhi's Printing Press: Experiments in Slow Reading*, Cambridge, MA: Harvard University Press, 2013; E. J. Yeo, 'Gender and Homeland in the Irish and Jewish Diasporas, 1850–1930', in M. Schrover and E. J. Yeo, eds., Gender, *Migration and the Public Sphere*, 1850–2005, Abingdon: Routledge, 2010, pp. 14–37.

23 Herren et al., *Transcultural History*, pp. 55–56.

24 Deacon et al., *Transnational Lives*, p. 2.

25 L. Frost and H. J. Maxwell-Fraser, *Chain Letters: Narrating Convict Lives*, Melbourne: Melbourne University Press, 2001.

26 C. Anderson, *Subaltern Lives: Biographies of Colonialism in the Indian Ocean World, 1790–1920*, Cambridge: Cambridge University Press, 2012.

27 P. Scully, 'Peripheral Visions: Heterography and Writing the Transnational Life of Sara Baartman', in D. Deacon, P. Russell and A. Woollacott, eds., *Transnational Lives*, Basingstoke: Palgrave Macmillan, 2010, pp. 27–40.

28 Saunier, *Transnational History*, pp. 118, 130–34.

29 Herren et al., *Transcultural History*, p. 13.

PART I

Gendered histories of transnational networks and connections

1
INDIAN FEMINIST PANDITA RAMABAI AND TRANSNATIONAL LIBERAL RELIGIOUS NETWORKS IN THE NINETEENTH-CENTURY WORLD

Clare Midgley

This chapter focuses on the pioneering Indian feminist Pandita Ramabai. Offering a fresh transnational perspective on her life, it seeks to throw new light on the inter-related feminist and faith journeys of a foundational figure in the global emergence of modern feminisms. In the process, it aims to offer new insights into the significance of informal cross-cultural networks of association during the nineteenth-century age of empire.

In an essential corrective to colonial discourse celebrating the British as emancipators of oppressed Indian women, early feminist postcolonial scholarship emphasized the suppression of Indian women's agency under the twin oppressive forces of colonial domination and indigenous patriarchal power.[1] It also developed a highly critical analysis of western women's engagements with Indian women, arguing that these were characterized by an 'imperial feminist' approach in which British women sought full citizenship by positioning themselves as the saviours of victimized Indian women, women who were given no space to speak for themselves.[2] This scholarship suggested a negative answer to the question famously posed by Gayatri Spivak in relation to the history of Indian women: 'Can the subaltern speak?' It also implied that the unequal power structures inherent in colonialism rendered impossible cross-cultural interchanges between British and Indian women based on mutual respect rather than assumptions of western superiority.

Recent research in Indian women's history has, however, suggested a more complex and nuanced answer to the question of subaltern agency under colonialism. Exposing the depth and range of nineteenth-century Indian women's activism from the mid-nineteenth century onward, it has shown how colonial legal reform, the spread of Christian missionary education, the emergence of indigenous social reform movements and intercultural contacts could open up opportunities for female empowerment rather than simply reshaping patriarchal power.[3] This research has been accompanied by a growing recognition of the limitations of analyzing

14 Clare Midgley

Indians' lives during the nineteenth century through the rigid binary categories of colonial collaborator/anticolonial nationalist: indeed, Padma Anagol, studying the emergence of feminism in India, has concluded that 'privileging the politics of colonialism and nationalism has led scholars to miss the real dynamic of change in gender relations.'[4] In tandem, recent scholarship approaching the history of South Asia from a transnational perspective has brought into focus hidden histories of cross-cultural friendship, intellectual exchange and co-operation within informal and alternative webs of association that operated within and beyond the bounds of the British Empire and were positioned outside official imperial networks and western-directed missionary societies.[5] The challenge, now, is to clarify the extent to which such transnational spaces of interaction helped facilitate Indian agency under colonialism and how much cross-cultural relationships remained shaped by imperial power and colonial discourse. This chapter on Pandita Ramabai seeks to advance the project of writing such critical transnational histories of South Asia by moving beyond their current focus on male actors and anti-imperialist alliances to explore female agency and cross-cultural collaboration on issues of social reform.

In her lifetime, Ramabai became a renowned but controversial figure on the western Indian, Indian national and international stages. A high-caste Hindu who became a member of the reformist Brahmo Samaj and then an independent-minded Christian, she became a pioneer of Indian women's agency beyond the domestic familial sphere: the first Indian woman to speak out in public about the oppression of women in colonial India, the first to travel overseas for education without being accompanied by a male family member, the founder of the first women's organiza-tion run by Indian women themselves and of the first school for high-caste Hindu widows and the first woman to address the Indian National Congress – and later the founder of the internationally renowned Mukti Mission.[6] After her death in 1922, the *Times of India* lauded her as one of the 'makers of modern India', while her early Christian biographers presented her as a saintly figure.[7] In contrast, she was denigrated by some Hindu nationalists for her willingness to engage with the colonial government, her conversion to Christianity and her solicitation of western funding. More recently, Indian feminist activists and scholars have reevaluated her contributions, presenting her as a founding mother of Indian feminism.

A great deal of excellent research has been published on Pandita Ramabai over the past twenty years.[8] However, little attention has been paid to her involvement in an established transnational web of religious liberals and social reformers. This chapter brings into focus and evaluates the significance of her positioning within this web, which connected members of a trans-Indian network comprising the influential Bengali-based organization for religious and social reform, the Brahmo Samaj, and its Bombay-centred sister organization, the Prarthana Samaj, with a transatlantic network of British and American religious liberals who identified as Unitarians or Transcendentalists.[9] Characterized by collaboration between groups whose roots lay in the very different religious traditions of Hinduism and Christian-ity, the history of co-operation among this cross-cultural web of reformers contrasts sharply with the much more familiar history of bitter conflict between orthodox

Hindu religious leaders and evangelical Protestant missionaries in India. This conflict was sparked by the missionary push to gain converts and by their denigration of Hindu religious culture, which they claimed was characterized by the mistreatment of women.[10] In contrast, Indian and Anglo-American religious liberals found common ground in their rejection of doctrinaire approaches to establishing religious truth and in their commitment to social reform, with a particular emphasis on improving the position of women in both 'East' and 'West'.

In the mid-1860s women began to emerge as important actors within this transnational network. British Unitarian social reformer Mary Carpenter entered into an extended period of collaboration with Brahmo men to promote Indian women's education, and Unitarian women took leading roles in the National Indian Association, which was set up by Carpenter and the Brahmo leader Keshub Chunder Sen during Sen's visit to Britain in 1870.[11] At the same time, Brahmo women themselves began to publish their own writings in Bengali and to meet outside the family to discuss their own social position. In the 1880s they were among the first women in the Indian subcontinent to gain university degrees, to train as doctors and to act as delegates to the Indian National Congress.[12] In an overlapping chronology of interconnected developments, women from Unitarian and Transcendentalist backgrounds played pioneering roles in British and American women's entry into higher education and the medical profession, and their public involvement in social reform, and became leading lights in the women's suffrage movement.[13]

This chapter, then, explores Ramabai's involvement in a transnational network that drew together Indian, British and American men and women in a web of mutual hospitality, friendship, intellectual interchange, spiritual community and practical collaboration. It evaluates how significant the network was in offering her practical and moral support in developing her work with Indian women and the part it played in the evolution of her religious beliefs and her feminist ideas. To what extent, it asks, did this support provide Ramabai with an effective alternative to western-directed evangelical missionary networks? How, too, did it facilitate her negotiation of intersecting hierarchies of gender, race, religion, class and caste within and between colonial India, imperial Britain and the United States? In tandem, the chapter considers how Ramabai's agency as an Indian woman activist altered the dynamics of collaboration on the 'woman question' among Indian, British and American members of this transnational liberal religious network. Did Ramabai's high public profile as an activist on the regional, national and transnational stage undermine the discursive construction by both western feminists and Indian male social reformers of the Indian woman as silent, passive and victimized? How did it impact on the transnational network's engagement with the 'woman question', and on the positioning of Indian women under British colonialism and within Indian nationalism?

These issues are investigated by exploring Ramabai's travels and intersecting faith and feminist journeys over the twenty-year period when she engaged with liberal religious networks.[14] The first part of the chapter focuses on Ramabai's life and work in colonial India and imperial Britain between 1878 and 1886, from

16 Clare Midgley

her initial encounters with the Brahmo Samaj and collaboration with the Prarthana Samaj, to her conversion to a Unitarian form of Christianity following her travel to Britain in 1883. The second part considers the new opportunities that opened up for her from 1886 when she moved outside the orbit of British imperial power relations to engage with Unitarians, Transcendentalists and feminists in the United States. It then explores her complex positioning as Christian, feminist, Indian nationalist and transnational activist after she returned to western India in 1889 to found a school for high-caste Hindu widows, an institution that was reliant both on American financial backing from the Unitarian-led Ramabai Association and local support from the Hindu reformist Prarthana Samaj.

Ramabai's faith and feminist journey between colonial India and imperial Britain, 1878–1886

When Ramabai first encountered the Brahmo Samaj in Calcutta in 1878, she was an orphaned young woman of twenty who had led an unorthodox early life. She had been born Ramabai Dongre in the state of Karnataka in western India. The year was 1858, when Britain finally succeeded in violently suppressing the Great Rebellion of 1857–1858 and imposed Crown Rule on the subcontinent. Her father was a devout Brahmin – a member of the high, priestly, caste of Hindus. However, he broke with tradition in teaching his wife to read Sanskrit (the language of the Hindu scriptures), enabling her to then educate Ramabai, and he also rejected the custom of child marriage for his daughter. He led his family into the life of wandering pilgrims, who eked out a living by reciting Hindu religious text to villagers. It was an exhausting and impoverished life, and both parents died of starvation and disease during a famine in Madras Presidency in 1874. Ramabai and her brother continued to travel around India as pilgrims and preachers, finally reaching Calcutta, the capital of Bengal Presidency and the hub of British colonial government, in 1878.[15]

It was Ramabai's encounter with the Brahmo Samaj in Calcutta that propelled her into public prominence, fostered her developing concern for the social position of women and led her into a new religious orientation which placed her within a cross-India and transnational liberal religious network. The Brahmo Samaj (Society of the Worshippers of the One True God / Supreme Being) was founded in the city by Rammohun Roy in 1828. Roy sought to reform Hindu religious culture from within. He was a monotheist, and he saw religious and social reform as inextricably linked, being particularly concerned with improving the position of women. While continuing to define himself as a Hindu, Roy was an admirer of Jesus Christ as an outstanding ethical teacher. He fostered close links with leading British and American Unitarian Protestants through extended correspondence and the exchange of publications, initiating a transnational web of religious liberals and social reformers, members who considered themselves kindred spirits despite their contrasting cultural backgrounds. Roy paid an extended visit to England in 1831, partly to deepen his connections with Unitarians. Following his death in Bristol in 1833, his tomb became a point of Brahmo pilgrimage.[16]

Keshub Chunder Sen, the charismatic Brahmo leader whom Ramabai encountered on her arrival in Calcutta, revived Brahmoism as an outward-looking activist movement in the 1860s. His new organization, the Brahmo Samaj of India, reconnected with western Unitarians and Transcendentalists and sent out missionaries to spread its message of religious and social reform throughout India. Sen was important to Ramabai in encouraging her to break fully with orthodox Hindu prescriptions on women reading sacred texts. However, encountering Sen at the time of his controversial decision to give his under-age daughter in marriage to the Maharajah of Cooch Behar, Ramabai showed her independence from her male mentor by publicly aligning with Sen's Brahmo critics in opposition to child marriage.[17] In 1880, in a final break with orthodox Hinduism, she married a fellow Brahmo in an intercaste marriage, marking her rejection of the caste system.[18] Encouraged by Brahmos, Ramabai spoke at public meetings on religion and the position of women and her learning and eloquence astounded the male intellectual elite in the city, leading her to be publicly honoured as 'Pandita' (woman scholar) and 'Saraswati' (goddess of learning). She also inspired Brahmo women, who presented her with an address praising her 'independence of spirit' and describing her as an exemplary contemporary Indian woman of learning.[19]

Involvement with the Brahmo Samaj opened Ramabai's eyes to the transnational liberal religious network to which the group belonged as she became aware of Sen's close co-operation in Calcutta with American Unitarian missionary Charles Dall.[20] She had also read about Sen's visit to England in 1870, and his collaboration in promoting Indian women's education with the Unitarian social reformer and educationalist Mary Carpenter.[21] Of more immediate significance was the cross-India link that Brahmos had with the Prarthana Samaj, a closely related religious and social reform organization founded in the 1860s following a missionary visit by Sen to Bombay.[22] Receiving news from their Brahmo contacts about Ramabai's activities in Bengal, the group became convinced that she could play a vital role in improving the position of women in western India. This proved a lifeline to Ramabai when her husband died of cholera in 1882. She took up the group's invitation to work for it, supporting herself and her young daughter by promoting women's education under its auspices.[23]

Ramabai rapidly gained a high profile in western India by giving public lectures on the position of women and founding the Arya Mahila Samaj [Indian Ladies' Society]. This society was run by Indian women and was open to members throughout India. It aimed to unite women in a campaign to improve their own condition through education and opposition to child marriage. This was a radical and ambitious step, giving a space for reform-minded women to organize outside the oversight of their male relatives in the Prarthana Samaj: as an organization run by and for Indian women, it was perhaps the first feminist organization in the subcontinent.[24]

18 Clare Midgley

Ramabai's growing national fame as an activist on the 'woman question' was at odds with the positioning of Indian women – both in colonial discourse and in the writings of Indian social reformers – as silent victims needing to be saved by others, and her activities began to shift these paternalistic positions. She began to occupy the activist position previously taken by Sen's Unitarian collaborator, the British reformer Mary Carpenter – who died in 1877, the year before Ramabai encountered the Brahmo Samaj. The radical wing of the Brahmo Samaj, which had earlier presented western Unitarian women such as Carpenter to Bengali women as role models of women's engagement in wider society beyond the home, now urged them to follow Ramabai's example by actively participating in efforts for the 'true uplifting of women's position in our society'.[25] The colonial government, which has earlier looked to Carpenter for advice on developing Indian female education, also now turned to Ramabai, giving her an advisory role in the development of the imperial government's policy on female education.[26] Testifying in 1882 before the Hunter Education Commission as a representative of the Arya Mahila Samaj, Ramabai stressed the importance of Indian women's *own* agency, both in running schools and acting as school inspectors, and she pressed the government to open up medical training to Indian women.[27]

Ramabai's own sense of agency was clearly enhanced by these endorsements from both Indian reformers and colonial officials, and in 1883 she took the bold step of travelling to the imperial metropole to seek training as a doctor and funding to advance the Arya Mahila Samaj's project of founding of a home for 'widowed and helpless women' in Poona.[28] Ramabai's time in Britain also marked a new stage in her faith journey. To the consternation of her colleagues in the Prarthana Samaj, before she left India Ramabai had begun to seriously question whether their reformist Hindu monotheism satisfied her religious needs, and she was becoming increasingly attracted to Christianity.[29] This was perhaps the reason why, rather than seeking support from the National Indian Association, which had close links to the Brahmo Samaj, she instead took up an invitation from an Anglican sisterhood working in Poona, the Sisters of the Community of St Mary the Virgin: they offered to fund her extended visit to Britain in return for her undertaking to teach Marathi at their British home base in Wantage to Sisters training for missionary work in western India.[30]

In Wantage Ramabai came under the religious authority of the Established Church of England, a Church that also functioned as the British religious establishment in colonial India. Her commitment to Anglicanism seemed complete when, after spending only five months in the Community of St Mary the Virgin in Wantage, she was baptised as Mary. However, she was no humble or obedient convert. In the face of intense pressure from the Church authorities to conform, she remained determined to develop her own distinctive understanding of Christianity from an Indian perspective and to maintain her own agenda for improving the position of Indian women. In this battle, her continuing sense of connection to the Brahmo Samaj, and her new friendships with the group's leading British liberal religious supporters, were to prove vital sources of strength. Asserting her spiritual independence from her Anglican mentors, Ramabai represented her decision to become a Christian, not as a dramatic conversion experience brought about through the agency of the Wantage Sisters but as a result of her growing conviction that the 'Brahmo religion' was in fact rooted not in Hindu scriptures but in Christ's teaching.[31] This was not as eccentric as it might sound: Rammohun Roy had revered Jesus Christ as an ethical leader, and Keshub Chunder Sen had positioned him as an Eastern prophet of universal religious significance.[32] In addition, Ramabai adopted a Unitarian form of Christianity, not Anglican Trinitarianism, a religious position whose close affinity to Brahmoism had been stressed by both Roy and Sen.[33]

Ramabai's continuing links with Brahmos and her Unitarian Christian positioning became a focus of intense concern from Sister Geraldine, her religious mentor at Wantage, who was outraged by her refusal to accept the doctrine of the Holy Trinity. The Sister had her own plans for Ramabai: she wanted her to return to India to work with the Sisterhood as an Anglican missionary educator of women, and she would not fit the role unless she was prepared to obey the authority of the Anglican Church. The Anglican Sister expressed her worries about Ramabai's correspondence with 'her old Brahmo friends' in India and the indications that she had 'some idea of working with them in the future'.[34] She was equally determined to keep Ramabai apart from Unitarians in Britain, writing later that she believed Ramabai's 'keen delight in intellectual fencing and her pride and vanity were dangerously inflated by her getting hold of points of controversy from her non-Conformist friends'.[35] She tried to convince Ramabai that Unitarians were heretics because 'they denied the Divinity of our Lord'.[36] Ramabai, however, responded by criticizing her mentor's religious sectarianism as inappropriate to the Indian environment, echoing a criticism made of western missionaries by many Indian Christian converts.[37]

In her fight with the Anglican establishment to define her own understanding of Christianity and retain the freedom to shape the direction of her future work for women in India, Ramabai's liberal religious contacts in the imperial metropole provided her with vital emotional, spiritual and intellectual support.[38] Her key backers were all long-standing friends of the Brahmo Samaj who were already familiar with her work in India: F. Max Müller, a liberal Anglican who was a leading Sanskrit scholar at Oxford University, and the feminists Sophia Dobson Collet, a religious liberal from a radical Unitarian family, Elizabeth Adelaide Manning, the Unitarian President of the National Indian Association, and Frances Power Cobbe, a Transcendentalist who had earlier befriended Keshub Chunder Sen. Müller invited Ramabai to stay with his family in Oxford and arranged for her to attend some medical lectures at the university.[39] Collet, who had learned Bengali and formed links to Brahmo women from the 1860s and had reported on Ramabai's activities in India in her capacity as editor of *The Brahmo Year-Book*, supplied her with several of Sen's works, including his famous lecture on Christ, which Ramabai then urged Sister Geraldine to read.[40] Manning, who had reported to a British audience on Ramabai's activities in India in the *Journal of the National Indian Association*, sent books received from her Brahmo contacts in India.[41] Cobbe, who had once described herself to her Bengali friends as a 'Brahmika' [female Brahmo], also befriended Ramabai, later recording in her autobiography that Ramabai had come to visit her in London 'and impressed me most favourably' with her commitment to securing education and freedom for her Indian sisters.[42]

Ramabai also drew direct inspiration from the life and work of the founder of the Brahmo Samaj, Rammohun Roy, who had himself spent several years in Britain some fifty years before her own visit. In the *Journal of the National Indian Association*, writing under the pseudonym Veritas [Truth], she reported her visit to Roy's funerary monument in Bristol as a 'pilgrimage' to Roy's 'shrine', thus asserting her continuing reverence for Brahmoism following her conversion to Christianity. She rested this on both religious and feminist grounds, praising the organization as 'an important agent in cultivating . . . a purer religion' and noting that Roy 'always supported the claims of women'. Ramabai was also deeply impressed by the way in which Roy had retained his Indian identity during his years in Britain. Referring to the striking full-length oil portrait of the Bengali reformer that was on public display in Bristol, she pointed out in her article that it showed that 'He never changed his dress; and I consider that his own native costume was entirely becoming to him.'[43] Despite her conversion, Ramabai had retained the white sari considered culturally appropriate for Hindu widows rather than adopting a western style of dress, a visible sign that for her, becoming a Christian was not synonymous with becoming westernized – or, as Indian themselves put it, denationalized.[44]

Strengthened by her visit to Roy's tomb, she wrote to Sister Geraldine asserting that, like Roy, her own obedience was to the Word of God, not to priests, and attributing the roots of her own mission to Indian women to the example of Brahmos rather than Christians. Ramabai went on to mount a powerful attack on Sister Geraldine's colonial stereotype of all Indian women as 'hedged', or kept in seclusion from men, pointing out that this did not apply to Marathi Brahmin women like herself. Asserting her right to a transnational public role – and implicitly calling into question Christian missionary claims that British women were much more emancipated than their Indian sisters – she also challenged Sister Geraldine's opposition to her wish to address mixed audiences in Britain. Calling into question the Victorian ideology of 'separate spheres' that shaped the Sisterhood's positioning within the Anglican Church and informed its missionary work in India, she told Sister Geraldine that, in India, she had addressed both mixed and all-male audiences and taught young men as well as women.[45]

In the end, Sister Geraldine had to acknowledge defeat. Writing to Ramabai in September 1885 to terminate her role as her religious mentor, she stated rather bitterly, deploying the standard missionary contrast between the heathen darkness of India and the light of western Christianity: 'We grieve that one of India's daughters whom we hoped God was training to carry a ray of light back to that benighted land should be returning to that darkness without the light of Truth.'[46] Challenging this negative colonial image of her homeland, Ramabai found sufficient spiritual and intellectual space in Britain to define her own distinctive Unitarian Christian and Indian feminist position and to resist the Anglican Church's attempt to impose its authority on her. As we have seen, this was not simply the result of her strong-mindedness as an individual, though this is very evident. She had been able to hold on to her sense of self and agency as an Indian woman partly through maintaining a strong sense of connection to Brahmoism, a connection underpinned by the transnational liberal religious network connecting the Brahmo Samaj with British Unitarians.

The actualization of Ramabai's feminist project between the United States and India, 1886–1898

While Sister Geraldine had failed to turn Ramabai into a Christian missionary, she had managed to block her access to the public platform which might have enabled her to gain support from the British public for her own plans to promote the education of Indian women.[47] Ramabai did not gain official organizational backing from British Unitarians or the National Indian Association, and she also failed to gain funding from the imperial government. It was only when she travelled to the United States that she was able to secure a public platform and access financial support in the west. In moving outside the orbit of British imperial power she had moved from an Anglican-dominated religious environment to one where Unitarians were far more politically powerful and socially influential. The support that she was now able to access from this liberal religious network proved crucial in enabling her to lay the grounds for her return to India to set up a new educational establishment for women.[48]

Her travel to the United States came about because her distant cousin, Anandibai Joshi, had in 1833 gained American sponsorship to train as a doctor at the Women's Medical College in Philadelphia. Over the course of her final year in Britain, Ramabai received letters from the Dean of this college, Rachel Bodley, inviting her to travel across the Atlantic to attend Joshi's graduation as the first Indian woman to qualify as a doctor overseas; Bodley also suggested that Ramabai extend her visit to inform American women about the condition of women in India.[49] Ramabai, having been set free of any sense of obligation she may have felt toward Sister Geraldine, seized on this invitation as offering an ideal opportunity to gain support in America for the promotion of Indian women's education.[50]

On her arrival in the United States in 1886, Ramabai found herself able to mix freely with leading religious liberals, feminists, social reformers and educationalists. She now firmed up her plans for improving the lives of women in India: building on the original plan of the Arya Mahila Samaj to open a home for widowed women, she decided that the distinctive contribution she could make would be to open an independent boarding school in western India for child widows who, like herself, came from high-caste Hindu backgrounds. In 1887 she wrote *The High-Caste Hindu Woman* to elicit American public support for her project. Ramabai's text, as Meera Kosambi noted, offered 'an incisive feminist analysis of the upper-caste woman's seamless oppression through all stages of her life'.[51] Its stress on Hindu women as victims of Hindu patriarchal oppression might be interpreted as reinforcing the western missionary stereotype of the Indian woman as helpless silent victim needing rescue from her western sisters, and Ramabai may have consciously sought to evoke this image as an effective way of gaining financial support in America. However, Ramabai also simultaneously combated this stereotype by her insistence that it was only through Indian women's *own* agency, rather than through the actions of Indian men or western women, that female emancipation would be achieved in the subcontinent. She thus implicitly presented her project as a progression from the earlier pattern of collaboration between the Brahmo leader Keshub Chunder Sen and the Unitarian social reformer Mary Carpenter, in which Indian women had been positioned as the focus of educational efforts rather than involved in an active leadership role:

> In a country where castes and the seclusion of women are regarded as essential tenets of the national creed, we can scarcely hope for a general spread of useful knowledge among women, through either men of their own race or through foreign women. All experience in the past history of mankind has shown that efforts for the elevation of a nation must come from within and work outward to be effectual.[52]

What was required for the general diffusion of education among Indian women, Ramabai argued, was for 'a body of persons from among themselves, who shall make it their life-work to teach by precept and example, their fellow-countrywomen'.[53]

Ramabai appealed for Americans to support her plan to address the absence of institutions anywhere in India to provide shelter and education for high-caste Hindu widows, who, not allowed by their relatives to remarry, were socially ostracized and often reduced to a state of homelessness and destitution following the death of their husbands. She wanted to pioneer schools that would enable these women to earn their own living, rather than remaining helpless dependents. In so doing, she was building on Brahmos' long-standing commitment to widow remarriage and to sheltering, educating and training destitute and ill-treated widows.[54] Ramabai had identified a gap in provision which she felt she could fill as an Indian woman who herself came from a Brahmin background and who, despite being a Christian convert, was willing to respect caste prescriptions and create a free religious environment rather than a Christian institution. She stressed that neither the secular schools promoted by Carpenter nor foreign mission schools were suitable for high-caste Hindu widows as they were open to women of every caste, and the widows feared either losing caste or being converted to Christianity in them.[55]

Ramabai's school plan involved reformist Hindus in the role of managers and westerners in the role of assistants, in a complete reversal of the usual imperial pattern of western managers directing Indian subordinates.[56] Instead of seeking funding through the colonial government, as she had earlier unsuccessfully attempted to do in Britain, Ramabai now sought to put her plan into action by drawing on voluntary support from the United States, inviting American women and men to pledge funding for a fixed ten-year period to get the school established.[57] In direct response to Ramabai's appeal, the Ramabai Association was founded in Boston in December 1887, and Ramabai herself drummed up support throughout the United States by conducting a series of extensive lecture tours, taking on the prominent public role that she had been unable to assume in Britain. These activities resulted in the formation of sixty-three local Ramabai Circles around the country and a substantial annual pledge of $5,000 to support her planned widows' home over an initial ten-year period, with an additional $11,000 collected for the building of the school.[58]

In negotiating the establishment of the Ramabai Association, Ramabai deliberately turned down offers from evangelical clergymen to take the lead, instead turning to a prominent American Unitarian with a long-standing interest in religious and social reform in India, the Rev Edward Everett Hale, considering him to be best placed to set up the group as a non-missionary organization with no specific denominational affiliation.[59] She also gained important backing for her project from the leading Transcendentalist and feminist Caroline Healey Dall, wife of the American Unitarian missionary in Calcutta, Charles Dall, who channeled the proceeds from the sale of her biography of Dr Anandibai Joshi to support Ramabai's school.[60] Leading American religious liberals thus provided Ramabai with vital support for developing her project of Indian women's education outside western missionary – and British imperial – control.[61]

Transnational channels of communication between American Unitarians and Bengali Brahmos also proved an important means through which Ramabai connected with new Brahmo religious writings that bolstered her independent Christian position. Her American Unitarian friends introduced her to *The Oriental Christ*, a book by Sen's close associate Protap Chunder Muzumdar that had made a deep impression on them when it was published in Boston in 1883 during Muzumdar's tour of the US to raise funds to promote Brahmoism in India.[62] Ramabi's own enthusiasm for the book, when reported back to Brahmos in Bengal, contributed to their renewed optimism that she would be able to work effectively with non-Christian women on her return to India, a possibility that they had earlier felt was sabotaged by her close association with Anglican missionaries. As the editors of the Brahmo women's journal *Bamodhodini Patrika* reported enthusiastically, Ramabai's time in America was enabling her to 'retain a sense of individual freedom in Christianity' and to 'propagate the eastern practice of Christianity', developments which would enable her future work 'towards the advancement of our country'.[63] Ramabai's warm welcome when she arrived in the US in 1886 also made Brahmos realise Indian women as well as Indian men could play a part in 'strengthening ties between their country and America'.[64]

Ties with the US were important to Brahmos not only because of their long history of links with American Unitarians but also for political reasons. The history of the foundation of the US as a republic formed from a set of former British colonies that had won their independence, made it an inspirational model to some early Indian nationalists, including the Brahmos who were among the founders of the Indian National Congress in 1885. Ramabai herself became an important promoter of the American model in Indian nationalist circles on her return to India in 1889, when she published a book in Marathi giving her impressions of America, *The People of the United States*. She contributed her own distinctive radical reformist, feminist and liberal religious perspective on society in America, arguing against the western missionary claim that there was an automatic link between the spread of Christianity and improvements in the position of women by pointing out that most denominations in the west preached that women should be obedient to men and did not allow female preachers. Developing Brahmo arguments, she stressed the universal applicability of Christ's own teachings and argued that, 'The religion which had led to women's high state' could not be claimed as 'our' religion by western Christians, but was simply 'the holy doctrine' or 'doctrine of Christ'. Updating the analysis offered by British Unitarian writer Harriet Martineau fifty years earlier in her book *Society in America*, Ramabai attributed the progress that had been made in the United States to the successful fights against slavery and the oppression of women fought by radical abolitionist feminists, rather than to the innate superiority of western civilization.[65]

By this point Ramabai's feminism had developed to encompass a commitment to female political representation, a stance probably influenced by hearing about women's suffrage campaigns in a range of western nations when she attended the founding meeting of the first transnational women's organization, the International Council for Women, in Washington in 1888, a conference at which the Unitarian abolitionist and feminist Susan B. Anthony played a leading role.[66] Ramabai viewed the recently formed Indian National Congress as an ideal platform for bringing about improvements in the position of women. However, the leader of the Prarthana Samaj, M.G. Ranade, on whose co-operation she was depending to establish her school in Bombay, was opposed to women's active participation in the Congress. Determined not to allow Indian male social reformers to set limits on her feminist agenda, in her speech at the inauguration of the school, she stressed the importance of women representing their own interests within Congress by making an analogy with the problems caused by Indians' exclusion from the British Parliament:

> Just as we do not have an Indian citizen as our representative in the British Parliament, which naturally is ignorant about the real state and situation in India, likewise we womenfolk have not been given an opportunity to place our representative in the Parliament of India; as a result you men have no idea of the plight of us women.[67]

Ramabai was calling for women's suffrage to be made an integral component of the development of Indian nationalism. With the support of the 'female emancipationist' wing of the Brahmo Samaj, she took her place in one of the first groups of female delegates to Congress. She attended its meeting in Bombay in 1889 as the representative of the Arya Mahila Samaj and addressed the gathering of over 2,000 delegates. She also participated in the National Social Conference, a complementary conference on social reform founded by Ranade. There, speaking against forcible shaving of the heads of widows, she again drew attention to the inconsistency in Ranade's position, noting: 'A great deal had been said, in that very Hall, about Government allowing the people the right of speech; all their women asked for was the same privilege.'[68]

Alongside promoting her feminist agenda within the Indian National Congress, Ramabai rapidly put into operation her plans for setting up her school for widows, having taken steps to heal the religious rift with the Prarthana Samaj that had occurred when she converted to Christianity in 1883. To achieve this, she publicly distanced herself from the western Christian missionary agenda, articulating her own understanding of Christianity as distinct from missionary teaching by explaining that she accepted only Christ's teachings, not the whole of the Bible, as the Word of God. She also promised that she would offer a secular educational curriculum in the school and take care to avoid all propaganda promoting any particular religion.[69] As a result, members of the Prarthana Samaj agreed to take a leading role on the Indian Advisory Board of the school. With their assistance, and drawing on funding from the Ramabai Association in America, the Sharada Sadan opened in Bombay as a residential school for high-caste Hindu widows.[70]

Ramabai's collaboration with the Prarthana Samaj inevitably alienated her from the wider Indian Christian community in Maharashtra, which publicly attacked her Unitarian religious beliefs and alliance with the 'Theists' of the Prarthana Samaj.[71] Further controversy with local Christians arose when a Brahmo woman activist arranged for Ramabai to address a women's meeting in a Hindu temple. In defending her actions, she further articulated her own distinctive liberal religious position as an Indian Christian who continued to respect the good Hindu lessons in morality that she had learned from her parents.[72] Ramabai also came under sustained attack from the opposite side of the religious divide. During this time B. G. Tilak and his supporters were spreading an anti-Christian, anti-Muslim, Hindu revivalist brand of Indian nationalism through western India. Tilak was strongly opposed to any British legislative interference in the Hindu household, seeing this as a violation of a sacred space that should remain untainted by western cultural contamination. Ramabai became a target of his attack in 1890 when she was involved in organizing a memorial to Queen Victoria signed by 2,000 Maharashtrian women in support of the introduction of the colonial government's Age of Consent Bill, which aimed to raise the legal marriage age for Indian women to 14.[73]

Even more problematic for Ramabai were the religio-cultural tensions that arose between the American leadership of the Ramabai Association and the Indian Advisory Board of the Sharada Sadan. These tensions provide a good example of the conflicts that could arise within transnational networks when individuals positioned in very different local cultural contexts attempted to work together on collaborative projects. While co-operation had initially been facilitated by the long history of American Unitarians' connection with the Prarthana Samaj's brother organization, the Brahmo Samaj, the issue of caste soon became a source of conflict. Members of the Prarthana Samaj believed the Sharada Sadan should rigorously observe all the caste rules of Brahminism to ensure that the home remained

26 Clare Midgley

accepted by Hindus as suitable for high-caste Hindu widows. In contrast, Ramabai's supporters in the Ramabai Association in America saw caste as a social evil and opposed strict adherence to caste rules. The resultant conflict became a power struggle between the western financial backers of the school and its local Indian governing committee and resulted in the resignation of Prarthana Samaj members from the advisory board in 1890.[74] Ramabai found a way around this problem by relocating the school to Poona, but in 1893 all the Prarthana Samaj members of the new advisory board resigned after coming under sustained attack from Tilak and his followers when rumours spread that, under Ramabai's influence, several girls were planning to convert to Christianity at the Sharada Sadan.[75]

In the end, then, orthodox Hindus' worries about retaining caste purity and fears of Christian conversion led to the foundering of an educational project which Ramabai had tried to frame in such a way as to avoid the two flashpoints which had caused so many western educational initiatives among upper-caste Hindu women to founder. Responsibility for the demise of the Sharada Sadan, however, lay partly with Ramabai herself, as she had begun to invite girls at the school to join her in Christian prayer if they so wished. This was linked to the opening of a new phase in her own faith journey: she was moving away from the rationalist Unitarian Christianity that sat relatively comfortably alongside the reformist Hinduism of the Prarthana Samaj as she experienced an intense Christian spiritual reawakening. When she visited America in 1898 to report to the Ramabai Association at the end of the agreed ten-year funding period for her school, the Association was reconstituted as an evangelical Protestant organization, with Unitarians dropping out. With the organization's support, on her return to India Ramabai inaugurated the Mukti Mission outside Poona. Her new religious orientation was accompanied by a shift from working with small numbers of high-caste widows to working with thousands of lower caste girls and women, many of whom had been left destitute or orphaned by famine. The phase of Ramabai's life with which we have been concerned here had come to an end, and another phase was beginning.[76]

Conclusion

This chapter has offered a retelling of the story of the central twenty years of Pandita Ramabai's life that draws attention to the importance of her involvement in a transnational web of religious liberals and social reformers comprising members of the Bengal-based Brahmo Samaj, their close associates in the Bombay-centred Prarthana Samaj and a transatlantic Anglo-American network of Unitarian Christians. It has shown how this long-standing web of connections created crucial national and transnational spaces within which Ramabai was able to gain spiritual support at different stages of her faith journey from Hinduism through Brahmoism to Unitarian Christianity and practical support in developing and actualizing her feminist agenda for empowering Indian women. Ramabai's story also reveals the difficulties and challenges of moving between religions and cultures for an Indian woman activist in the late nineteenth century, an era of British imperial power and rising Indian nationalism and a time of intense conflict between Christian missionaries and Hindu revivalists. It exposes the complex set of specific challenges she faced in each of the distinct but interconnected national arenas of colonial India, imperial Britain and republican America, arenas within and among which she sought to pursue her intertwined faith and feminist journeys. It also reveals the feminist dimensions of the attraction the US held for liberal Indian nationalists at this period as an alternative space through which to engage with the west outside the dynamic of British imperial power relations.

This case study illuminates the transnational context within which debates on the 'woman question' and feminist activism developed in the late nineteenth-century world. Liberal religious networks, it is clear, provided one important set of spaces within which these debates and actions took place. My main focus here has been on the Brahmo-Unitarian network's impact on Ramabai in her development as a pioneering Indian feminist. I have sought to address Tanika Sarkar's call for explanations of Indian feminism as 'a modern Indian phenomenon, and not simply as a foreign implant' by helping to create a more 'complex framework of understanding' of 'the relationship between gender and modernity', which moves beyond the dynamics of the colonizer / colonized binary to take into account the 'vastly enhanced communication and transport recourses' that 'brought local, national and global identities into interaction' and 'allowed for a questioning of the fundamental premises of the ideologies of gender difference'.[77] It can be concluded that Ramabai's faith and feminist journeys within the transnational spaces created by this network enabled her to develop and enact the conviction that it was Indian women, not the Indian male reformers or western feminists from whom she gained support, who were best placed to take the lead in improving the lives of their sisters. As she modeled through her own life, Indian women could achieve this by setting up woman-run organizations and becoming social reformers, educationalists and representatives of women in the political arena of the India National Congress.

Studying Ramabai's place within the *informal transnational web* connecting Brahmos with Unitarians, helps us appreciate that the emergence of modern feminisms was a transnational, not simply a western, phenomenon. This is a truth that tends to be obscured when we simply focus on the *formal international organizations* of women that emerged at the end of the nineteenth century – which were indeed western dominated.[78] Ramabai's life, and those of other Brahmo women active in women's organizations and as pioneering university students and doctors, also suggests a *chronology* which undermines a diffusionist western invention / eastern imitation model of modern feminist development. Instead, the mid-1860s to mid-1890s emerge as a crucial period in the transnational story of feminist mobilization both within and between India, Britain and the US.

In this context, it is of course equally important to explore the Brahmo-Unitarian network's impact on the development of modern feminisms in both Britain and the US. While it has not been possible to pursue this angle within the scope of this chapter, we can note that, with the appearance of Ramabai and a number of other Indian women on the transnational stage in the late nineteenth century, western recognition of the potential of Indian women's *own* agency to bring about improvements in women's position in India began to dawn. As Ramabai's

28 Clare Midgley

life suggests, conversations and friendships developed between Brahmo women and British and American liberal Christian and theist women, and these were based on a recognition of common ground in approaches to religion and commitments to improving the position of women. This sense of identification, which bridged Hindu-Christian and colonizer-colonized divides, jostled uneasily with contemporary British imperial and broader western discourses that, in both their evangelical missionary and secular feminist inflections, represented Indian women as silent and passive victims who needed to be saved by western men and women.[79] In Ramabai's own writings, stressing both Indian women's potential for agency and their victimization, and in her attempts to assert leadership on the transnational stage as an Indian woman rescuer of her oppressed Indian sisters while drawing on the support of western activists, we see her own inevitably complex positioning in relation to these contesting western perceptions and agendas.

Notes

1 K. Sangari and S. Vaid, eds., *Recasting Women: Essays in Colonial History*, New Delhi: Kali, 1989; J. Krishnamurthy, *Women in Colonial India: Essays on Survival, Work and the State*, New Delhi: Oxford University Press, 1989; L. Mani, *Contentious Traditions. The Debate on Sati in Colonial India*, Berkeley: University of California Press, 1998. For the theoretical underpinnings of this scholarship see G.C. Spivak, 'Can the Subaltern Speak?' in C. Nelson and L. Grossbert, eds., *Marxism and the Interpretation of Culture*, Hampshire: Macmillan, 1988, pp. 271–313.

2 A. Burton, *Burdens of History. British Feminist, Indian Women and Imperial Culture, 1865–1915*, Chapel Hill: University of North Carolina Press, 1992; C. Midgley, *Feminism and Empire. Women Activists in Imperial Britain, 1790–1860*, London: Routledge, 2007; P. Parmar and V. Amos, 'Challenging imperial feminism', *Feminist Review*, 17, 1984, 3–19.

3 R. Kumar, *A History of Doing,* New Delhi: Kali, 1993; N. Kumar, ed., *Women as Subjects: South Asian Histories*, New Delhi: Stree, 1994; B. Ray, ed., *From the Seams of History: Essays on Indian Women*, New Delhi: Oxford India, 1995; G. Forbes, *Women in Modern India*, Cambridge, UK: Cambridge University Press, 1996; P. Anagol, *The Emergence of Feminism in India, 1850–1920*, Aldershot: Ashgate, 2005. For early critiques of postcolonial feminist scholarship for denying Indian women's agency see A. Loomba, 'Dead women tell no tales: Issues of female subjectivity, subaltern agency and tradition in colonial and postcolonial writings on widow-immolation in India', *History Workshop Journal*, 36, 1993, 209–227; J. Nair, 'On the question of agency in Indian feminist historiography', *Gender & History*, 6:1, 1994, 82–100; for a lucid recent statement of alternative approaches, stressing Indian men's and women's agency in the reshaping of gender relations in colonial India see T. Sarkar, 'Gendering of Public and Private Selves in Colonial Times', in D. M. Peers and N. Gooptu, eds., *India and the British Empire*, Oxford: Oxford University Press, 2012, pp. 284–312.

4 Anagol, *The Emergence of Feminism*, p. 182.

5 E. Boehmer, *Empire, the National and the Postcolonial 1890–1920: Resistance in Interaction*, Oxford: Oxford University Press, 2002; L. Gandhi, *Affective Communities. Anticolonial Thought, Fin-de-Siècle Radicalism, and the Politics of Friendship*, Durham, NC: Duke University Press, 2006; D. Ghosh and D. Kennedy, eds., *Decentring Empire. Britain, India and the Transcolonial World,* Hyderabad: Orient Longman, 2006; S. Bose and K. Manjapra, eds., *Cosmopolitan Thought Zones. South Asia and the Global Circulation of Ideas*, Basingstoke: Palgrave Macmillan, 2010; S. Kapila, *An Intellectual History for India*, Cambridge: Cambridge University Press, 2010.

6 Ramabai wrote a short autobiography 15 years before her death: Pandita Ramabai, *A Testimony of Our Inexhaustible Treasure,* Kedgaon: Pandita Ramabai Mukti Mission, 10th

ed., 1977 [reprint of original edition Kedgaon: Mukti Press, 1907]. There is no definitive modern biography but useful accounts include P. Sengupta, *Pandita Ramabai: Her Life and Work*, London: Asia Publishing House, 1970; S. M. Adhav, *Pandita Ramabai*, Madras: The Christian Literature Society, 1979.

7 'Pandita Ramabai – Courage and Spirituality', *Times of India*, 7 April, 1922; N. McNicol, *Pandita Ramabai*, Calcutta: Associated Press, 1926.

8 M. Kosambi, 'Multiple contestations: Pandita Ramabai's educational and missionary activities in late nineteenth-century India and abroad', *Women's History Review*, 7:2, 1998, 193–208; M. Kosambi, 'Tracing the voice: Pandita Ramabai's life through her landmark texts', *Australian Feminist Studies*, 19:43, 2004, 19–28; A. Burton, 'Colonial encounters in late-Victorian England: Pandita Ramabai at Cheltenham and Wantage 1883–6', *Feminist Review*, 49, Spring, 1995, 29–49; A. Burton, *At the Heart of Empire. Indians and the Colonial Encounter in Late-Victorian Britain*, Berkeley: University of California Press, 1998, pp. 72–109; U. Chakravarti, *Rewriting History. The Life and Times of Pandita Ramabai*, New Delhi: Kali for Women, 1998; G. Viswanathan, *Outside the Fold. Conversion, Modernity and Belief*, Princeton, New Jersey: Princeton University Press, 1998, pp. 118–152.

9 D. Kopf, *The Brahmo Samaj and the Shaping of the Modern Indian Mind*, New Delhi: Atlantic, 1996; S. Lavan, *Unitarians and India: A Study in Encounter and Response*, Boston: Skinner House, 1977.

10 For an early stage of this conflict see Mani, *Contentious Traditions*.

11 For differing interpretations of the collaboration between Sen and Carpenter see Antoinette Burton, 'Fearful bodies into disciplined subjects: Pleasure, romance, and the family drama of colonial reform in Mary Carpenter's 'Six Months in India', *Signs*, 20, 1995, 545–574; Clare Midgley, 'Mary Carpenter and the Brahmo Samaj of India: A transnational perspective on social reform in the age of empire', *Women's History Review*, 22:2, 2013, 363–386. See also Sarkar, 'Gendering of Public and Private Selves', pp. 291–293 for a reevaluation of liberal middle-class religious and social reform movements such as the Brahmo Samaj as having a more transgressive impact on Hindu gender orthodoxies than earlier interpretations of them as 'denationalised' agents of western cultural hegemony have allowed.

12 M. Borthwick, *The Changing Role of Women in Bengal 1849–1905*, Princeton: Princeton University Press, 1984; M. Karlekar, *Voices from Within. Early Personal Narratives of Bengali Women*, Delhi, Oxford University Press, 1991; M. Bhattacharya and A. Sen, *Talking of Power: Early Writings of Bengali Women from the Mid-nineteenth Century to the Beginning of the Twentieth Century*, Kolkata: Stree, 2003; G. Murshid, *Reluctant Debutante: Response of Bengali Women to Modernization, 1849–1905*, Rajshahi: Rajshahi University, 1983.

13 K. Gleadle, *The Early Feminists: Radical Unitarians and the Emergence of the Women's Rights Movement, 1831–51*, Basingstoke: Palgrave, 1995; R. Watts, 'Rational Religion and Feminism: The Challenge of Unitarianism in the Nineteenth Century', in S. Morgan, ed., *Women, Religion and Feminism in Britain*, Basingstoke: Palgrave, 2002, pp. 24–39; J. Rendall, '"A Moral Engine"? Feminism, Liberalism and the English Woman's Journal', in J. Rendall, ed., *Equal or Different: Women's Politics 1800–1914*, Oxford: Blackwell, 1987, pp. 112–140; D. M. Emerson, ed., *Standing Before Us: Unitarian Universalist Women and Social Reform 1776–1936*, Boston: Skinner House Books, 2000; T. K. Wayne, *Woman Thinking: Feminism and Transcendentalism in Nineteenth-Century America*, Lanham: Lexington Books, 2005.

14 My framing of Ramabai's travels and life as an intersecting faith and feminist journey draws inspiration from Alison Twells, '"An Africa of religious life": Fredrika Bremer's American faith journey, 1849–1851', *Journal of Women's History*, 25:1 (Spring 2013), 158–181.

15 Pandita Ramabai, *A Testimony*, pp. 1–9.

16 For evaluations of Roy's significance as a religious and social reformer see B. C. Robertson, *Raja Rammohun Roy: The Father of Modern India*, New Delhi. 1995; D. Killingly, *Rammohun Roy in Hindu and Christian Tradition*, Newcastle upon Tyne: Grevatt & Grevatt, 1993; V. C. Joshi, ed., *Rammojun Roy and the Process of Modernization in India*, Delhi: Vikas, 1975. For Roy's impact in Britain see L. Zastoupil, *Rammohun Roy and the Making of*

30 Clare Midgley

Victorian Britain, New York: Palgrave Macmillan, 2010. For the transnational commemoration of Roy see C. Midgley, 'Transoceanic commemoration and connections between Bengali Brahmos and British and American Unitarians', *The Historical Journal*, 54:3, Sept 2011, 773–996.

17 Sen led a successful campaign for the colonial government to introduce a special Brahmo Marriage Act, setting the minimum marriage age as 14, but his daughter was just below that age when he agreed to her marriage, causing outrage among his supporters in both India and Britain (see Kopf, *The Brahmo Samaj*, pp. 324–329). For a translation of the text of Ramabai's address to Brahmo women, see McNicol, *Pandita Ramabai*, pp. 44–45.

18 Ramabai, *A Testimony*, pp. 21–22.

19 Pandita Ramabai, *A Testimony*, pp. 21–22; McNicol, *Pandita Ramabai*, pp. 42–44, which includes a translation of the address from Bengali women.

20 For Dall's mission to Calcutta see Lavan, *American Unitarians and India*, pp. 81–103.

21 S. Dobson Collet, ed., *Keshub Chunder Sen's English Visit*, London: Strahan & Co., 1871. Ramabai refers to Sen's account in an article she later published in Britain about her visit to Rammohun Roy's tomb: Veritas, 'My pilgrimage to Bristol', *Journal of the National Indian Association*, 179, Nov. 1885, 554.

22 C. Heimsath, *Indian Nationalism and Hindu Social Reform*, Princeton: Princeton University Press, 1964, pp. 72–112.

23 M. Kosambi, *Pandita Ramabai's Feminist and Christian Conversions. Focus on Stri Dharma-Neet,* Bombay, India: Research Centre for Women's Studies, SNDT Women's University, 1995, pp. 45–47.

24 For the formation of the Arya Mahila Samaj see Sengupta, *Pandita Ramabai Saraswati*, pp. 348–51; for the organization in the wider context of social reform and the 'woman question' in Maharastra see Anagol, *The Emergence of Feminism;* Chakravarti, *Rewriting History*.

25 *Bamabodhini Patrika* [Journal for the Enlightenment of Women], Jan 1883, 2–3. I would like to thank Sahana Bajpaie for this and other translations from the journal. For a discussion of the journal's use of western Unitarian women as role models see Clare Midgley, 'Liberal religion and the "woman question" between east and west: perspectives from a Bengali women's journal', *Gender & History*, 25:3, Nov. 2013, 445–460.

26 See W. W. Hunter, *England's Work in India*, London: Smith, Elder & Co., 1881, pp. 46–52 for Hunter's positive views of the Brahmo Samaj, pro-Unitarian position, negative views on Christian missionaries, and interest in Ramabai's activities in Bengal.

27 M. Kosambi, trans. and ed., *Pandita Ramabai's American Encounter. The Peoples of the United States (1889)*, Bloomington: Indiana University Press, 2003, p. 59, p. 242, note 13.

28 Ramabai arranged to meet the former Governor of Bombay following her arrival in London, seeking to gain his support in promoting this appeal for support to Queen Victoria and the British Prime Minister – see 'The Cry of Indian Women', letter from Pandita Ramabai, London 11th June 1883 to Sir Bartle Frere, reproduced in M. Kosambi, ed., *Pandita Ramabai Through Her Own Words: Selected Works*, New Delhi: Oxford University Press, 2000, pp. 105–114.

29 Adhav, *Pandita Ramabai*, pp. 7–8, 10.

30 See Kosambi, *Pandita Ramabai Through Her Own Words*, p. 8–9.

31 Letter from Pandita Ramabai to Canon Butler, 3rd July, 1885, printed in A. B. Shah, ed., *The Letters and Correspondence of Pandita Ramabai. Compiled by Sister Geraldine,* Bombay: Maharashtra State Board for Literature and Culture, 1977, p. 74.

32 R. Roy, *The Precepts of Jesus,* Calcutta: Baptist Mission Press, 1820; K. C. Sen, *Jesus Christ: Europe and Asia,* 3rd ed., Calcutta: Indian Mirror Press, 1869.

33 Adhav, *Pandita Ramabai*, pp. 129; for a discussion of Roy and Sen's reverence for Christ see M. M. Thomas, *The Acknowledged Christ of the Indian Renaissance*, London: SCM Press, 1969, pp. 1–37; 56–81.

34 Letter from Sister Geraldine, C. S. M. V Wantage to the Rev. C. Gore [n.d.], reproduced in Shah, ed., *The Letters,* p. 82. Ramabai's correspondence with Sister Geraldine on religious matters, selected from notebooks compiled by Sister Geraldine, can be followed in detail in this publication.

35 Sister Geraldine's preface in Shah, ed., *The Letters*, p. 4.
36 Letter from Sister Geraldine, CSMV at Bath to Pandita Ramabai, October 1885, printed in Shah, ed., *The Letters*, p. 102.
37 Letter from Pandita Ramabai to Sister Geraldine, Cheltenham, 7 November 1885, printed in Shah, ed., *The Letters*, p. 112.
38 This support is underplayed in existing scholarship – see, for example, Burton, *At the Heart of Empire*, pp. 72–109.
39 F. Max Muller, *Auld Lang Syne. Second Series. My Indian Friends*, London and Bombay: Longmans, Green and Co., 1899, pp. 121–129. For Müller's continuing interest in Ramabai's work see *The Life and Letters of the Right Honourable Friedrich Max Müller*, ed. by his wife, 2 vols, London, New York and Bombay: Longman, Green, and Co., 1902, Vol. 2, pp. 217–218 and 252–253.
40 'Puna Prarthana Somaj' in *The Brahmo Year-Book for 1882*, London and Edinburgh: Williams and Norgate, p. 48; letter from Pandita Ramabai to Sister Geraldine, Ash Wednesday, 1884, printed in Shah, ed., *The Letters*, pp. 23–24.
41 Letter from Pandita Ramabai to Dorothea Beale, [?1885] in Shah, *The Letters*, p. 120.
42 *Bamabodini Patrika*, Aug.–Sept. 1869, pp. 76–77; Frances Power Cobbe, *Life of Frances Power Cobbe*, London: Swan Sonnenschein & Co, 1904 ed. [original ed. 1894], p. 495; Frances Power Cobbe, 'The Hindoo Marriage Law', *Times* (London), 1 Oct 1887:6 [The Times Digital Archive, accessed 23 August 2013].
43 Veritas, 'My pilgrimage to Bristol'. Before she came to Britain, Ramabai had been working on translating into Marathi a Bengali-language biography of Roy written by a Brahmo, Nagendranath Chatterji (see *The Brahmo Year-Book for 1882*, p. 48). Images of Roy's funerary monument and portrait are included in Midgley, 'Transoceanic commemoration'.
44 For the question of dress reform among Brahmo women see Murshid, *Reluctant Debutante*, pp. 241–9. A photograph of Ramabai and her daughter during their time in England, taken from the archives of the Pandita Ramabai Mukti mission, forms a frontispiece to M. Kosambi, trans. and ed., *Pandita Ramabai's American Encounter*.
45 Letter from Pandita Ramabai to Sister Geraldine, 12 May 1885 printed in Shah, ed., *The Letters and Correspondence of Pandita Ramabai.*, pp. 58–61. For Maharashtran women's greater freedoms in comparison to Bengali women see Anagol, *The Emergence of Indian Feminism*, pp. 80–81.
46 Letter from Sister Geraldine, CSMV at Bath to Pandita Ramabai, Oct. 1885. Shah, *The Letters*, p. 107.
47 In the final stage of her time in Britain Sister Geraldine arranged for Ramabai to teach Sanskrit at Cheltenham Ladies' College, but there she remained under intense scrutiny from the imperial Anglican establishment, who pressed the school's Anglican principal, Dorothea Beale, to ensure Ramabai did not gain a public platform – see Burton, *At the Heart of Empire*, pp. 72–109.
48 This support is skated over in existing scholarship: see, for example, Lavan, *Unitarians and India*; Kosambi, *Pandita Ramabai's American Encounter*.
49 Letter from Prof. Rachel L. Bodley, Dean, Women's Medical College, Philadelphia, to Pandita Ramabai, 28th December 1885, printed in Shah, ed., *The Letters*, pp. 164–166.
50 Letter from Pandita Ramabai to Dorothea Beale, Cheltenham, 12 December 1885, reprinted in Shah, ed., *The Letters*, pp. 163.
51 Kosambi, *Pandita Ramabai's American Encounter*, p. 22.
52 Pandita Ramabai Sarvasvati, *The High-Caste Hindu Woman*, 2nd ed., Philadelphia: J. B. Rodgers, 1887, p. 106.
53 Ibid.
54 Borthwick, *The Changing Role of Women in Bengal*, pp. 142–145.
55 Ramabai, *The High-Caste Hindu Woman*, pp. 110–114.
56 Ibid., p. 114.
57 Ibid., p. 117.
58 Kosambi, ed., *Pandita Ramabai's American Encounter*, p. 23. The work of the Association, and its monitoring of Ramabai's activities when she returned to India, can be traced in

32 Clare Midgley

its annual reports – see, for example, *Report of the Annual Meeting of Ramabai Association held March 11, 1891*, Boston: Lend a Hand Co., 1891.

59 'A statement by Sister Geraldine, C. S. M.V., Wantage', printed in Shah, ed., *The Letters*, pp. 191–192.

60 Caroline Healey Dall, *The Life of Dr. Anandabai Joshee, A Kinswoman of the Pundita Ramabai*, Boston: Roberts Brothers, 1888, p. iv.

61 For American women missionaries in India see M.C. Singh, *Gender, Religion and 'Heathen Lands'. American Missionary Women in South Asia (1860s–1940s)*, New York: Garland Publishing, 2000.

62 Letter from Pandita Ramabai to Dorothea Beale, Philadelphia, April 1886, sending her the gift of *The Oriental Christ*, printed in Shah, ed., *The Letters*, p. 171; Lavan, *Unitarians and India*, pp. 131–135.

63 'Samayik prasanga' [Current affairs], *Bamabodhini Patrika*, November 1886.

64 *Bamabodhini Patrika*, May 1886, p. 62.

65 Kosambi, trans. and ed., *Pandita Ramabai's American Encounter*, pp. 170–171.

66 Kosambi, *Pandita Ramabai's American Encounter*, p. 36; Leila J. Rupp, *Worlds of Women: The Making of an International Women's Movement*, Princeton; Princeton University Press, 1997 discusses the domination of this and other early 'bourgeois' international women's organizations by elite white women.

67 *Indu Prakash*, 18 March, 1889, as quoted in Sengupta, *Pandita Ramabai Saraswarti*, p. 183. Dadabhai Naoriji became the first Indian to be elected to the British Parliament in 1892.

68 Sengupta, *Pandita Ramabai Saraswarti*, pp. 192–195; *The Times of India*, 30 December, 1889.

69 Adhav, *Pandita Ramabai*, p. 183.

70 Shah, ed., *The Letters*, p. xxi.

71 Rev. Babu Padamunju, article in *Dnyanodaya*, 48, March 1889, 102, as quoted in English translation in Adhav, *Pandita Ramabai*, p. 183.

72 Adhav, *Pandita Ramabai*, pp. 187–88. Ramabai's response, which Adhav translates from the Marathi, appeared in *Dnyananodaya*, 48, 25 July, 1889, p. 237.

73 M. Kosambi, *At the Intersection of Gender Reform and Religious Belief: Pandita Ramabai's Contribution and the Age of Consent Controversy*, Bombay: Research Centre for Women's Studies, S.N.D.T. Women's University, 1993; Anagol, *The Emergence of Feminism*, pp. 209–218.

74 Adhav, ed., *The Letters*, p. xxiv.

75 Shah, ed., *The Letters*, p. xxiv.

76 For accounts of her second conversion experience and life as an evangelical Protestant running the Mukti mission see Ramabai, *Testimony*; Sengupta, *Pandita Ramabai Saraswati*, pp. 227–296; McNicol, *Pandita Ramabai*, pp. 79ff.

77 Sarkar, 'Gendering of Public and Private Selves', pp. 286, 284.

78 L. J. Rupp, *Worlds of Women: The Making of an International Women's Movement*, Princeton, NJ: Princeton University Press, 1997.

79 For a discussion of US female missionary imperialism see Mary A. Renda, 'Conclusion. Doing Everything: Religion, Race and Empire in the US Protestant Women's Missionary Enterprise', in B. Reeves-Ellington, K. K. Sklar and C. A. Shemo, eds., *Competing Kingdoms: Women, Mission, Nation, and the American Protestant Empire*, Durham, NC: Duke University Press, 2010, pp. 384–385.

2

THE INTERNATIONAL LABOUR ORGANIZATION, TRANSNATIONAL WOMEN'S NETWORKS, AND THE QUESTION OF UNPAID WORK IN THE INTERWAR WORLD[1]

Susan Zimmermann

When women's and gender history emerged as a branch of historical writing in its own right in the 1970s and 1980s, the question of women's unpaid labour played a key role in both historical inquiry and conceptual debate. In contrast, this important theme is rather marginalized in the new global labour history, in recent transnational and intersectional gender history, and in the literature on gender in global governance. This chapter addresses this gap in the literature, seeking to develop a more inclusive global labour and gender history. It focuses on the development of gendered international labour policy in the interwar period which touched upon the question of unpaid labour in the service of social reproduction. I explore how these international policies on unpaid work were developed by the International Labour Organization (ILO) with reference to broader transnational arguments and debates, debates in which women's networks played key roles.

The ILO was established in conjunction with the League of Nations in the aftermath of World War I. Its founders declared that lasting peace had to be based 'upon social justice'. The ILO was to contribute to achieving this double goal through international labour Conventions and Recommendations aimed at the improvement of the conditions of labour everywhere in the world.[2] In the interwar period the ILO formed a key point of reference for transnational activism, sustained by many different individuals, networks, groups and organizations who aimed to bring about social reform and betterment in the world of work. Women's committees and organizations were prominently represented in this transnational activism and in the unfolding transnational argument on unpaid labour. They did not have, however, any formalized access to the ILO, which, through its tripartite institutional framework, brought together governments and representatives of both employers and workers. The newly established organization quickly developed into an important machine for creating and monitoring the implementation of international labour legislation. The politics of the ILO and the related transnational debates contributed to the evolution of gendered global governance on a variety of levels. The

34 Susan Zimmermann

influence and 'soft power' of the ILO in framing discourse and politics over labour issues internationally and within many countries and territories went well beyond the actual adoption, ratification and implementation of international labour standards. The transnational debates on international labour policies played some role in generating this broader impact, and they made their own contribution to shaping a transnational discourse on gendered labour policy. In addition, the politics of the ILO brought about policy innovation in labour law. When preparing new international instruments, the International Labour Office, the permanent body of the ILO seated in Geneva, carefully studied preexisting territorial legislation and practice, but it then added its own political thumbprint. In this process of internationalizing labour law, the ILO contributed to the globalization and interlinking of divergent territorially grounded social policies relating variously to paid and unpaid labour.

Focusing on the international policies of unpaid work developed by the ILO, and the related debates, this chapter explores why and how they were characterized by divergent standards and approaches as they related to two unequal worlds of paid work: to 'free' wage labour as originating in the industrial revolution in the Global North and increasingly spreading over the globe, and to 'unfree' labour in the Global South originating for the most part in the economic policies of the Western imperial powers. I argue that 'thinking together', as elements of a common global politics of unpaid labour, these different standards and approaches reveals otherwise invisible transnational connections that were constitutive of the emerging gendered global governance in the arena of labour policy. In addition, such 'thinking together' sheds new light on the precarious status of social reproduction in modern capitalist society and on its precarious relationship with both 'free' and 'unfree' paid labour. My chapter, in other words, aims to develop a more inclusive framework for thinking about gendered global labour history by foregrounding the international policies of unpaid work as they related to different world regions and to free and unfree labour.

The ILO in the interwar period was strongly dominated by the major European powers, many of whom ruled over large overseas empires. The organization pursued its policies on unpaid labour within the framework of two distinct sets of international labour standards. A first group of standards emerged in response to the conditions of free labour in the industrial and industrializing countries, still predominantly located in the Northern Hemisphere. In the period from the late 1920s to the outbreak of World War II, the ILO then developed a second set of international instruments aimed at restricting and regulating particularly oppressive forms of labour to which non-white populations in the Southern Hemisphere – including colonies, the mandates of the League of Nations, and a number of 'special' countries – were subjected. These forms of labour, which involved forced and contract labour in particular, were commonly associated with the term 'unfree' labour, though the ILO, throughout the interwar period, addressed them as 'native' or 'indigenous' labour; the related standards were deemed as referring to 'special' circumstances.[3] ILO labour standards belonging to both of these sets of instruments were in principle conceived of as globally applicable, while ILO Conventions became binding for a given territory only if the relevant authority decided to ratify them.

In this context, three elements of the international policies of unpaid work can be identified. The first comprised the protection of motherhood at work – maternity policies directed at women workers prior to and after confinement. The second element addressed the question of material support for the (otherwise) unpaid care activities carried out by woman workers, by other women, or by families – family policies. These two elements belonged to the group of policies which emerged with reference to free labour in the industrialized world; the related labour standards were deemed 'universal' and framed in such a way that, in principle, they could have also been implemented in contexts where unfree labour was put to use. The third element concerned the regulation of the relationship between unpaid work within the 'native community'[4] and paid work in non-self-governing territories – subsistence policies. These formed part of the second set of 'special' standards, which addressed extremely oppressive labour relations to which non-white populations were frequently subjected.

My analysis of how the international policies of unpaid work related to free and unfree labour is inspired by the insight that labour for social reproduction has been the constitutive 'other' of paid labour, and thus of both free and unfree labour, in the modern world. However, the relationship between unpaid work and paid labour has been asymmetric, variegated, and fraught with tension, and these tensions have had an important impact on the shape and development of free and unfree labour. The involvement of individuals, many of them women, in unpaid work has served to construct them as unreliable, or not fully available workers, a fact that in turn has contributed to their precarious status in the world of paid work. In parallel, unpaid work has served as a means allowing employers and societies to keep the cost of social reproduction, and thus wages to be paid and social expenditure, low. Finally, involvement in paid labour has tended to result in tremendous pressure on the work performed in the sphere of social reproduction. In industrial countries, measures aimed at easing that squeeze as a rule implied costly transformations of women's unpaid into paid care work. In regions with functioning subsistence agriculture, and thus a sphere of social reproduction relatively or partly independent from paid labour, the squeeze could also be eased by reducing the amount of paid work that was performed, a fact that in many cases has had visible repercussions in terms of particular forms of unfreedom in the world of paid work.

This chapter demonstrates how these tensions between paid and unpaid work lay at the core of the development, and the contention over, the international policies of unpaid work. Each of the following three sections is dedicated to one of the three core elements of these policies.

Motherhood at work: de/constructing the social meaning of maternity protection for the woman worker

The ILO's *Convention concerning the Employment of Women before and after Childbirth* (the Maternity Protection Convention, or C3) was one of six international labour standards adopted in 1919. It belonged to the large group of ILO labour standards which, while conceived of or defined as universal, had their origins in labour

36 Susan Zimmermann

conditions in the industrialized world. The Convention covered women workers in non-family businesses in both the industrial and commercial sections but did not cover women working in agriculture. It prescribed the following standards for these workers: six weeks of compulsory leave after confinement; up to six weeks of leave before confinement upon production of a related medical certificate; medical care in confinement; dismissal protection during the period of leave; a minimum standard of compensation for the loss of earnings during the leave, to be paid from social security or public funds; and last but not least, breaks at work for nursing mothers.[5]

The first ILO instrument which negotiated the relationship between maternity – here conceptualized as unpaid work – and paid labour thus constructed maternity as a sex-specific obstacle to, or handicap in, paid work. To protect the women concerned, C3 called for compulsory temporary exclusion of those women workers facing the handicap of maternity from the active labour force and their material support during this period. In confining the welfare aspect of its provisions to women engaged in paid employment, the Convention ensured that its focus, while construing paid labour and maternity as mutually exclusive, was on paid labour. It left open whether employers should – for example, through insurance schemes – at least indirectly co-finance the maternity benefit or whether funding should come directly from taxpayers and thus from society at large, through the state.

The International Labour Office conceived of the Maternity Protection Convention as a minimum standard and a core element of its program of sex-specific labour protection for working women. It rested on the principle that there were 'consequences in the field of labour of the physical differentiation between men and women'.[6] From the point of view of the Office and those other groupings within the ILO who supported the maternity policies enshrined in C3, the Convention simply acknowledged the inevitable social implications of this fact in the world of work and sought to ease the tension between childbirth and paid work. Conceived of as one element of the emerging international politics of unpaid work, C3, in separating out maternity from the whole range of unpaid work for the family and household that was shouldered in a disproportionate manner by women, aimed to ease the tension between (this one element of) unpaid work and paid labour without calling into question the fundamental subordination in modern society of the necessities of care work to the necessities of paid work.

For a long time, Albert Thomas, the Director of the International Labour Office, was convinced that C3 would not and could not ever be involved in the ongoing argument on special protection for women versus legal equality between the sexes in international labour law. This was so because even 'the partisans of absolute equality are obliged to recognise . . . that maternity is an inequality imposed by nature itself' and that 'the need of protecting motherhood . . . could not be better served than by a Convention prohibiting work before and after childbirth.'[7] Yet Thomas's hope that the ILO's maternity legislation could be kept out of the conflict over special labour protection for women was to be frustrated. From the late 1920s onward the International Labour Office was confronted with mounting

The International Labour Organization **37**

internationally concerted criticism of all elements of its sex-specific labour standards. The Open Door International (ODI), a feminist organization founded in 1929 and backed by the Equal Rights International (ERI, 1930/1931) – an organization which aimed to bring about an all-encompassing international equal rights treaty – pursued a politics of strict legal equality in labour law and was especially vocal in voicing this critique. The campaign for legal equality pursued by these new organizations contributed to the evolution of an elaborate transnational argument on international labour law, which engaged the ILO and some of its close associates and many international women's organizations and networks, including socialist and non-socialist groups. The ILO's maternity policies came under direct attack from 1930, when the Swedish government unsuccessfully attempted to get the ILO to revise C3, with the aim of individualizing and making more flexible the protection measures contained in the Convention. Workers' representatives in particular dismissed this request as simply weakening the existing standard, and Albert Thomas made clear that the International Labour Office judged such a course of action 'impossible'.[8]

The international network of feminists demanding legal equality in labour law came up with more definite and far-reaching alternatives to the ILO's maternity policies. The Open Door Council, a British organization founded in 1926 and strongly involved in the ODI later on, made it plain in 1928 that it was 'opposed to that part of the Washington Maternity Convention which forbids a woman to decide for herself whether or not she shall engage in paid work' as interfering with 'a woman's inherent human right to decide for herself'.[9] In this perspective any benefit aimed at enabling a woman for a certain time to focus on unpaid care for an infant had to be conditional on the woman worker's own decision to withdraw temporarily from the workforce. The ODI launched an initiative against the ILO's maternity policies on its foundation in 1929 and arrived at a definitive statement of its maternity policy in 1935.[10] The assumption 'that nothing could help the mother as a worker, vis-à-vis the employer, which put her in a different position from that of other workers' in the world of paid work formed its point of departure. Starting from this basis, the ODI came up with four interrelated fundamental principles. First, labour law was to handle pregnancy and confinement in the same way as other incapacitations for work by reason of accident or illness; 'where a medical certificate is required in the one case, it should also be required in the other.' Second, there should be no compulsory leave of absence to ensure women's legal autonomy to conclude contracts without gender-specific restrictions. Third, the ODI rejected all maternity-related regulations which would 'place special burdens on a woman's employer', among them maternity-related dismissal protection and regulations about (partial) wage continuation in the case of women's absence due to maternity. Their reasoning was that these burdens would, in practice, 'be borne by the woman herself', because any given employer would inevitably activate the well-known 'code on which he acts' when confronted with such provisions, by not hiring women, dismissing women upon the first sign of pregnancy and paying them lower wages. Fourth, the ODI explicitly excluded from its programme

38 Susan Zimmermann

motherhood-related benefits other than those given to childbearing women in direct connection with their status as incapacitated workers.[11]

The formula carved out by the ODI is remarkable when read against both the organization's overall program for creating gender-neutral labour law and the ILO's position regarding maternity-related labour protection. It is most probably the only instance when the ODI conceded that the law needed to reflect on or relate to pregiven sexual difference, namely to the fact that 'maternity places a disability on industrial workers.'[12] At the same time the ODI, in stark contrast to the ILO's approach, aimed to rebuild labour law in such a way that the social consequences of maternity as a pregiven sex-specific function would not assume any gender-specific social meaning in the world of gainful employment. Rather than aiming to reconcile women's paid work and maternity, as was the aim of C3, the ODI construed maternity in such a way that in the world of paid work it would not socially or legally differentiate women. While C3 construed the woman worker as a category distinct from the male worker, the ODI wanted to free women's paid work from the burden of engagement in maternity and thus, by assimilating female and male paid work, avoid the construction of women as a separate category of workers. Women, in other words, should be as free as men when engaging in free labour; free waged labour was conceptualized as free from any social consequences from becoming a mother.

When confronted with the ODI's initial initiative 'against the Maternity Convention' launched in 1929, Albert Thomas of the International Labour Office, in an internal document, condemned it as an 'absurdity, and, so I take the liberty to say, a monstrosity'.[13] In 1930 he declared publicly that because of the 'evil effects of industrial work on the health of working mothers when the conditions were not subject to regulations' he was not willing 'to accept any arguments against the value of a Convention for the protection of maternity such as had been put forward by certain feminist groups'.[14] In taking this position the International Labour Office drew on far-reaching support from many international women's organizations and committees, which disagreed with the stance of the ODI, and from international trade union and socialist movements and organizations.

The ILO managed to ward off all attacks against the standards set by the Maternity Protection Convention and C3 remained set in stone until 1952. C3 thus operated as an instrument that both internationalized and globalized a gender policy based on a particular conceptualization of the relationship between paid and unpaid work. The International Labour Office managed to effectively ignore alternative visions that insisted that it was possible, and good for woman workers, not to bestow social meaning on bodily sexual difference. Demands for more flexibility, individualization, and women's choice, some of which aimed at avoiding the construction of woman workers as 'different', and which were supported by a variety of equal rights groups in Europe and the US, were dismissed as lowering the standards of protection, i.e. widening the class gap in the world of work. The ILO, in other words, trusted that if labour – with the support of the ILO – was politically strong then employers could not turn the fact that the woman worker was constructed as different into woman workers' discrimination on the labour market and at the workplace. In contrast, those opposed to constructing the woman worker as different felt that it was impossible to avoid this consequence, and some of them were prepared to tolerate the lowering of labour standards to avoid such result.

Taking care of the family: how women's unpaid work did not enter international labour law

Another challenge to the ILO's policies of unpaid work arose from the related area of family allowance policy broadly defined, with regard to which there were deep divisions among women's networks and organizations which cultivated an interest in women's work.

Again with an implicit focus on industrial countries, the ILO deliberated possible international action that would, directly or indirectly, attach a measurable value to women's unpaid work insofar as it related to the care for children and construe it as a (partial) alternative to wage work. Already before World War I, related ideas had been advocated under the label of motherhood endowment or motherhood insurance by the women's movement in particular. This section discusses why and how in the interwar period the ILO did not commit itself to the internationalization of such policies, policies which would have challenged both the subordination of unpaid work to paid work and the disregard for the material value of unpaid work in the industrial world. When contrasted with the policies over unfree labour in the Global South, discussed in the following section, it will become apparent that the difference between how paid labour related to unpaid labour in the context of industrial societies as opposed to subsistence-based societies plays a key role in explaining the ILO's stance.

Support for motherhood endowment and family allowances was rooted in a range of concerns. While some feminists explicitly construed the allowances as 'attach[ing] value to women's unpaid work' and as a means to fight women's and children's poverty, the motives of other actors ranged from a concern for population policy to an endeavour to control wages.[15] What connected all of these concerns was that they acknowledged and focused on the investment of adults in the upbringing of children. This rationale clearly differed from the rationale behind the ILO's maternity policy as defined in C3, which, as discussed above, conceived of advanced pregnancy and confinement as a temporary obstacle to women's paid work, the enabling of which was its principle aim.

The ILO concerned itself from the very beginning with the question of family policies as differentiated from maternity policy in this way. However, already the actors concerned with the establishment of the International Labour Office in 1919/1920 explicitly conceded that the issue of policies on unpaid work relating to the family, which went beyond C3, 'will no doubt prove controversial' and that 'the solution . . . by means of Conventions will raise a whole series of important questions.'[16] The International Labour Office soon defined family allowances in the 'narrower sense' of 'regular payments supplementary to wages or salaries, varying

40 Susan Zimmermann

according to size of family, for the maintenance of its members'.[17] The 1924 report, 'Family Allowances. The Remuneration of Labour According to Need', while endorsing the inherited division of labour within the family, clearly recognized the idea that the care labour done by women of the labouring classes should be somehow materially valued.[18] However, the International Labour Office throughout the interwar period carefully avoided referring to women's 'family responsibilities' as work.

The interest of the International Labour Office in women's unpaid care work beyond maternity was sustained – insofar as the focus was on the Global North – by a number of factors.[19] The period following World War I witnessed the introduction or expansion of family allowance schemes in a number of mostly European countries, and both internationally organized women and academic researchers focused intensely on the issue. Another important factor, which from the middle of the 1920s onward sustained the interest of the Office in the subject of family allowances, was the fact that the League of Nation's Child Welfare Committee included this subject on its agenda.[20] The International Labour Office made sure from the beginning that it would be properly involved in what would turn out to be a continuous subject of study within the League's Committee.

However, while the International Labour Office did consider the generation of an additional universal international instrument – i.e. beyond its maternity-oriented policies – that would have intervened into the relationship of unpaid care work and work,[21] the Office never took the issue forward. Three key factors may explain this reluctance; all involved anxiety or disagreement over the question as to whether it was possible and advisable to transform some of women's unpaid care responsibilities into directly or indirectly paid work and who would shoulder the financial burden caused by this transformation.

The first of these impeding factors had to do with the status of the ILO as a tripartite institution with a mandate to internationalize labour and social policies and the ensuing pressure to accommodate the interests of member states and employers as well as workers. In its 1931 flagship publication, *The First Decade*, the Office pointedly described some of the related challenges. The publication discussed the allowances as a benefit that, in addition to the wage, was granted with reference to the family-related needs of the (implicitly male) worker. It constructed the allowances as one of a number of 'social charges', i.e. a societal commitment to compensate for the otherwise uncompensated or unpaid-for investment into the upbringing of children (which could take the form of women's unpaid work, of acquiring goods, and of paying for services). However, 'the idea' of family allowances was still 'far from being generally accepted in every country, and it is perhaps too early to think of international regulations'.[22] The Office would not embark on action toward an international standard on family allowances because too many amongst the industrialized member states of the ILO were not (yet) willing to take on the financial burden of the allowances defined as a 'social charge'. The alternative would have been to still conceive of allowances as a part of the employers' cost. However, employers as a rule were not prepared to pay wages compensating for family responsibilities, since they considered 'wages as the remuneration for work performed and as an element in . . . [the] cost of production'.[23] The question as to whether allowances should or might be financed by employers, or whether they formed an element of the 'social charges' to be shouldered by the society and the state, had indeed caused tension within the International Labour Office in earlier years. Workers' representatives insisted that family allowances, as long as they were paid by employers, were not to be considered social charges. The Governing Body of the Office in April 1931, by narrow majority, decided to consider even this type of allowance as falling into the category of 'social charges'.[24]

The second impeding factor had to do with the mandate of the ILO, and the interpretation thereof, defined in the Constitution as concerning the improvement of the 'conditions of labour' of 'workers'.[25] Family allowances, by contrast, constituted a social benefit that was not clearly tied to the working population. The International Labour Office was well aware of the ambiguity thus created and the political disagreement in the international argument on motherhood and family policies as to whether family allowances should be confined to wage workers. One hypothetical way of overcoming the difficulty would have been to reconfigure women's family responsibilities as work. Since such work was performed in all households, such a move would have enabled the ILO to claim responsibility for family allowances for all families rather than for working-class families alone. Yet such a redefinition was clearly unimaginable both for the ILO and the League of Nations. As a result, the Office, rather than trying to expand its competence as regards the allowances, made sure to carefully define its limits. It underlined that it could not 'claim exclusive competence' for 'public assistance systems . . . intended for . . . large families', i.e. a portion of the general population, 'since these assistance services provide benefits for persons other than actual or former wage-earners'.[26] In its study of social services it underlined that the services studied – amongst them those tackling the 'risk' of 'family responsibilities' – 'should be established on behalf of classes of the population consisting mainly of wage earners and persons of small means working on their own account'.[27]

The third factor contributing to the reluctance of the International Labour Office to move forward on the issue of family allowances had to do with those international (and national) trade union and socialist organizations and their respective women's committees, which served as key collaborators of the International Labour Office in terms of representing workers' interests. The Women's Committee of the International Federation of Trade Unions (IFTU), the most important representative of workers' interests in the ILO, never embraced family allowances as an organization, though representatives of the Committee were clearly aware of the pressure under which working-class women laboured for their families. The IFTU women aligned themselves with the argument within the trade union movement that the allowances, especially when they didn't form part of the wage system, 'would encourage employers to refuse higher wages, on the ground that family needs were being met by other means'.[28] The IFTU women wished to ease women's 'double burden' of paid and unpaid work, and they wanted women's family work

42 Susan Zimmermann

to be materially acknowledged. But they thought this was best achieved by raising male wages and thus through the employers' contribution, rather than through social benefits which, at best, would be only partly financed by employers. Reifying women's family responsibilities as a gendered universal of social life, they believed that married woman workers would (and should) be enabled to at least temporarily interrupt work, and this could be achieved 'if their husbands earned enough to maintain the family'. One essential condition for raising men's wages was the fight against women's low wages, since low-paid women's work was responsible for the overall 'squeezing of wages'.[29] The IFTU women did not discuss the possible connection between women's low wages and their family work.

In parallel, the IFTU itself, while at first positively considering – within the framework of social insurance – 'family allowances' as one base demand,[30] in 1932 had to acknowledge that the 'differences of opinion' regarding this matter could not be reconciled,[31] and the demand was dropped. This development was connected to controversial debate within the British labour movement on the subject, which in turn impacted the position taken by the International Advisory Committee of Women (IACW) of the Labour and Socialist International. The IACW, which pursued a mandate much broader than its trade-union-based sister committee, the IFTU Women's Committee, regularly discussed policies related to women's paid and unpaid work and the 'double burden'. In one resolution adopted at their 1931 conference, the socialist women characterized women's care work as 'non-occupational, domestic work for society' and as a 'precondition' of their paid work.[32] The representative of the British Independent Labour Party (ILP) on the Committee worked hard, despite the ongoing controversy, to internationalize the demand for family allowances.[33] Yet after the demand was defeated in Great Britain[34] the IACW similarly gave up on it.[35] Instead, the 1931 IACW conference declared itself in favour of various means of easing the unpaid care work of the working woman to enable her 'to fulfill her socially necessary duties'.[36] The IACW never again considered the allowances an issue ripe for decision making. The International Labour Office thus could not count on support from the international trade union and socialist movement for action regarding a possible international instrument on family allowances.

It was this combination of factors which also led the International Labour Office not to take up the challenge, when it was confronted in the latter half of the 1930s, with renewed pressure from equality-oriented women's organizations to recognize women's unpaid work in the context of industrialized societies in the Global North. It did not respond, for example, to the demands of the ERI that 'Woman as Wife, Mother and Home Maker' should be considered a 'worker' for legislative purposes, or that family allowances and the state endowment of motherhood should give 'practical recognition of the money value of the work done by wives', and that mothers should in their 'own right have a claim upon the State for the means of rearing the children' when necessary.[37] Nor did it respond to ODI's 1935 demand for gender-neutrality in any policy aimed at supporting parents of infants.[38]

The anticipation voiced in 1920 in the Governing Body of the ILO that the problem of family policy 'will no doubt prove controversial' proved to be true. The tangible reluctance in many countries, among them influential European countries, and within the labour movement toward introducing benefits compensating for otherwise unpaid family work and family responsibilities, the unwillingness to consider as work women's investment in the family, and controversy as to who exactly – employers, tax payers, or contributory social systems – should shoulder hitherto uncompensated costs of bringing up children can be identified as the major factors that explain the ILO's lack of action over this area of unpaid work by women.

Taking care of the subsistence of communities and families: how women's and men's unpaid work entered international labour law

The ILO was thus reluctant to engage with family policies within the framework of its universally applicable international standard-setting framed with reference to conditions of work in industrialized countries in the Global North. Yet at the same time the organization did engage from the late 1920s onward in the creation of a set of 'special' international labour standards for 'native' or 'indigenous' workers in the Global South, which encompassed the issue of unpaid work. These standards involved the third element of the new international politics of unpaid work, namely subsistence policies.

Three amongst the four core Conventions, or at least related Recommendations, which together developed this set of instruments on 'native' labour, explicitly dealt with the relationship between unfree paid labour and subsistence work. These were the 1930 *Convention concerning Forced or Compulsory Labour* (Forced Labour Convention, C29), the 1936 *Convention concerning the Regulation of Certain Special Systems of Recruiting Workers* (Recruiting of Indigenous Workers Convention, C50), and the 1939 *Convention concerning the Regulation of Written Contracts of Employment of Indigenous Workers* (Contracts of Employment [Indigenous Workers] Convention, C64). The instruments on 'native' labour built closely on and made selective use of the various traditions of colonial and imperial regulation of labour relations in dependent territories. In addition, the International Labour Office sought the continuous and authoritative advice of the Committee of Experts on Native Labour, established as the Office embarked on the preparation of these 'special standards'.[39]

The instruments addressed the relationship between subsistence labour and paid unfree labour with reference to the 'native community' as a whole, in relation to individual workers, and in relation to their families. Forced labour and (recruitment into) contract labour often involved prolonged[40] or at least repeated absence of the workers from home. Where large quantities of such labour were performed, this caused a considerable reduction of the pool of labour available for the sustenance of the 'native community' and the individual families of migrant labourers and could threaten the survival or at least the functioning of the subsistence economy.[41] The ILO's instruments on 'native' labour addressed this tension on three distinct levels.

44 Susan Zimmermann

On a first level, C29 and C50 – regulating forced labour and recruitment into contract labour, respectively – both dealt in relation to the 'native community', with the connection between 'native' labour and subsistence labour. C29 abolished forced labour for women and non-adults and tied the recourse to forced labour of able-bodied adult males to various restrictions and conditions. Among other things it fixed 'the proportion of the resident adult able-bodied males who may be taken at any one time for forced or compulsory labour' from a given 'community' to '25 per cent', so as to ensure 'the maintenance in each community of the number of adult able-bodied men indispensable for family and social life'. In fixing the proportion, account was to be taken of 'the economic and social necessities of the normal life of the 'community concerned', of the seasons, and' of the 'work which must be done by the persons concerned on their own behalf in their locality'. C50 concerned itself in a parallel manner with possible 'untoward . . . effects of the withdrawal of adult males on the social organisation of the population concerned', authorizing the competent authority to 'fix the maximum number of adult males who may be recruited in any given social unit' at a time.

C29 introduced a second element of subsistence policies which focused on the immediate families of the individual workers and the individual workers themselves rather than the 'native community' as whole. The limitation of the amount of such labour that could be imposed on each worker coerced into forced labour implicitly touched on possible responsibilities for subsistence work of these workers. This type of regulation was present in a whole number of labour codes of dependent territories and as such figured prominently in the report on forced labour which the International Labour Office laid before the International Labour Conference, in preparation of C29, in 1929.[42] Since, according to C29 as adopted in 1930, forced labour could be imposed only on men, the limitation of forced labour to a maximum of sixty days per adult male within the period of one year is to be read not only as a clause regulating forced labour but also as a gendered clause that could serve to keep intact the family economy 'behind' the workers coerced into paid labour in the service of public enterprise.

A third group of clauses – contained in the regulations on recruitment into contract labour and long-term contract labour adopted in 1935 and 1939 – focused on the relationship between individual workers and their families in an additional manner. This concerned the reattachment of familial subsistence labour to contract workers who worked at a distance from their place of origin. With regard to such 'resettlement' of family members, C50 stipulated – vaguely – that in certain cases, 'the competent authority' might 'encourage recruited workers to be accompanied by their families, more particularly in the case of workers recruited for agricultural or similar employment at a long distance from their homes and for periods exceeding a specified duration'. C64 was accompanied by a Recommendation exempting from restrictions of the duration of absence from home those workers who were 'accompanied by their families', who settled 'near the place of employment'. Both of these regulations, while gender-neutral in legal terms, were clearly informed by a gendered vision of securing an immediate and continuous connection between the paid labour of the 'native' unfree worker imagined as male and labouring at a large distance from the place of origin and the care and subsistence labour provided by his family.[43]

The ILO's instruments on 'native' labour thus regulated the relationship between the subsistence economy and paid labour – in the form of forced, recruited, and long-term contract labour performed by 'native' workers. They did so by stipulating the maximum proportion of workers that could be drawn from the 'native community' at any one time, the duration of the involvement of the individual 'native' worker in these forms of unfree labour, and in terms of reestablishing the connection between subsistence and paid labour at the place of work in the case of long-term and distant absence of the worker from home. While considerable conflict surrounded the framing of some of these clauses, with regard to the subsistence question, all actors substantially involved in the preparation of these instruments, including the Committee of Experts on Native Labour, the responsible officers at the International Labour Office, and the relevant delegates and advisors at various sessions of the International Labour Conference, were in basic agreement on three factors. They explicitly recognized the activities pertaining to the maintenance of the subsistence economy of the 'native communities' and families as work. They agreed that this work as a rule continued to be an essential condition for the survival and well-being of 'native' workers and their families and communities, once 'native' workers were drawn into the forms of 'unfree' paid labour addressed by the ILO's 'special' labour standards. And they acknowledged that there was an inherent tension between such labour and the necessities of the subsistence economy.

While accepting western-directed processes of colonial 'development' as a given, the ILO instruments on 'native' labour thus recognized the asymmetric and tense relationship between subsistence economies and the introduction of unfree forms of paid labour in the Global South. While in principle aiming for the transformation of unfree into free labour, the International Labour Office, in the meantime, sought to create instruments on unfree labour which aimed to control the tension between such labour and subsistence work. It did so because existing unfree labour relations took a form which would not otherwise enable the social reproduction of the workers involved. The 'labour necessary for the food production of the communities concerned' was considered one key principle in a list of general principles 'which underlie, or which should underlie, the regulation of forced labour, where it is still permitted'.[44]

These principles had been discussed at length during the very first meeting of the Committee of Experts on Native Labour in 1927.[45] Two coalitions of women's organizations had, prior to the meeting, submitted two parallel memoranda to the Director of the International Labour Office after representatives of the Office had proactively worked for the involvement of women's organizations. Both memoranda were distributed to the Experts at their first meeting. The signatory organizations represented – among women activists in industrial countries – a wide range of different approaches to women's labour. The first coalition, rallied behind the International Council of Women, made a firm case for gendered differential labour

46 Susan Zimmermann

protection and a policy of strengthening gendered family and social structures. By contrast, the second coalition, which brought together British women's organizations and included the major alliance of British trade union women,[46] avoided reference to family and tribal life and talked exclusively about work. Yet when it came to subsistence policies the women's memoranda, just like the ILO's Expert Committee, agreed that care had to be taken to address the needs of the subsistence economy whenever 'native' male workers were forced into paid labour in non-self-governing territories. The first memorandum affirmed the need to take into consideration the 'necessities of agricultural production' when regulating forced labour; the second one, in a parallel manner, referred to the 'village requirements in the matter of labour'.[47]

Against the background of this agreement in principle on the need to ensure the viability of the relationship between subsistence labour and paid (unfree) work, the International Labour Office made sure to add its own distinctive political thumb-print to the future instruments on forced labour and recruitment and the 'principles' attached to these instruments.[48] For example, although regulations on the proportion of males who could forcibly be taken away from any 'given community at one time' were rare in colonial legislation consulted by the Office, the 1929 Report on Forced Labour prepared by the Office made regulations of this kind into one of the principles which were to underlay the international regulation of forced labour.[49] In other cases, controversy between the various actors within the ILO resulted in the watering-down of initially envisioned regulations. The Committee of Experts on Native Labour strongly recommended resettlement, especially with a view to allotting 'plots of ground' to workers accompanied by their families in the event of agricultural long-distance employment.[50] Supporters of such policies suggested that resettlement could work as a solution to the persistent problem that 'the recruiters' harvest', i.e. the result of their activities, in some territories in the South of Africa dependent on a self-reliant 'barter subsistence economy', had long been 'neglect, depression and famine'.[51] Yet in the end, in C50, the stipulation about resettlement remained vague, in conformity to employers' interests in the Global South.

In the process of creating its 'special' labour standards for the Global South, the International Labour Office, after its initial consultations in 1927, never again initiated a dialogue with international women's organizations.[52] Subsistence policies did not play a role in the later interactions between the ILO and women's organizations on 'native' labour, even after these reintensified in the second half of the 1930s. At this later stage it was legal equality feminists who were most vocal when monitoring or intervening in the politics of the International Labour Office with regard to 'native' labour. The focus of these groups was on paid labour, or more precisely on 'the right to enter a contract of employment as a civil right',[53] or '[t]he right' of 'the Man in his capacity as a Worker or Earner . . . to sell his labour for gain without requiring authorization from a third party'.[54] Amongst the international women's organizations and committees which visibly tried to influence the politics of the ILO and the League of Nations, the St. Joan's Social and Political Alliance, a Catholic organization dedicated to the legal equality principle, was the only one to develop a pronounced interest in questions related to the status of 'native' women in general in its activism.[55] Yet even the most extensive related document in no way focused on 'native' women's involvement in the subsistence economy, mentioning their involvement in 'field work and domestic work' without further comment.[56] Neither in the records of the women's activism with a visible connection to the ILO nor in those of the International Labour Office do we find any traces of a possible aspiration to get 'native' women themselves involved in the making of regulations pertaining to paid or unpaid 'native' labour. The International Labour Office, in a note sent to some of the members of its Correspondence Committee on Women's Work, described 'native' women as 'know[ing] nothing of life outside their family and their Native villages';[57] the St. Joan's Social and Political Alliance saw them as 'for the most part inarticulate'.[58]

The documents about the origins of the ILO's instruments on 'native' labour demonstrate that the International Labour Office, driven by its wish to control certain forms of unfree labour in the service of public or private enterprise and to avoid the socially destructive consequences of any too excessive utilization of such forms of labour, put great emphasis on reference to subsistence work as one key justification for a number of the restrictions it aimed to include in its international instruments. The Experts sitting on the Committee for 'native' labour, who knew subsistence policies quite well from colonial legislation, supported this line of action in principle but sought to avoid far-reaching interference with colonial labour policies.

The easy agreement within the ILO as to the need to rely on subsistence policies in its instruments on unfree 'native' labour is astounding at first sight, considering the anxiety that characterized discourse and policies on family policy within and around the International Labour Office and the reluctance of the ILO to substantially engage with such policy. This difference between subsistence policies and family policy, as well as the fact that neither the ILO nor the actors in its orbit connected debate and discourse on family policy and subsistence policy with each other, are striking, especially considering that these two sets of policies addressed in a largely identical manner the pressure which involvement in paid, free, or unfree labour put on unpaid care or subsistence-oriented labour. The key to explaining this difference in approach lies in the divergent consequences that policies aiming to address the tension between paid and unpaid labour had or would have within each of these two sets of labour policy. Family policies, or more precisely family allowances, aimed to ease this tension by attaching a material benefit to hitherto unpaid care work, and this benefit had in substance to be financed by the state and/or employers, who in this way would recognize the value of unpaid work for society and in fact remunerate it. In contrast, acknowledging the value of unpaid subsistence labour did not result in any additional financial burden for private or public enterprise as it built on the 'native' subsistence economy. We need to put this distinction centre stage if we are to explain the difference in the ILO's approach to family policy as opposed to subsistence policy in the interwar period.

In the rare moments in the history of the ILO's engagement with the politics of unpaid work, when subsistence policy and family policy touched on each other,

48 Susan Zimmermann

this difference became blatantly apparent. In the Conference Committee on forced labour, sitting during the 1929 session of the International Labour Conference, the Belgian workers' delegate suggested that financial support might be granted to ensure 'the subsistence of the families of the workers'. Mr. Pauwel wanted the International Labour Office to inquire whether governments considered that 'a right' should be fixed 'of the wife to accompany her husband in the areas where such work is carried on . . . carrying with it the obligation on the authority which organises the work to furnish absolutely free food and lodging for the wife'. Yet no other workers' representatives supported such transformation of subsistence policy into family policy in the context of unfree labour in the colonies. The Advisor of the Dutch workers' delegate, Mr. Jadji Salim, resident in the Dutch East Indies, who probably had more realistic knowledge about the conditions of forced labour in the colonies, argued that 'it would not be fair to family life if families were herded together, as would happen.' The Conference Committee dropped Mr. Pauwel's suggestion without further discussion.[59]

Conclusion

This study discussed the evolution of the international policies of unpaid work, their particular character and the related international argument, and the role of diverse actors in shaping these policies.

With regard to the actors, we have seen that in developing these policies the International Labour Organization, interacting with a myriad of networks and individuals based overwhelmingly in the Global North, reworked various concepts and practices of labour and social policy preexisting in both the Global North and the Global South. While non-socialist women's organizations involved in this process largely had to rely on the goodwill of the International Labour Office, international committees of socialist and trade union women, through their connection with the International Federation of Trade Unions and other workers' organizations, had, as long as this connection worked smoothly, a somewhat stronger leverage. As regards the global divide between North and South, political developments and claim-making related to industrial countries in some cases exerted tangible influence on the ILO's course of action, while in the process leading to the creation of the international instruments on 'native' labour the ILO relied heavily on colonial expertise. With the support of workers' delegates the International Labour Office managed to a degree to remould this heritage, so as to set – amongst other things with reference to the needs of the subsistence economy – certain limits on the exploitation of 'native' labour.

As to the character of the international policies of unpaid work developed by the ILO, it can be argued (with a degree of exaggeration) that the first of the three elements of these policies, namely maternity policy, focused on the woman-specific burden maternity put on paid work, while the other two elements, family policies and subsistence policies, focused on unpaid work in its relation to free and unfree

The International Labour Organization **49**

labour in the service of private and public enterprise. Maternity policy, in other words, was about enabling a woman's paid work despite her bodily 'handicaps', while the other two sets of policies were about acknowledging or transforming unpaid work aimed at the sustenance and reproduction of family and community.

The argument over maternity politics evolved around the question of how to create a situation where women's involvement in unpaid labour did not lead to a woman-specific vulnerability or powerlessness within the world of paid work. The ILO's discourse of maternity as a 'natural' function and a 'handicap' to women's paid work contributed to both the gendered reification of women's bodies as an inherently problematic presence in the world of paid work and society at large and to the cultural devaluation of all work other than paid work. Women's organizations that favoured legal equality sought instead to suppress gender-specific difference in the world of paid work, including that stemming from women's involvement in unpaid work by assimilating women's paid work with that performed by men. However, this approach was also problematic, involving a refusal to acknowledge that this might make woman workers vulnerable in a different manner.

The ILO's family policies and subsistence policies both acknowledged that engagement in unpaid labour restricted the capacity to engage in – free or unfree – wage labour. Yet these two sets of policies differed fundamentally in terms of how to address the related tension between paid work and unpaid care labour. Family policies sought to enable care labour by directly or indirectly supporting it financially. In contrast, subsistence policies did not involve material investment by the colonial state or employers in non-self-governing territories; instead they sought to restrict the amount of (unfree) wage labour to be performed by members of 'native' families and communities. This difference is one of the key factors that explain why, in the context of the industrial countries, the ILO did not in the end develop family policies that would have eased the strained relationship between unpaid care work and free wage labour, which placed an especial burden on women. In contrast, some women's organizations strongly argued in favour of family allowances with a view to easing – but as a result also reifying – women's 'double burden', while the ODI alone came up with a gender-neutral vision of societal support for unpaid family work. As to subsistence policies, the tension within the ILO between colonial and imperial interests on the one hand and the policies pursued by the Office and the workers' side on the other were rooted in disagreement as to how much pressure could be exerted on the 'native' subsistence economy without endangering its function as a costless breeding ground for labour exploited in the service of profit and colonial development. The vision that, in the context of colonial labour relations as shaped by the ILO's instruments on 'native' labour, 'native' women more than 'native' men would be associated with unpaid labour was never questioned within the ILO and was shared by many women's organizations.

The distinctions among maternity policy, family policy, and subsistence policy were barely ever questioned in the international argument over unpaid work in the interwar period. At the same time, taken together, the related concepts mirrored,

50 Susan Zimmermann

politically reified, and sought to ease the strained and tense relationship between unpaid labour on the one hand and free and unfree labour for capitalist and public enterprise on the other.

In a long-term perspective, the development together-apart of the three elements constituting the new international politics of unpaid work can be read as a significant contribution to the generation of two problematic traits of gendered global governance – characteristics which also all too often continue to colour feminist scholarship on the past and present of women's labours. Thinking separately about women's work in the contexts of free and unfree labour has helped to create and sustain the unrealistic vision that the future of women's labour in the Global South would entail their involvement in free paid labour alone. The process of making distinctions between and thinking apart the three elements of the international politics of unpaid work has been instrumental in keeping invisible and unacknowledged the exploitation of care and subsistence labour as subordinated to free and unfree paid labour in all parts of the world.

Notes

1 An extended development of the issues covered in this chapter will be included in Chapter 6 of my book manuscript in progress. I am grateful to Kathryn Kish Sklar for her instructive reading of that chapter (http://people.ceu.edu/sites/people.ceu.hu/files/profile/attachment/1634/zimmermanninternationallabourstandardsch6finalforweb_0.pdf) and to Clare Midgley for her comments on the first version of this text. These conversations helped make my argument more explicit.
2 The Constitution of the ILO was contained in all Paris peace treaties. The Versailles Treaty, Part XIII 'Labour'. Online: http://avalon.law.yale.edu/imt/partxiii.asp
3 The term 'native' was widely used by the ILO but not in its international labour standards. The introduction of the term 'indigenous' in the instruments on 'native' labour from 1936 onward served to point to the limited scope of application of these instruments while avoiding racialization in the legal language of the ILO. Reference to 'special circumstances' was made already in the Constitution of the ILO.
4 While this term did not appear in the legal language of the ILO, it was used in official publications of the International Labour Office.
5 All ILO Conventions and Recommendations are available on ILO, *NORMLEX. Information System on International Labour Standards*. Online: www.ilo.org/dyn/normlex/en/f?p=NORMLEXPUB:12000:0::NO::::. All quotations from ILO instruments and factual information about the contents of these instruments are taken from this source.
6 ILO, *Women's Work under Labour Law. A Survey of Protective Legislation* (Studies and Reports. Series I, no. 2), Geneva: ILO, 1932, p. 1.
7 League of Nations (hereafter LoN), *International Labour Conference* (hereafter ILC), *Eleventh Session Geneva 1928*, vol. 2, *Report of the Director Presented to the Conference*, Geneva: ILO, 1928, pp. 60, 147.
8 *Minutes of the 49th Session of the Governing Body of the International Labour Office, Geneva, June 1930*, Geneva: no publisher given, 1930, pp. 103, 495–500.
9 Restrictive Legislation and the Industrial Woman Worker. A Reply by the Open Door Council to the Statement by the Standing Joint Committee of Women's Industrial Organisations, printed brochure (February 1928), and other documents contained in D 611/2010/01, International Labour Office Archives (hereafter ILOA).
10 The related 1935 Resolution and discussion are documented in ODI, Report of the Fourth Conference in Copenhagen, August 19–23, 1935, Pamphlet Collection, Women's

The International Labour Organization **51**

Library @ LSE (hereafter WLL). The following quotes taken from this document are on pp. 29–34, 57–60 (in part in italics).

11 ODI, Report 1935, pp. 8, 57–8, (in part in italics i.o.); ODI, Second Conference, Stockholm, August, 1931, Resolutions Adopted, pp. 9–11, both Pamphlet Collection, WLL.

12 The Vote, 4 December 1931, WN 1000/6/19, jacket 1, ILOA.

13 This statement most likely was Albert Thomas's. Memo to M. Phelan 04/09/1929, WN 1000/7/1, ILOA, jacket 1 (French i.o.).

14 Reception of Delegation from the Equal Rights International by the Director (30 September 1930) (incl. quote); Equal Rights 15 (1930) no. 42, 25. October 1930, both WN 1000/18/1, jacket 1, ILOA.

15 J. Lewis, 'Models of Equality for Women. The Case of State Support for Children in Twentieth-century Britain', in G. Bock and P. Thane, eds., *Maternity and Gender Policies. Women and the Rise of the European Welfare States, 1880s-1950s*, London, New York: Routledge, 1991, pp. 73–92, esp. p. 88; S. Pedersen, *Family, Dependence, and the Origins of the Welfare State*, Cambridge: Cambridge University Press, 1993, chapters 4 and 5.

16 *Minutes of the Second Session of the Governing Body of the International Labour Office held in Paris, 26–28 January 1920*, no place given: ILO, 1920, p. 30.

17 Johnston to Mlle Collin 15/12/1926, I 4061/7/2 → 4061/12/3, ILOA.

18 ILO, *Family Allowances. The Remuneration of Labour According to Need* (Studies and Reports, Series D, no. 13), Geneva: ILO, 1924, esp. pp. 6–7, 14–16, 21.

19 Zimmermann, see endnote 1.

20 J. Droux, 'From Inter-agency Competition to Transnational Cooperation: The ILO Contribution to Child Welfare Issues during the Interwar Years', in S. Kott and J. Droux, eds., *Globalizing Social Rights. The International Labour Organization and Beyond*, Houndsmills, Geneva: Palgrave Macmillan, Geneva, 2013, pp. 262–279.

21 ILO, *The ILO. The First Decade*, London: Allen & Unwin and ILO, [1931], pp. 172–173.

22 Ibid.

23 ILO, *International Survey of Social Services* (Studies and Reports, Series M, no. 11), Geneva: ILO, 1933, pp. VII–XXIII.

24 *Minutes of the 52d Session of the Governing Body of the International Labour Office, Geneva, April 1931*, no place given: no publisher given, pp. 284–90.

25 The Versailles Treaty, Part XIII 'Labour'.

26 LoN, Advisory Committee on Social Questions, First Session, 15th April 1937, Future Work of the Committee, Suggestions of members of the Advisory Committee, p. 43 (statement of the representative of the Office), L 10/5/1, ILOA.

27 ILO, *International Survey*, p. XV.

28 This is Pat Thane's summary phrasing, referring to Great Britain. 'Visions of Gender in the Making of the British Welfare State: The Case of Women in the British Labour Party and Social Policy, 1906–1945', in Bock and Thane, *Maternity and Gender Policies,* 93–118, p. 111. For the IFTU women see For the meeting of the International Committee of Trade Union Women, 1st and 2nd October 1929, Guiding Principles, By Gertrud Hanna, MSS.292/62.14/5, Trades Union Congress Archives, Modern Records Center, University of Warwick (hereafter TUCA-MRC-UW).

29 IGB, *Protokoll des IV. Ordentlichen Kongresses des Internationalen Gewerkschaftsbundes. Abgehalten im Grand Palais, Paris, vom 1. bis 6. August 1927. Nebst Berichten über die Konferenz der Internationalen Berufssekretariate und über die Internationale Arbeiterinnenkonferenz*, Amsterdam: IFTU, 1927, pp. 240, 265, 269–70 (German i.o).

30 IFTU, *Congress Stockholm 1930. The Activities of the International Federation of Trade Unions 1927–1930*, Amsterdam: IFTU, 1931, esp. pp. 314, 357, 389.

31 Trades Union Congress, General Council, Report of 'Meeting of the IFTU 04–05/01/1932; Extract from the Minutes of the Executive Meeting, 09–10/06/1932, both MSS.292/915.2/3, TUCA-MRC-UW.

32 *Vierte Internationale Frauenkonferenz der S.A.I. Wien, 23.–25. Juli 1931. Bericht des Sekretariats an die Frauenkonferenz und Protokoll der Verhandlungen der Frauenkonferenz*

52 Susan Zimmermann

(Vierter Kongreß der Sozialistischen Arbeiter-Internationale. Berichte und Verhandlungen [Abteilungen III und IX]) Berlin, Zürich: Verlag des Sekretariats der sozialistischen Arbeiter-Internationale Zürich. In Kommission bei: J. H. W. Dietz Nachf., no year given, pp. IX/93–4 (German i.o.).

33 *International Information Women's Supplement* (hereafter *IIWS*), 7, 1930, no. 1 (January), p. I.I./32; Motion by Dorothy Jewson, ILP Women's Committee, inv.-no. 4428; Adler to Präsidium, 21/09/1929, inv.-no. 4505, both Labour and Socialist International Archives (hereafter LSI Archives), International Institute of Social History (hereafter IISH), Amsterdam.

34 *IIWS* 7 (1930), pp. I.I./527–530, I.I./630–633; Thane, 'Visions of Gender', in Bock and Thane, *Maternity and Gender Policies*, pp. 111–2; see also J. Hannam and K. Hunt, *Socialist Women. Britain, 1880s to 1920s*, London, New York: Routledge, 2002, pp. 73–77.

35 Zur Tagesordnung der Internationalen Frauenkonferenz Wien, 1931, Familienunterstützungen; Vorschläge des Präsidiums, Vierte Internationale Frauenkonferenz der S.A.I., both inv.-no. 4364, LSI Archives, IISH; *IIWS* 8, 1931, pp. II./10–1; *Vierte Internationale Frauenkonferenz der S.A.I. 1931.*

36 Ibid., pp. IX/93–4 (German i.o.).

37 Elsie Maitland to Director 28/09/1937, and attached Statement . . . (italics i.o.) WN 6/01/1, jacket 3, ILOA.

38 ODI, Report 1935, pp. 57–60; ODI, The Policy with Regard to Maternity of the Open Door International for the Economic Emancipation of the Woman Worker, both Pamphlet Collection, WLL.

39 S. Zimmermann, '"Special Circumstances" in Geneva. The ILO and the World of Non-Metropolitan Labour in the Interwar Period', in J. van Daele, M. Rodriguez Garcia, G. van Goethem and M. van der Linden, eds., *ILO Histories. Essays on the International Labour Organization and its Impact on the World During the Twentieth Century*, Bern etc.: Peter Lang, 2010, pp. 221–250, pp. 232–241.

40 The types of labour discussed here involved, to various degrees, long–distance travel and thus long–term absence, and the ILO instruments implicitly or explicitly took note of this fact.

41 Labour performed within the 'native community' or the family economy, of course in many cases, also included the production of goods for sale. The ILO instruments themselves were explicit neither about this distinction nor about the relationship between the latter type of labour on the one hand and forced or contract labour on the other.

42 *ILC, Twelfth Session Geneva 1929, Forced Labour, Report and Draft Questionnaire*, Geneva: ILO, 1929.

43 Originally, the Office had planned sex-specific restrictions on the recruitment of women and paternalistic control over certain groups of women for long-term contract labour. S. Zimmermann, 'The Politics of Globalizing Gendered Labor Policy: International Labor Standards and the Global South, 1919–1944', in E. Boris and S. Zimmermann, eds., Women's ILO. Transnational Networks, Working Conditions and Gender Equality, Houndsmills, Basingstoke and Geneva: Palgrave Macmillan and ILO, forthcoming 2017.

44 *Forced Labour Report 1929*, pp. 256, 271 (the principle in italics i.o.).

45 International Labour Office, Thirty-Seventh Session of the Governing Body, Berlin, October 1927. Third Item of the Agenda, Report of the Committee of Experts on Native Labour, p. 4, D 737/100/3, jacket 1, ILOA; *Forced Labour Report 1929*, pp. 256–294.

46 None of the coalitions included proponents of those organizations that by then were most vocal in terms of pursuing an agenda of strict legal equality between women and men. This likely was related to the fact that the major intention of the initiative as a whole was the sex-specific abolition of forced labour. Aberdeen et al. to Thomas, 14/05/1927, and Woodman to Thomas, 01/06/1927, both N 206/1/01/1, ILOA; S. Zimmermann, 'Night Work for White Women and Bonded Labour for "Native" Women? Contentious Traditions and the Globalization of Gender-Specific Labour Protection and Legal Equality Politics, 1926 to 1939', in S. Kimble and M. Röwekamp, eds., New Perspectives

The International Labour Organization **53**

on European Women's Legal History, Milton Park and New York: Routledge, forthcoming 2016.

47 Lady Aberdeen et al. to Dear Sir [Albert Thomas], 14/05/1927; Dorothy Woodman to Director [Albert Thomas], 01/06/1927, and attached Memorandum on Forced Labour; Elise Zimmern to Harold Grimshaw, 19/05/1927, all N 206/1/01/1, ILOA; Zimmermann, 'Night Work', in Kimble and Röwekamp, *New Perspectives*.

48 *ILC, Nineteenth Session Geneva 1935, The Recruiting of Labour in Colonies and in Other Territories with Analogous Labour Conditions, Report IV*, Geneva: ILO, 1935, pp. 255–60; *ILC, Twenty-Fourth Session Geneva 1938, Regulation of Contracts of Employment of Indigenous Workers, Report II*, Geneva: ILO, 1937, pp. 217–222.

49 *Forced Labour Report 1929*, pp. 79, 244.

50 *Recruiting of Labour Report 1935*, pp. 120–124. This theme had been present already at the very first meeting of the Experts in 1927, International Labour Office, Eighth Sitting of Committee of Experts on Native Labour, 11/07/1927, afternoon, p. 123, N 206/2/1/5, ILOA.

51 *ILC, Nineteenth Session Geneva, 1935, Record of Proceedings*, Geneva: ILO, 1935, p. 414; ILO, *ILC, Twentieth Session Geneva, 1936, Record of Proceedings*, Geneva: ILO, 1936, pp. 279, 604, 609, 618–620, 624–625, 771.

52 It did so, however, in the context of appointing one woman, with a thorough knowledge of colonial affairs, to the Committee of Experts on Native Labour, Zimmermann, '"Special Circumstances"', in Van Daele et.al., *ILO Histories*, p. 237.

53 ODI, The Modern Line of Attack on Women's Civil Rights. An Examination of Confused Thinking, p. 2, Archive Nationaal Bureau voor Vrouwenarbeid, inv. no. 469 (bold type letters i.o.), Atria, Institute on Gender Equality and Women's History, Amsterdam.

54 ODI, Status of Women, as contained in LoN, Nationality and Status of Women, Geneva, August 30th, 1935, p. 41, LoN Collection, Box 94, IISH.

55 S. Zimmermann, 'Liaison Committees of International Women's Organisations and the Changing Landscape of Women's Internationalism, 1920s to 1945', in K. Kish Sklar and T. Dublin, eds., *Women and Social Movements, International. 1840 to Present*. Online: http://wasi.alexanderstreet.com/.

56 St. Joan's Social and Political Alliance, Status of the women of native races, 30 May, 1937, contained in LoN, Nationality and Status of Women, Geneva, 30 August, 1935, here p. 58, LoN Collection, Box 94, IISH.

57 Alice Cheyney to Mary Anderson, 19/11/1938, attachment, WN 12/01/8, ILOA.

58 LoN, Nationality and Status of Women, 1935, p. 56, LoN Collection, Box 94, IISH.

59 Twelfth Session of the ILC, Committee on Forced Labour, Eighth Session, 7 June 1929, pp. 11–2, D 612/800/1, ILOA.

3

REIMAGINING GREENHAM, OR THE TRANSNATIONALITY OF THE NATION IN ACTIVIST WOMEN'S NARRATIVES IN 1980s JAPAN[1]

Ulrike Wöhr

> At that time . . . I fervently admired [the women of Greenham Common]. I absolutely wanted to go and visit [the Camp]. Women crocheting ropes and weaving spider webs . . . I had always participated in men's movements, always feeling awkward . . . 'Unfettered thought and spontaneous action' – magnetized by this image I set out [for Greenham Common].[2]

This is how a woman from Hiroshima recently recalled feelings and events of the early 1980s. The Greenham Common Women's Peace Camp (hereafter, Greenham), which she visited in October 1983, was founded in September 1981, when a group of women chained themselves to the fence of the US Army Air Force base at Greenham Common, in the UK, to protest against the placement of cruise missiles at the base.[3] Greenham epitomizes the upsurge of the European peace movement after the NATO Double-Track Decision of 1979, in which European governments consented to the deployment of American middle-range nuclear weapons in Western Europe.[4] These events had their counterpart in Japan. Starting in 1980, the Liberal-Democratic government's efforts to abolish the Renunciation of War clause of the Japanese Constitution, a greatly increased military budget and the impending deployment of US nuclear cruise missiles in the Pacific region sparked mass protests exceeding the milieu of the leftist peace movement. One conspicuous feature of this new, autonomous peace activism was the large number of female participants.[5]

To many of these women, the merging of feminism and peace activism that characterized the European movement was an alluring phenomenon.[6] Indeed, Greenham, which exemplified this coalescence, had already become something like a spiritual home to some Japanese women within the first year of its establishment.[7] What did this yearning, which is also expressed in the opening quote, signify in terms of intersecting gendered and racialized power relations, in national and transnational contexts? How were historical and contemporary power constellations addressed or negated, reproduced or challenged in the process of reimagining Greenham in Japan? How did contacts with Greenham impact the activism of women in Japan?

I approach these questions from an insight that emerged from my analysis of sources pertaining to communications between Greenham and Japan – namely, that such exchanges across national borders could be involved in constructing, rather than dissolving, ideas of the national. This insight relates to what Merry Wiesner-Hanks calls one of the 'iconic conclusions' of transnational history, namely, 'just how transnational nationalism has been'. Or, as Jane Rendall argues, 'a transnational approach' needs to understand movements across national boundaries 'in relation to the emergence of national identities and nation states, and to regional and global identifications'.[8] Moreover, I found the specific ways in which such identities were imagined in my sources to be inflected by larger discursive formations structured by binary tropes like East/West (or Orient/Occident), First World/Third World and nation/state, which are, again, imbued with notions of advancement/backwardness or masculinity/femininity. This suggests the applicability and, indeed, the necessity of an intersectional approach to these narratives, revealing how colonialism and issues of race and power impacted women's transnational connections in specifically gendered ways. My analysis in this chapter illuminates the extent to which gendered, nationalized and racialized self-concepts of 'Japanese women', empowering oppositional positions within Japan, emerged from transnational communications and how these self-concepts, in turn, produced diverse conceptions of a transnational community of women.

I begin by tracing this transnationality of the nation in the broader context of two key competing oppositional discourses in postwar Japan, the first focused on universalizing discourses, the second on the authentic ethnic nation. In the following section, I map the more immediate discursive background to the narratives surrounding Greenham, analysing how an imagined entity of Japanese women, seen as participating in a transnational community of women, was pitted against masculinized inner oppressors like the established peace movement and the state, thereby illustrating how binaries like nation/state and Orient/Occident were conceptualized in oppositional discursive traditions in Japan. In the remainder of the chapter, I take a closer look at the politics of meaning at work in the reimagining of Greenham by Japan's autonomous peace activists. My focus is on the 'contact moment' of July and August 1984, when Hiro Sumpter, one of the Greenham campers, visited Japan and was hosted by grassroots women's groups around the country. Drawing on contemporary accounts by participants in this exchange and from interviews conducted with some of these women, I explore the complex interaction of discourses of sameness and difference that contributed to creating an imagined community of Japanese women activists for peace in the context of transnational contact with Greenham Common activists in England.

Just as I use 'transnational' to signify a relational approach rather than a scale,[9] I introduce the term contact moment not to denote a temporal unit but to refer to Katsuhiko Suganuma's adaptation of Marie Louise Pratt's concept of the 'contact zone'. This term best expresses my interest in how, in the examined transnational encounter, subjectivities constituted by binary paradigms and generic concepts pertaining to culture, gender, nationality and race were rearticulated and modified, 'however asymmetrical the imposed power dynamics might look in their inception'.[10] The notion of contact moment resembles that of point of intersection, or intercrossing, in the approach to transnational history as *histoire croisée*, or crossed history. This perspective is, most significantly, distinguished by its consideration of intercrossing entities, 'not merely … in relation to one another but also through one another'.[11] It views intercrossing as a dynamic, reciprocal and self-reflexive process, which not only changes the involved entities but also contributes to generating the object of research in an empirical and epistemological sense.[12] This constructivist stance corresponds to my inquiry into how women in Japan imagined Greenham and constructed their own identities, in relation to this almost utopian entity. It also bears on my historiographical interest in the prerequisites for a particular intercrossing to emerge as an object of memory or research. I return to these issues in my conclusions.

The transnationality of the 'ethnic nation'

Engagements with Greenham took place within the broader context of feminist and related intellectual and activist endeavours in Japan, extending back to the early postwar period. The discursive field surrounding the transnational imaginations and interactions examined in this chapter comprised two competing strategic approaches. One invoked supposedly universal standards and values to substantiate its assertions or claims; the other resorted to the 'ethnic nation' – true Japaneseness – as a source of authenticity and potency. While the former, which has been dubbed a politics of externality, tended to be expressed in terms of rights and implied an alignment with the West,[13] the latter referred to culture or history and signified a (re)turn to Japan or Asia.[14] Here the Japanese ethnic nation was brought into play against the Japanese state, which was presented as an inauthentic and adversarial agent in collusion with US imperialism in Asia and imposing a reckless and devastating course of industrialization on the Japanese people. Both discourses were imbued with gendered tropes. Women as housewives and mothers figured either as the impeccable protagonists of postwar democracy[15] or as quintessential 'inhabitants of daily life' (*seikatsusha*) and tokens of authenticity or rootedness in tradition.[16]

Invocations of the ethnic nation proliferated in the context of protests against the renewal of the US-Japan Security Treaty (1960) and within New Left formations like the anti-Vietnam War movement, which emerged during the 1960s. Japan's women's liberation (*ūman ribu*) movement began in 1970 in protest against what its members castigated as the misogyny and masculinism of the New Left. Nevertheless, its radical feminist critique of contemporary Japanese society and the Japanese state was infused with anti-imperialism, pan-Asianism and a quest for indigenous feminist traditions, bespeaking their inheritance of the New Left discursive tradition of pitting the ethnic nation against the state.[17]

Previous research on women's movements in postwar Japan might suggest that major transformations in feminist politics up to the 1980s can be identified with shifts from an externalist phase until around 1960, when liberal democracy, bestowed on Japan by the US occupation authorities, was believed to guarantee peace and women's rights; to an ethnic nationalist awakening since the late 1960s, when women's liberation and its predecessors brought postwar democracy into question; and back to externalism since the mid-1970s, when the UN's Decade for Women and its Conferences on Women created opportunity structures that boosted transnational networking and domestic lobbying activities in reference to international standards.[18] However, the new research presented in this chapter suggests that no such clear distinctions can be made. Rather, it indicates that these discursive strategies were often utilized simultaneously and in combination.[19] Ostensibly externalist rhetoric was imbued with references to the ethnic nation; conversely, constructions of the ethnic nation were made with reference to transnational images and discourses. Japanese activists' invocations and imaginations of Greenham provide prime examples of this confluence of externalist and ethnic nationalist tropes. Indeed, I argue, the dichotomy of external versus internal is as misleading as that of transnational versus national, as one is constructed through reference to the other.

The history of Japan since its forced 'opening' to the West in the mid-nineteenth century is the background against which *both* ethnic nationalist ideas *and* the impulse to emulate the West have emerged.[20] Differences between feminisms and gendered nationalisms in Western and non-Western contexts have long been recognized in connection with colonial and postcolonial power relations.[21] However, we have also been cautioned not to essentialize these differences and construct Third World or non-Western women as archetypal victims or as politically immature.[22] In regard to late twentieth-century Japan, for example, numerous commentators have emphasized that culturalist or traditionalist arguments were commonly invoked to curb social and political change.[23] I argue, first, that such discursive practices (surrounding culture and tradition as well as ethnicity, race or gender) are productive, or generative of new identities and ways to relate to others rather than simply repressive and limiting. Second, these discourses should be approached with a decentralized, 'capillary' concept of power – as invested in and emanating from institutions and social relations at the local and everyday levels[24] and with a view of Japanese women as agents participating in the production and strategic deployment of these discourses.

The Japanese case cannot simply be tagged as postcolonial. Japan's modern history, proceeding from narrowly escaping colonization by accomplishing modernization (or Westernization) and, in turn, invading and colonizing other nations, to postwar occupation and then to economic and cultural dominance in Asia, is a reminder of the fluidity of regional and global power constellations. Japan's relationship with its Asian neighbours, in particular, has interplayed with Japanese women's activism and feminist theorizing. In the prewar and early postwar periods in Japan, there was a strong tendency to connect with or favour women's movements and feminist ideas associated with the West and to imagine a world-spanning community of women based on gender universalism (the assumption that 'gender oppression [is] universally experienced by women no matter what their social location').[25] However, with the advent of 'women's liberation' – which occurred in the wake of the anti-Vietnam War movement's discursive turn to Asia – solidarity with other Asian women became a key focus of women's activism in Japan. Arguably, there were two contrasting approaches among activists. The first involved imagining a postcolonial community of Asian women, thereby including Japanese women among the victims of colonial and sexual exploitation by the West.[26] The second emphasized Japanese women's complicity in the victimization of other Asian people before and after 1945.[27] Narratives of the first kind could result in erasing or downplaying Japan's historical role as invader and colonizer and tie in with a discourse of Japan as victim that was enabled by the very memory of the atomic bombings of Hiroshima and Nagasaki.[28] The second approach involved a 'focus . . . on mutuality and coimplication'[29] or a 'recognition of mutual imbrication in structures of inequality', implying the awareness 'that [one's] own privilege is linked in a structured way to the lack of privilege of other women'.[30]

Binaries like external/internal, East/West or Japan/Europe – no less than male/female – are, of course, contested and unstable categories defined by 'discursive boundaries [that] change with historical conditions'.[31] Nevertheless, in Japan, 'the archetypal binary trope' of Japan and the West has continued to exist as 'the primal means of cross-cultural referencing'.[32] In that sense, the discursive situation of women's movements in Japan has indeed been different from the situation of European or 'white' North American movements, whose own national, racial or ethnic belonging has tended to constitute a default category.[33] Yet the reception of Greenham in Japan cannot simply be understood as an effort to forge a global alliance or to learn from an advanced culture.[34] Rather, I aim to show in the following sections of this chapter that Greenham was appropriated in complex ways, bringing forth and shaping the national through references to and input from the transnational.

Japan's established peace movement, gender, and the 'West'

> The peace that we call for is not simply a state of warlessness. Peace means building a world free of colonialism, racism, poverty and sexism. We confirm that we will better attain peace when we acknowledge the part that women have played by taking the initiative and promoting movements at the grassroots, in many countries; when political power is shared between men and women; and when we politically combine the efforts made by individuals to resist violence and oppression of all kinds.[35]

This quote from the so-called Tokyo Manifesto of the 1983 annual World Conference against Atomic and Hydrogen Bombs (*Gensuikin sekai taikai*) invites us to reflect on the relationship between women and the established peace movement in

Japan and on the transnational dynamics of this relationship. As mentioned above, the early 1980s were marked by the emergence of a new autonomous peace movement characterized by the participation of large numbers of women and the quest for new forms of organization and action. The above-quoted passage may be read as the established peace movement's response to this phenomenon.

Women played an important role at the grassroots of Japan's peace and anti-nuclear movement, from its beginnings in the 1950s.[36] However, in the movement the strings were increasingly pulled by the male-dominated political parties and unions, and members were mainly recruited and mobilized through these and other constituent organisations, few of which stated peace as their primary goal.[37] After a schism between organizations controlled by the Japanese Communist Party (JCP) and other groups – many of them affiliated with the Japan Socialist Party (JSP) and the General Council of Trade Unions of Japan (*Sōhyō*) – manifested in the early 1960s,[38] non-affiliated women's organizations were among the most zealous advocates of reconciliation and unity. Without their mediation efforts, the period of collaboration between 1977 and 1985, when the two political camps rejoined in organizing the annual World Conferences, might have been much shorter.[39]

What remained largely unchanged and unchallenged, in spite of these achievements by women, were the top-down organizational structure and the male dominance prevalent in both camps of the peace movement. The subordination of women within the movement was, however, not a unidirectional process. Indeed, their commitment as mediators as well as earlier actions protesting partisanship within the peace movement reflect women's own construction of the feminine as harbouring a natural concern for peace and representing the authentic voice of the people. This entailed not only the denial of women's implication in the war system but also the reinscription of gender difference, confining women to 'daily life' and restricting their political subjectivities to those of 'housewives' and 'mothers'.[40]

By acknowledging women's contributions, the 1983 manifesto gestured toward the new autonomous wave of women's peace activism as well as toward the many women who had not yet taken to the streets but whose voices found expression, in such outlets as the concerned female readers' letters which abounded in Japanese newspapers at the time.[41] Paradoxically, its mention of 'the part that women have played . . . at the grassroots' can be seen to reinscribe the gendered identity of the female peace activist.[42] However, the proclamation also seemed to promise a new age, where gender discrimination and power sharing between men and women were addressed not only as societal and global issues but also in a self-reflexive way in relation to the movement itself. It was the first time in the history of Japan's post-war peace movement that women or gender relations were explicitly mentioned in the manifesto of a World Conference. Though unfortunately, in the following year, the reference to sexism was dropped, perhaps reflecting the superficial concern for this issue among the movement's leadership.[43]

The passage in the 1983 manifesto also has an eminently transnational dimension. Its inclusion was, apparently, the result of the fervent advocacy of Rebecca Johnson, one of the figureheads of Greenham, who had been invited to represent

60 Ulrike Wöhr

the Camp at the World Conference.[44] During her stay in Japan, Johnson also spoke at local gatherings and repeatedly criticized Japan's peace movement for its out-dated style and male domination, blaming these factors for its stagnancy and failure to appeal to the masses. These comments were quoted by feminist critic and activist Kondō Kazuko, in the afterword to her translation of the book *Greenham Women Everywhere* (London, 1983/Tokyo, 1984), thus authenticating an imagined appeal by Greenham women to the 'women of Japan', who were 'still constrained by Confucianism', to 'take the lead in the peace movement'.[45]

These communications, taking place in a triangle composed of the male leadership of the Japanese peace movement and two eminent feminist activists, bear witness to complex and subtle negotiations of power relations surrounding gender, nationality and culture. On the one hand, all participants seem to agree that the gender order prevailing in the movement must be considerably changed, if not reversed. There also seems to be concordance regarding the relative positioning of Europe and Japan on an evolutionary scale of both gender relations and movement cultures: Japan was framed as backward and in need of learning from an advanced Europe. On the other hand, Johnson's invitation as a foreign delegate to Congress presumably reflected movement leaders' groping for ways in which to expand their constituency;[46] her critique was opportunely used to endorse one Japanese feminist's call to her readers, women of Japan, to liberate themselves and unite in pursuit of a higher goal. To these actors, the implicitly discriminating idea of a less advanced Japan was thus a useful strategic construct.

The communications analyzed above can be seen to exemplify the discursive strategy of prioritizing the West, or the universal, over Japan, or the particular. I suggest, however, that this discourse was not self-contained or pure, in that its objective was not to dissolve Japan, just as the acknowledgement of women's contributions did not aim to dissolve women as gendered entities but, rather, actively imagined a subject called women of Japan.

Reference to an external model and constructions of the ethnic nation (in opposition to the state) also interact in Kondō's afterword.

> If those women who have already raised their voices [against nuclear weapons] would hold hands, just like the women of Greenham, and form a human chain around the oceans of Japan, then the Tomahawk missiles would not be able to approach Japan.[47]

In this evocative image of how the Japanese archipelago and its oceans could be protected from the deployment of American missiles, tactics associated with Greenham women (whose 1982 action to 'Embrace the Base' had made them famous in Japan, as elsewhere) are adopted to prevent the whole of Japan from being turned into a US military base. This image can also be read as a fantasy about women as the protectors – rather than the protected. Moreover, these protectors are imagined not as a state-run army but as a kind of non-violent female militia emerging from the people. As such, they guard the nation against the external aggressor in the form of US imperialism but are also capable of mobilizing against an oppressive Japanese state. This is implied by Kondō's reference to the recent success of women's protests against a law amendment that would have made it harder to obtain an abortion.[48]

Japan in Greenham in Japan: ambiguous boundaries

To further illuminate the politics of meaning at work in the reimagination of Greenham among Japan's autonomous women peace activists, I now focus on the contact moment of July and August 1984, when Hiro Sumpter (hereafter Hiro), one of the peace campers at Greenham Common, visited Japan, showing the film *Carry Greenham Home* and speaking about Greenham at more than twenty localities across the country.[49] These meetings were mostly arranged by women from loosely connected grassroots groups organizing around concerns ranging from nuclear weapons to consumers' issues and subsequently dubbed 'The Network Connecting Grassroots Voices for Peace' (*Kusanone no heiwa no koe o tsunagu nettowāku*; hereafter: Grassroots Network).[50]

My discussion is, mainly, based on participating groups' and individuals' accounts of the above-mentioned events, which were circulated by the means of a self-published pamphlet and various newsletters.[51] Narratives published in this type of media are often informed by an informal style associated with the verb *kataru* (narrating, telling, talking in an informal manner),[52] connoting 'a creative reworking of the meanings of . . . experiences, often in interaction with peers and audiences'.[53] I do not, however, consider these types of sources to be more authentic than others. Rather, I take the very representation of such narratives as authentic voices to point to the pervasiveness of a discourse of authenticity and to indicate women's gendered agency in its production. By framing their communications as telling or sharing (*dashiau*) opinions and stories, rather than as arguing about or discussing issues, these actors constructed a difference between male and female speech, affirming both the liberating and connecting effects of 'female' ways of communication.[54]

The pamphlet entitled 'Talking [*kataru*] with Hiro from the Greenham Peace Camp' suggested that the act of *kataru* had the power to connect women across continents and nations. Yet in contrast to Rebecca Johnson, who unequivocally represented Europe, Hiro was a Japanese woman living in England. This circumstance might have served to simply bridge or level out perceived differences between Britain and Japan, or between Greenham women and activist women in Japan. However, Hiro's national, cultural or racial belonging emerges as a prevalent theme in most of the oral and written recollections of those who met her. The contact moment with Greenham was thus structured by a proliferation rather than an ignoring of questions of national, cultural or racial difference.

One conspicuous motif in the renderings of Hiro's character and appearance was that of strangeness associated not only with foreignness but also with gender deviance or ambiguity. Hiro was, for example, portrayed to have 'un-Japanese [*Nihonjinbanare shita*] facial features',[55] and someone remembered being stunned by her 'sturdy' (*gotsui*) physique.[56] Her attire, which apparently set her apart from

62 Ulrike Wöhr

her audience, was described in detail – purple T-shirt, yellow-green trousers and white sneakers.[57] One of the women who hosted Hiro commented on how, in the communal bath, she used her towel to cover her breasts instead of her pubic area, proving that she was 'not Japanese'.[58] The manner in which Hiro expressed herself in Japanese was also frequently mentioned. The way she 'faltered' in her speech[59] and her 'awkward Japanese'[60] were seen to indicate the degree of her separation from Japan. Someone emphasized the briskness and decisiveness of her speech,[61] and some even described her as 'tense', 'scary' or 'distant'.[62] Again, the fact that her name – not just the family name of her English husband, Sumpter, but also her given name – was rendered in *katakana* phonetic script rather than in its original Chinese characters doubtless also underscored the perception of Hiro as foreign.

However, foreignness was only one major way in which Hiro was portrayed in accounts of her visit. The other portrayal, in complete contrast, stressed familiarity and shared identity. In many instances, Hiro was introduced by variations of the epithet, 'the only Japanese woman of Greenham',[63] affirming her difference from the white majority of Greenham women and, conversely, her propinquity to her audience in Japan. Emphases on likeness and affinity also extended to physical attributes. A woman who had actually visited Greenham and had met Hiro there described her as 'delicate' – in notable contrast to her above-quoted portrayal as 'sturdy'. She also stressed that seeing a photograph of Hiro 'with her long black hair down' (Figure 3.1), among the many photos of white women in a pamphlet introducing the Camp, first provoked her desire to go there.[64] Constructions of familiarity were thus imbued with gendered images of Hiro as a Japanese woman.

The contradictory portrayal of Hiro's personality, physique and behaviour is reminiscent of Zygmunt Bauman's figure of the ambivalent stranger, who is '*neither/nor*, that is, simultaneously, *either/or*'.[65] In modernity, strangers are needed and continuously constructed as the screen on which 'the ambivalence which saturates the whole of social space' is projected, focusing diffuse anxiety and enabling a however fragile sense of security and orientation.[66] The preoccupation of these actors with Hiro's belonging thus suggests a concern regarding their own belonging and a desire to retain or restore the 'ordering power of the opposition'[67] – between Europe and Japan, or Greenham women and Japanese women.

Assertions of such an opposition were also prevalent in imaginations of Japan that did not refer to Hiro. It was, for example, suggested that the cultural climate (*fūdo*) of Japan was opposed to the adherence to higher principles deemed to characterize the life and actions of the women of Greenham. In addition, Japanese women, identified as housewives (*shufu*), were described as very much restricted by rules of propriety, by the neighbours' eyes and by their husbands' will, in implicit contrast to the situation in Britain.[68]

Constructing sameness through difference

Why, then, was ethnic, racial or cultural otherness constructed, to the point of over-determination, despite the fact that the much-professed aim of inviting someone

FIGURE 3.1 Hiro Sumpter. Photograph by Lesley McIntyre, published in *The Greenham Factor* (London: Greenham Print Prop, 1983). Reproduced with permission from Lesley McIntyre.

from Greenham was to 'unite as women'? One possible factor was the deeply engrained notions of Japan's backwardness or inferiority vis-à-vis the West, which have been discussed above, as well as apprehensions about Western women's racism, concerns which were reinforced by Hiro's own accounts of her experiences in England. In an interview conducted during her stay in Japan and published shortly afterward, Hiro spoke about her own encounter with racism in England and suggested that this was an experience she shared with other Japanese women living in

64 Ulrike Wöhr

foreign marriages abroad.[69] In addition, one of the women who had actually visited Greenham from Japan admitted that her idealized image of the Camp was somewhat tainted by what she perceived as racial discrimination against Hiro, who, she felt, was taken advantage of by some of the white women, who used her as a cook and caretaker.[70] In this light, insistences on difference in the narrations surrounding Greenham might be understood either as 'translations' of Western colonialist discourse[71] or as instances of 'reverse Orientalism'.[72] While not denying the applicability of such interpretations, I would like to take them one step further and ask what may have been the historically specific purpose of such translations, in view of the two particular contexts sketched earlier in this chapter: the circumstances of women's activism for peace, in the early 1980s, and discursive traditions constructing the ethnic nation as a source of opposition against the state.

As indicated above, women's autonomous peace activism in early 1980s Japan developed in response both to what was conceived as the Japanese state's alignment with US imperialism in Asia and as a result of long-standing dissatisfaction with the male-led established peace movement. Small activist circles and individuals sharing these concerns emerged all over Japan, and the formation of the Grassroots Network constituted one attempt to connect these individuals and groups to create more visibility and impact. Already in December 1980 a women's peace rally drawing more than 1,500 participants had been organized by loosely connected groups and individuals in Tokyo, resulting in the formation of the Liaison Group of Women Opposed to War (*Sensō e no michi o yurusanai onnatachi no renrakukai*; hereafter Liaison Group), which subsequently organized events and demonstrations at regular intervals.[73] Yet the affiliates of the Liaison Group remained limited to groups from the Kantō region, centred on Tokyo and Yokohama. Moreover, some women seem to have been alienated by what they perceived as the Liaison Group's leading members' elite background and lack of a more radical feminist commitment.[74]

The Grassroots Network started out as an alternative endeavour within the Tokyo-centred autonomous women's peace movement. It was, from the beginning, characterized by a wide geographical spread and diversity in terms of the issues addressed by its members – in contrast to the single-issue politics of the Liaison Group. The Network's Tokyo-based initiators turned to Greenham not only as a model for women's mobilizing against nuclear weapons but also as a radical feminist experiment.[75] Furthermore, they included women like Kondō Kazuko, who had ties to the post-New Left activist scene. Kondō's involvement in the antinuclear power movement, in particular, can be seen to have contributed to the transregional orientation of the Grassroots Network. At least six of the involved groups, from the southernmost to the northernmost of Japan's main islands, were concerned with nuclear power or nuclear waste.[76] Other focal concerns included nuclear weapons, ecology, consumers' and feminist issues. This regional and thematic variety also suggests the possibility of groupings and dissent. The issues of nuclear power and nuclear waste, for example, connoted such a difference of perspective, as they were conceived as problems of the energy-devouring centre exploiting the periphery, which had to cope with nuclear plants and disposal sites.[77] Again, not all of the participants shared the initiators' radical feminist convictions. More than a few identified as 'housewives' or were, at least, living that reality.[78]

Indeed, diversity — framed as a multitude of individuals' distinct qualities — was hailed as one of the Grassroots Network's essential and meaningful characteristics, flourishing in encounters (*deai*) between women (*onna*), based on 'trust' rather than on 'organization'.[79] However, in view of the diversity and even opposing viewpoints of the *onna* involved in the Network, it seems clear that the development of trust and mutual understanding was not a matter of course. In this context I would suggest that identity politics emphasizing Japan or Japanese women was subconsciously or sometimes consciously utilized to aid the construction of a community of grassroots women in Japan — one which united women beyond differences in outlook and across spatial and regional divides. Indeed, a community of Japanese women was visualized through the inscription of the twenty-three venues of events featuring Hiro onto a map of Japan, on the cover of the pamphlet documenting her visit (Figure 3.2).

We can thus conclude that the emphasis on difference from Greenham or Europe was not so much intended to reiterate the Japan/West binary, per se, but rather to establish an imagined community of Japanese women. This interpretation echoes existing analyses of nationalisms as discourses of difference between

FIGURE 3.2 Cover of pamphlet documenting Hiro Sumpter's visit to Japan (edited by Gurīnamu no Hiro-san to kataru kai, Tokyo, 1984). Reproduced with permission from Kondō Kazuko.

66 Ulrike Wöhr

the home and the foreign nation.[80] However, I would argue that the narratives examined above also followed another pattern, namely, invocation of the ethnic nation as an authentic realm opposed to an exploitative and colonizing state. In many of the self-portraits penned by groups from the Grassroots Network there are images of an oppressive state in the guise of bullying policemen, the 'triangular system' of government, bureaucracy and big business or the central power turning the periphery into nuclear and military wastelands.[81] There was also criticism of the state's colonization of women's bodies and sexuality via eugenic population control and the marriage system.[82] Many of the groups, moreover, grounded their opposition to the state or the 'system' in the sphere of the family and the home, referred to as 'daily life'. Sometimes this female-identified sphere was explicitly set against the sphere of 'politics', but more often it was represented as the very source of political consciousness and subjecthood. Some women's activities had begun with concerns about the disappearance of locally grown rice from their kitchens or pollution from synthetic household detergents. One group proclaimed that 'the rice scoop [symbolizing the realm and the authority of the Japanese housewife] is stronger than the sword.'[83]

As explained above, the profoundly gendered space of daily life had already been carved out in opposition to the state by New Left and post-New Left movements. In the Grassroots Network, Hiro's ambiguous presence as objective onlooker *and* sympathetic companion with an authentic grasp of Japan seems to have facilitated the interpretation of this sphere of daily life as distinctly and authentically Japanese. One woman, for example, recounted how talking to Hiro, who had come 'from so far away' but felt 'like an old friend', had confirmed her belief in the importance of conserving not only the local environment but also a traditional lifestyle and food culture.[84] If we understand such articulations to pertain to the oppositional discourse of daily life and the ethnic nation, this suggests that the imagined distance and alterity of Greenham – as mediated by Hiro – empowered grassroots activists in Japan in their struggle against the state.

Boundaries in transnational space: separating or connecting?

Thus far, I have discussed the perceived otherness of Greenham only in terms of how it was utilized in the construction of an ethnic national community of Japanese women. However, as Xiangming Chen reminds us, borders – whether material or symbolic – 'can be either barriers or bridges. They both separate and connect'.[85] The borders delineating Japan, in the accounts of Hiro Sumpter's visit, are no exception. Indeed, every single assertion of difference between the women of Greenham and Japanese grassroots women could be read to imply a desire to move beyond that difference. This is exemplified by the rereading of a successful local antipollution movement of the early 1970s, led by women of the fishing village of Kazanashi, as 'Japan's Greenham'.[86] This association was first made by Hiro, but within the Grassroots Network her idea was embraced with enthusiasm. It is not difficult to see how this interpretation connected Japanese women in a community of struggle across space and time and, at the same time, affirmed the bond between activist women in Britain and Japan. Another compelling example is the aforementioned spatial rendering of the projected community of Japanese women in the form of a map (Figure 3.2). This drawing shows the Japanese archipelago encircled by a double-headed serpent. Its body can be seen to mark Japan's maritime borders, but snakes were also symbolic of Greenham (just like the spider web in the top left corner of the same drawing).[87] The snake in this drawing epitomizes the ambivalence of boundaries by signifying Japan's separateness and, at the same time, attesting to a desire to bridge the gap separating it from Europe. Again, the persona of Hiro herself might be seen to form an ambiguous boundary between Greenham and Japan, in a similar way to the serpent. These observations correspond with Suganuma's view of contact moments as being structured by binary oppositions and, at the same time, revealing their discursive limits. Moments of cross-cultural or transnational contact could thus be described as nodes in processes of identity formation wherein binaries function as facilitators of self-reflexive processes or desires that actually point beyond fixed oppositions and categories of identity.[88]

The question remains of what the binary of Japanese women versus Greenham or Western women implied in regard to other Asian or non-Western women. Arguably, the decoration of the serpent's body with what might be called a tribal pattern points to a world neither Western nor Japanese. From the perspective of *histoire croisée*, seemingly simple linear transfers may in fact be 'movements between various points in at least two and sometimes several directions'.[89] As mentioned above, oppositional discourses of the ethnic nation in modern Japan developed in close affinity to pan-Asian ideas, and from the time of the anti-Vietnam War movement of the 1960s there was a growing consciousness of 'co-implication' or 'mutual imbrication' in an unequal global order. Issues addressed by groups from the Network included Japanese men's sex tourism to other Asian countries, the trafficking in Asian women within Japan, and the unequal structures through which Japanese women contributed to the economic exploitation of other Asian women.[90] There were also representations of a wider 'Asia' within Japan. These included the Korean resident singer-songwriter, who performed at one of the events featuring Hiro and was introduced as an activist against fingerprinting on Korean residents' alien registration cards, and the Filipina activist for democracy who joined a rally in solidarity with Greenham organized by Osaka women.[91] One group in the Network also explicitly challenged the representation of Japan as the 'only nation ever to have been atom-bombed', a trope that characterized the rhetoric of the postwar peace movement. Instead, the group looked at radioactive contamination from nuclear testing in the South Pacific, moving beyond the Japanese experience of victimization.[92]

In the accounts of the Grassroots Network, to draw closer to Asia could also mean to identify as Asian, in opposition to Europe, or the West, as for example when Hiro was dubbed Greenham's 'only Asian' – rather than its 'only Japanese' – activist.[93]

68 Ulrike Wöhr

Such imaginations of a larger community of non-Western or non-white women reverberate with Hiro's narration of her own experience with racial discrimination in England as well as with one of my informant's impression that, even at Greenham, Hiro was being treated as racially inferior. Incidentally, this woman – an atom bomb survivor and peace activist from Hiroshima – greatly sympathized with Selma James and Wilmette Brown, the central figures of the King's Cross Women's Centre in London, who stood for the infusion of antiracism into the feminist movement and the peace movement.[94] Although such narratives could be seen to tie in with constructions of collective victimhood that have tended to erase past and present realities of Japan as a colonizing and victimizing nation, we should still take these experiences and perceptions seriously. Indeed, the account of Hiro's relegation to a service role parallels better-known criticism of how some white women at Greenham treated black women.[95]

Conclusion

We may conclude that – at this particular point in the transnational history of women's movements – the thought and activism of women in Japan were still very much bound by the binaries of Orient/Occident and First World/Third World, albeit in changing and diverse ways that implied the possibility of shifts in the borders separating those categories. A key element in these discourses was the never wholly suppressible ambiguity of Japan itself, projected on and mirrored by Hiro, the visitor from Greenham, who was neither/nor and, simultaneously, either/or, in terms of the intersections of gender, race, nationality and culture. However, it seems that, at this point in time in the 1980s, the Grassroots Network's trajectory pointed more toward the elimination of such ambiguity, in pursuit of an activist community of Japanese women. Indeed, the connections made in the summer of 1984 evolved into a women-only network, which, after the Chernobyl accident of 1986, made nuclear power its central concern.[96] In contrast, transnational networking during the decade following Hiro's visit seems to have remained sporadic among these actors and dependent on individual efforts.

This tendency runs counter to Valentine Moghadam's periodization of late-twentieth-century women's transnational networking into before and after the watershed of the UN World Conference on Women held in Nairobi, Kenya, in 1985. According to Moghadam, this event marked a shift from a situation in which women's movements were still mostly nationally based and nationally oriented, and feminists were deeply divided by ideologies and Cold War realities as well as by differences between developed and developing countries to the emergence of a new collective identity as women and new forms of organizing across national borders.[97] While this analysis may adequately capture a general trend, my example of one transnational dynamic in mid-1980s Japan points not only to possible non-simultaneities in such global processes but casts doubt on the evolutionary optimism implied in Moghadam's narrative. Indeed, my observations regarding the contact moment of 1984 and beyond suggest that the purported watershed of

Reimagining Greenham **69**

1985 has not rendered intersectional analyses of gender and race (or ethnicity, or nationality) obsolete. Also, my analysis could serve to complement Moghadam's perspective on women and the transnational. While she limits her use of the term to women's networking on a global scale, mainly after 1985,[98] I have demonstrated the relevance and productivity of an approach that moves beyond the binary of national versus transnational, focusing on intercrossings or contact moments where the transnational and the national, masculinity and femininity, Occident and Orient, First World and Third World are not simply interacting but constituting or reconstituting each other in a polycentric dynamic that cuts across these binaries. My research also suggests that paying attention to intercrossings or contact moments helps to understand how the transnational impacts women's movements, beyond the existence of transnational networks.

Although the topic of this chapter has been the reimagining of Greenham in Japan, I would like to close by shifting our gaze and ask how Greenham and the women's peace movement in Europe might have been implicated in the failure of the Grassroots Network to develop more substantial transnational ties. When I tried to track the paths of Hiro and of the numerous Japanese women who visited Greenham, I was struck by the absence of practically any trace of their existence in the works on Greenham that I consulted and what this seemed to indicate about the asymmetry of the relationship between Greenham women and the Japanese activists. Intercrossing is not a historical given, which only needs to be recorded. According to the theorists of *histoire croisée*, '[i]t requires an active [and one may add: inspired] observer to construct it.'[99] Seemingly, to the protagonists and historians of Greenham, the Japanese women's peace movement was much less inspiring than vice versa. I would suggest that two new approaches to the historiography of the European women's peace movements, and of Greenham in particular, could help throw light on this asymmetry. First, there could be a historical analysis of the racial politics of these movements as 'white majority women's movements';[100] second, there could be an examination of how these movements may have participated in potentially exploitive[101] ways of citing Hiroshima and Nagasaki, turning those who died or suffered as a result of the atomic bombings into passive victims. The narratives by activist women in 1980s Japan, which I analyzed in this chapter, are crying out for such complementary research.

Notes

1 I would like to thank Andrea Germer, Hilaria Gössmann, Vera Mackie, Angela Coutts, Mark Pendleton and the editors of this volume for their many helpful comments and their encouragement.
2 Interview with H. H., conducted in Hiroshima, 31 May 2013. This and all other translations are my own.
3 E.g., J. Liddington, *The Road to Greenham Common*, New York: Syracuse University Press, 1989; S. Roseneil, *Disarming Patriarchy*, Buckingham: Open University Press, 1995.
4 L. Wittner, *Toward Nuclear Abolition*, Stanford: Stanford University Press, pp. 63–168.
5 Glen D. Hook, 'The ban the bomb movement in Japan', *Social Alternatives*, 3:2, 1983, 35–39; Yoshitake T., 'Sensō e no michi o yurusanai onnatachi no renrakukai', in Kōdō

suru kai kiroku henshū iinkai, ed., *Kōdō suru onnatachi ga hiraita michi*, Tokyo: Miraisha, 1999, pp. 238–245. See also the section of this chapter titled 'Constructing Sameness through Difference'.

6 On the 'feminization' of the European peace movement, see Gurīnamu no Hiro-san to kataru kai (hereafter: Kataru kai) (ed.), *Gurīnamu pīsukyanpu no Hiro-san to kataru: Kusanone no heiwa no koe o tsunagu nettowāku*, photocopied pamphlet, Tokyo, 1984, p. 32. Cf. also B. Davis, 'Europe Is a Peaceful Woman, America Is a War-Mongering Man?', *Themenportal Europäische Geschichte*, 2009. Online: www.europa.clio-online.de/Portals/_Europa/documents/B2009/E_Davis_Europe.pdf

7 Two members of an Osaka women's group campaigning against nuclear power, for example, visited Greenham during the summer of 1982 (interview conducted in Osaka, 3 March 2013).

8 M. E. Wiesner-Hanks, 'Crossing borders in transnational gender history', *Journal of Global History*, 6, 2011, 374; J. Rendall, 'A Transnational Career? The Republican and Utopian Politics of Frances Wright (1795–1852)', in O. Janz and D. Schönpflug, eds., *Gender History in a Transnational Perspective*, New York: Berghahn, 2014, p. 153. Cf. also V. Mackie, 'The language of globalization, transnationality and feminism', *International Feminist Journal of Politics*, 3:2, 2001, 188–189.

9 To avoid confusion I use other terms, like 'global' or 'world-spanning', to signify scale.

10 K. Suganuma, *Contact Moments: The Politics of Intercultural Desire in Japanese Male-Queer Cultures*. Hong Kong: Hong Kong University Press, p. 19.

11 M. Werner and B. Zimmermann, 'Beyond comparison: *Histoire Croisée* and the challenge of reflexivity', *History and Theory*, 45, 2006, 38.

12 Ibid., 38–44.

13 Cf. J. Gelb, *Gender Policies in Japan and the United States: Comparing Women's Movements, Rights, and Politics*, New York: Palgrave Macmillan, pp. 4–8.

14 See K. Doak, 'What is a nation and who belongs? National narratives and the ethnic imagination in twentieth-century Japan', *The American Historical Review*, 102:2, 1997, 304–308; A. Germer, '"The inner and the outer domain": Sexuality and the nation-state in Japanese feminist historiography', *Social Science Japan Journal*, 9:1, 2006, 61–68; S. Avenell, *Making Japanese Citizens: Civil Society and the Mythology of the Shimin in Postwar Japan*, Berkeley: University of California Press, 2010, pp. 133–137.

15 See L. Yoneyama, *Hiroshima Traces: Time, Space and the Dialectics of Memory*, Berkeley: University of California Press, 1999, pp. 190–191; V. Mackie, *Feminism in Modern Japan*, Cambridge: Cambridge University Press, 2003, pp. 122–131.

16 E.g., Matsui Y., 'Hankōgai undō ni tachiagaru onnatachi', in 'Nihon ni okeru seisabetsu' hakusho kankō iinkai, ed., *Nihon no onna wa hatsugen suru*, vol. 1, Tokyo: 491, 1975, pp. 81–88; Cf. Avenell, op. cit., pp. 226–228.

17 Cf. S. Shigematsu, *Scream from the Shadows: The Women's Liberation Movement in Japan*, Minneapolis: University of Minnesota Press, 2012, pp. 33–62, 70–72, 86–87; Germer, op. cit., passim; A. Germer, *Historische Frauenforschung in Japan: Die Rekonstruktion der Vergangenheit in Takamure Itsues "Geschichte der Frau"*, München: Iudicium, 2003, pp. 356–367.

18 Many studies on Japanese women's movements in the postwar period suggest the applicability of such a tripartite scheme, although each author frames it somewhat differently. E.g. Mackie, op. cit. (2003); Gelb, op. cit.; Shigematsu, op. cit.; I. Lenz, 'From Mothers of the Nation to Embodied Citizens', in A. Germer, V. Mackie and U. Wöhr, eds., *Gender, Nation and State in Modern Japan*, London: Routledge, 2014, pp. 211–229.

19 For a similar argument, cf. I. Lenz, 'From mothers of the nation to global civil society: The changing role of the Japanese women's movement in globalization', *Social Science Japan Journal*, 9:1, 2006, passim.

20 Cf. Doak, op. cit., 284–299; Germer, op. cit., 2006, 52–54.

21 E.g., D. Kandiyoti, 'Identity and its discontents: Women and the nation', *Millenium: Journal of International Studies*, 20:3, 1991, 429–443; P. Chatterjee, *The Nation and its Fragments: Colonial and Postcolonial Histories*, Princeton: Princeton University Press, 1993, pp. 116–157.

Reimagining Greenham **71**

22 V. Amos and P. Parmar, 'Challenging imperial feminism', *Feminist Review*, 17, 1984, 3–19; C. T. Mohanty, 'Under western eyes: Feminist scholarship and colonial discourses', *Feminist Review*, 30, 1988, 65–88.

23 Cf. Gelb, op. cit., p. 6, and the studies quoted ibid.

24 Cf. M. Foucault, *Power/Knowledge: Selected Interviews and other Writings (1972–77)*, ed. by C. Gordon, New York, Pantheon Press, 1980, p. 96.

25 Quote taken from B. Roth, *Separate Roads to Feminism: Black, Chicana, and White Feminist Movements in America's Second Wave*, Cambridge: Cambridge University Press, 2004, p. 188; on transnational feminisms in modern Japan see, e.g., B. Molony, 'Crossing Boundaries: Transnational Feminisms in Twentieth-century Japan', in M. Roces and L. Edwards, eds., *Women's Movements in Asia*, London: Routledge, 2010, pp. 93–105.

26 Cf. Germer, op. cit., 2006, passim; U. Wöhr, 'Japanese Comfort Women – Sex Slaves or Prostitutes? An Issue of Feminist Politics and Historiography', in C. Derichs and S. Kreitz-Sandberg, eds., *Gender Dynamics and Globalisation*, Berlin: LIT Verlag, 2007, pp. 116–117.

27 Cf. Iijima A., 'Naze "Shinryaku=sabetsu to tatakau Ajia fujin kaigi" datta no ka' [1996], in *Aru feminisuto no hansei*, Tokyo: Inpakuto shuppankai, 2006, passim; Mackie, op. cit. (2003), pp. 148–149; Shigematsu, op. cit., pp. 12–13, 47–50; Iijima A. and A. Germer, 'From Personal Experience to Political Activism in the 1970s: My View of Feminism', in A. Germer, V. Mackie and U. Wöhr, eds., *Gender, Nation and State in Modern Japan*, London: Routledge, 2014, pp. 296–297.

28 Cf. Yoneyama, op. cit., p. 12.

29 C. T. Mohanty, '"Under western eyes" revisited: Feminist solidarity through anticapitalist struggles', *Signs*, 28:2, 2002, 522.

30 Mackie, op. cit. (2001), 195.

31 T. de Lauretis, 'Introduction', in T. de Lauretis (ed.), *Feminist Studies/Critical Studies*, Bloomington: Indiana University Press, p. 8.

32 Suganuma, op. cit., p. 87.

33 Cf. R. Frankenberg, *White Women, Race Matters: The Social Construction of Whiteness*, London: Routledge, 1993.

34 Indeed, Japan had its own non-violent antimilitary women's peace camp, which was initiated two decades before Greenham and was introduced, at length, in a 1983 British publication on women's peace movements around the world: L. Caldecott, 'At the Foot of the Mountain: The Shibokusa Women of Kita Fuji', in L. Jones, ed., *Keeping the Peace: A Women's Peace Handbook*, London: Women's Press, 1983, pp. 98–107.

35 Gensuibaku kinshi Nihon kyōgikai (hereafter: Gensuikyō) (ed.), *1983 Gensuibaku kinshi sekai taikai to Gensuikyō kōdō no kiroku*, vol. 2, Tokyo: Gensuikyō, 1983, p. 104.

36 Maruhama E., *Gensuikin shomei undō no tanjō*, Tokyo: Gaifūsha, 1911; V. Mackie, 'From Hiroshima to Lausanne: The World Congress of Mothers and the Hahaoya Taikai in the 1950s', *Women's History Review*, forthcoming.

37 Apart from the unions, some of the larger organizations included, for example, the Housewives' Association (Shufuren), the Federation of Regional Women's Organisations (Chifuren), the Japan Youth Association (Nisseikyō) and the Consumers' Co-operative Union (Seikyōren).

38 As a result, the decimated, now JCP-controlled Japan Council against Atomic and Hydrogen Bombs (Gensuibaku kinshi Nihon kyōgikai, or Gensuikyō) continued to exist under its original name, while groups affiliated with Sōhyō and the JSP reorganized as Japan Congress against A- and H-Bombs (Gensuibaku kinshi Nihon kokumin kaigi, or Gensuikin), in 1965. See Wada N., *Genshiryoku to kaku no jidaishi*, Tokyo: Nanatsumori shokan, 2014, pp. 71–81; Yoneyama, op. cit., pp. 21–22.

39 For a critical account of these mediations, see Gensuibaku kinshi Nihon kokumin kaigi, ed., *Gensuikin undō no saisei o motomete*. Tokyo: Gensuibaku kinshi Nihon kokumin kaigi, 1984, passim. About how various women's groups dealt with the schism, see Kondō Y., Saitō T., Sumiya S., and Kanō M., 'Zadankai: Fujin undō no bunretsu o megutte', in Onnatachi no genzai o tou kai, ed., *Kōdo seichō no jidai, onnatachi wa*, Tokyo: Inpakuto shuppankai, pp. 126, 133 and passim.

72 Ulrike Wöhr

40 Cf. Yoneyama, op. cit., pp. 202–208; M. Todeschini, 'The Bomb's Womb? Women and the Atom Bomb', in Veena Das, A. Kleinman, M. Lock, M. Ramphele, and P. Reynolds, eds., *Remaking a World: Violence, Social Suffering, and Recovery*, Berkeley: University of California Press, 2001, pp. 148–149; Muta K., *Jendā kazoku o koete*, Tokyo: Shin'yōsha, 2006, pp. 151–159.
41 Cf. Yoshitake, op. cit., 1999, p. 239.
42 Cf. U. Wöhr, 'Gender and Citizenship in the Anti-nuclear Power Movement in 1970s Japan', in A. Germer, V. Mackie and U. Wöhr, eds., *Gender, Nation and State in Modern Japan*, London and New York: Routledge, 2014a, pp. 230–254.
43 See the texts of the manifestos in Gensuikyō, op. cit., p. 104; and Gensuikyō, ed., *Gensuibaku kinshi sekai taikai to Nihon Gensuikyō kōdō no kiroku 1984*, vol. 2., Tokyo: Gensuikyō, 1984, p. 96.
44 Cf. Wada, op. cit., p. 145.
45 Kondō K., 'Yakusha atogaki', in A. Cook and G. Kirk, ed., *Gurīnamu no onnatachi*, Tokyo: Hachigatsu shokan, 1984, pp. 248–249.
46 About the political and contested nature of international delegates' invitations to the World Conferences, see Yoshikawa Y., *Shimin undō no shukudai*, Tokyo: Shisō no kagakusha, 1991, pp. 82–83.
47 Kondō K., op. cit., p. 250.
48 Ibid., p. 251.
49 According to Hiro's letters to her Japanese hosts, transcriptions of her speeches and interviews and my communications with people who knew her, she (née Ishii Hiroko) was born in Japan around 1941, moved to England around 1972, was, for a number of years, married to an Englishman, and had a son. She joined women's and antinuclear groups in the late 1970s, started living at Greenham in summer 1982 and later went on to North America as an activist against uranium mining. Hiro died of cancer in 1993. Cf. U. Wöhr, 'Greenham and the Politics of Race and Ethnicity: A Photo of Hiro Sumpter', *History Workshop Online*, 2014b. Online: www.historyworkshop.org.uk/radical-objects-a-photo-of-hiro-sumpter
50 Kataru kai, op. cit., cover.
51 Additionally, I refer to contemporary coverage in the general press and to later recollections by individual participants, in interviews as well as published sources.
52 Kataru kai, op. cit., cover page and p. 1.
53 Todeschini, op. cit., p. 134. See ibid. for implications with regard to discourses of female atom bomb survivors.
54 See, e.g., the 'Newsletter of the Delta Women's Group', *Deruta onna no kai nyūsu* (hereafter: *Deruta nyūsu*) 2, 1982, 1; and Nani ga nandemo genpatsu ni hantai suru onnatachi, 'Ari no mama ni, nobiyaka ni jūyonen', in T. Miwa and N. Ōsawa, eds., *Genpatsu o tomeru onnatachi*, Tokyo: Shakai shisōsha, 1990, pp. 160–161.
55 Kataru kai, op. cit., p. 5.
56 Emails by T. H., dated 13 and 22 April 2013 (follow up on interview conducted in Osaka, 3 March 2013).
57 Kataru kai, op. cit., p. 3.
58 Interview with H. H. and H. M., conducted in Hiroshima, 21 July 2013.
59 Kataru kai, op. cit., p. 4.
60 Ibid., p. 9.
61 Ibid., p. 3.
62 Ibid., pp. 5, 14, 25.
63 E.g., Ibid., pp. 12, 17, 19.
64 Interview with H. H., conducted in Hiroshima, 31 May 2013. See the photo in *The Greenham Factor*, London: Greenham Print Prop, no date or pagination. Also cf. Wöhr, op. cit., 2014b.
65 Z. Bauman, 'Modernity and ambivalence', *Theory, Culture & Society*, 7, 1990, 146.
66 Z. Bauman, *Postmodern Ethics*, Cambridge, MA: Blackwell, 1993, pp. 160–161.
67 Bauman, op. cit., 1990, p. 146.

68 Kataru kai, op. cit., pp. 11, 14; Cf. also Kondō K., op. cit., p. 247; and Hatakeyama H., 'Deruta no kai', unpublished manuscript, 1986, p. 1.
69 H. Sanputā and Kondō K., 'Gurīnamu kara Nihon no onnatachi e', *Sekai*, 10, 1984, 224–225; reprinted in Kataru kai, op. cit., p. 29.
70 Interview with H. H., conducted in Hiroshima, 31 May 2013.
71 R. Sakamoto, 'Japan, hybridity and the creation of colonialist discourse', *Theory, Culture & Society*, 13:3, passim.
72 C. Ueno, 'In the feminine guise: A trap of reverse orientalism', *U.S.-Japan Women's Journal*, 13, 1997, passim.
73 Yoshitake, op. cit., 1999, pp. 240–244.
74 Emails by K. K., dated 25 and 26 July 2013 (follow-ups on interview conducted in Tokyo, 30 March 2013).
75 Kataru kai, op. cit., p. 32. Interview with K. K., conducted in Tokyo, 30 March 2013.
76 Kataru kai, op. cit., pp. 15, 18, 20, 21, 24; *Deruta nyūsu* 1, 1982, 1.
77 Kataru kai, op. cit., pp. 21, 24;
78 Kataru kai, op. cit., pp. 9, 14, 21, *Deruta nyūsu* 17, 1984, 2.
79 Kataru kai, op. cit. (2nd edition, 1985), first page after cover (unpaginated). On implications of *deai* and *onna* in feminist discourses, see Shigematsu, op. cit., pp. 16–17, 61; Wöhr, op. cit., 2014a, p. 244.
80 E.g., S. Blättler, 'Identity Politics: Gender, Nation and State in Modern European Philosophy', in A. Germer, V. Mackie and U. Wöhr eds., *Gender, Nation and State in Modern Japan*, London: Routledge, 2014, pp. 279–282.
81 Kataru kai, op. cit., pp. 10, 20, 24.
82 Ibid., p. 20.
83 Ibid., pp. 9, 14, 21.
84 Ibid., p. 21.
85 X. Chen, *As Borders Bend: Transnational Spaces on the Pacific Rim*, Latham: Rowman and Littlefield, 2005, p. xii.
86 Kataru kai, op. cit., pp. 13, 17; *Deruta nyūsu* 17, 1984, 2. On the Kazanashi struggle, see M. McKean, *Environmental Protest in Japan*, Berkeley: University of California Press, 1980, pp. 85–88.
87 Cf. Liddington, op. cit., p. 251; A. Feigenbaum, *Tactics and Technology: Cultural Resistance at the Greenham Common Women's Peace Camp*, doctoral thesis, Montreal: McGill University, 2008, pp. 134–145. Online: http://annafeigenbaum.com/wp-content/uploads/2013/08/April_2014_CV_public.pdf
88 Suganuma, op. cit., pp. 34–35, 177–181.
89 M. Werner and B. Zimmermann, op. cit., 37.
90 Kataru kai, op. cit., pp. 5, 17; *Deruta nyūsu* 18, 1984, 2.
91 Kataru kai, op. cit., pp. 17, 20.
92 Kataru kai, op. cit., p. 5. On the trope of the 'only nation' cf. J. Orr, *The Victim as Hero: Ideologies of Peace and National Identity in Postwar Japan*, Honolulu: University of Hawaii Press, 2001, pp. 36–70.
93 *Deruta nyūsu* 17, 1984, 1.
94 Deruta onna no kai (ed.), *Yōroppa – onnatachi no hankaku kōdō*, pamphlet, Hiroshima: Deruta onna no kai (no date; presumably published 1983 or 1984), pp. 4–5.
95 Amos and Parmar, op. cit., 16.
96 *Deruta nyūsu* 24, 1985; *8/9 Hiroshima onnatachi no tsudoi*, pamphlet, Hiroshima: Deruta onna no kai, 1987; K. Kondō, 'Gurīnamu no onnatachi kara Fukushima no onnatachi e', in K. Kondō and Y. Ōhashi, eds., *Fukushima genpatsu jiko to onnatachi*, Tokyo: Nashi no ki sha, 2012, pp. 164–176.
97 V. Moghadam, *Globalizing Women: Transnational Feminist Networks*, Baltimore: Johns Hopkins University Press, 2005, pp. 1, 5–6.
98 Ibid., pp. 3–4.
99 M. Werner and B. Zimmermann, op. cit., 39.
100 Feigenbaum, op. cit., p. 19.

74 Ulrike Wöhr

101 P. Boyer, 'Exotic Resonances: Hiroshima in American Memory', in M. J. Hogan, ed., *Hiroshima in History and Memory*, Cambridge: Cambridge University Press, 1996, p. 164. In the context of Greenham, for example, a badly deformed 'Hiroshima-baby' was used to illustrate the need of taking action (cf. Liddington, op. cit., 1989, p. 227). A pamphlet put out by a Greenham support group contained numerous references to the bombings of Hiroshima and Nagasaki, evoking the deaths and suffering, particularly of women and children. No mention, however, was made of the peace activism that many women from these cities engaged in (*The Greenham Factor*, op. cit.; cf. Wöhr, op. cit., 2014b).

PART II

Women's agency in the intersecting histories of imperialisms and nationalisms

4

'NEW WOMEN', AMERICAN IMPERIALISM, AND FILIPINA NATIONALISM

The politics of dress in Philippine mission stations, 1898–1940

Laura R. Prieto

> *"Beware of all enterprises that require new clothes."*
>
> – Henry David Thoreau

In 1937, Maxine Gonong appeared before the Methodist Episcopal Woman's Home Missionary Society (WHMS) annual meeting in Seattle, Washington. She was one of a great many guests and speakers over the several days of the meeting, and the minutes mention her only in passing. They do not note, for example, that she was a student at the University of Seattle, brought from the Philippines as part of the government-sponsored *pensionado* scholarship program. At this gathering, Gonong played a representative rather than an individual role. Whereas other missionaries merely told stories of 'other races and places', Dr. Walter Bundy introduced Miss Gonong, 'in a Filipino costume', as a living exemplar of his work in the Philippines. Whatever Gonong said publicly on the occasion is again not recorded. Her native dress is what left an impression, designating her as a transnational figure – unlike her male companion, Pio Daba, whose sartorial choice went pointedly unmarked.[1]

Gonong's appearance in front of the Woman's Home Missionary Society points to the significance and politics of dress within American imperialism. American Protestants had begun to evangelize in the Philippines in 1898, directly following the Spanish-American War when the US took possession of Spain's Pacific and Caribbean colonies. Methodist, Presbyterian, Baptist, and Congregationalist missionary societies from the US worked collaboratively to 'civilize and Christianize' the Filipino population, the majority of whom had converted to Catholicism over the centuries of Spanish rule. The missionaries shared the public purpose of American imperialism; as Minnesota Senator Knute Nelson put it, 'Providence has given the United States the duty of extending Christian civilization . . . not to enslave the

78 Laura R. Prieto

Filipinos but to uplift them.'[2] This self-styled 'benevolent assimilation' intended not (only) to dominate but to transform American colonial subjects. Religious missionaries and business enterprises thus became important partners alongside federal employees and the military in the American imperialist project. American women, especially women missionaries and teachers, were also key. A female presence signaled the purported benevolence of the enterprise, a transition from Krag rifles to schoolbooks as the means of pacification. Just as the concept of 'woman's work for woman' had typified nineteenth-century missiology, so did federal policy integrate American women as agents of imperialism who could reach and 'uplift' Filipinas in a way that men could not.

At the time the Baptist missionaries welcomed Gonong to their annual meeting, the Philippines was, at last, gaining its independence. Filipinos' organized colonial resistance dated back to the anti-Spanish Katipunan, formed in 1892. Filipino nationalists at first looked to the US as an ally in their war against Spain. When Spain was defeated and the US took possession of the Philippines for itself, many then turned their fight against American troops. The US declared victory in the ensuing Philippine-American War (1899–1902), a conflict that cost hundreds of thousands of lives. But guerrilla resistance continued for decades in Cavite and Mindanao.[3] Other Filipino nationalists tried to secure independence by working within the US government, holding American imperialists to their word that they always meant to transition toward Filipino self-government, once the colony had been properly tutored. Through the early twentieth century, Filipinos gradually took up civil service positions and became appointed officials under US occupation. In 1934, the Tydings McDuffie Act at last established an interim Filipino government of the Philippines. A referendum in 1935 accepted the new Constitution, establishing the Commonwealth of the Philippines. American colonial rule officially ended in 1946.[4]

This study examines gender, imperialism, and anticolonialism in the US–occupied Philippines through the lens of dress within mission communities. It extends the study of the politics of dress in other transnational Filipino networks.[5] Dress reveals the visual and material dimensions of power relationships. The complex history, religion, and politics of the archipelago make Filipino dress an especially rich marker of identity. Though the WHMS report referred to Gonong's 'Filipino costume' as a self-evident type of clothing, in reality Filipino styles of dress ranged widely, reflecting the diverse global influences from China, Islam, Spain, and the US on the Philippines' past. Gonong's particular Filipino costume was probably a *terno*, still popular in the 1930s but dating to the beginnings of the American occupation; the *terno* or butterfly dress integrated native Filipino fabrics with a Western silhouette, derived from Spanish styles. It also connoted the wearer's cultural identity, because dress comprised one of the few ways in which women could show public support for Filipino nationalism. Though the *terno* was well known, missionaries in the field would have been familiar with many other sorts of indigenous – and syncretic – clothing. Mission stations were cultural borderlands where success depended on persuading, not coercing, local populations to adopt Protestant Christianity.

Photographs do more than augment the verbal references to dress in archival records. As both images and objects, photographs possess a dual visuality and materiality.[6] They attest, immediately and vividly, to the combinations of accommodation and resistance at work in what Filipinas and American women chose to wear – how Filipinas adopted elements of American dress and how American women on occasion wore Filipina dress. Photographs simultaneously served as a form of exchange, connecting local Filipino missions to a global community. They linked readers of missionary literature to Bible women at distant outposts and donors to Filipina schoolgirls. Missionaries relied on visual evidence to demonstrate their success in evangelization and Americanization.

This essay argues that Filipina and American women expressed complex identities through dress, even within the clear power dynamics of empire; they thus redefined modern womanhood with local materials for a global stage. The chapter begins with an examination of the politics of dress within the context of empire and missions. Then it turns to Protestant mission stations in the Philippines specifically, tracing the bodily practices and cultural meanings attached to clothing there. Missionaries promoted American styles as markers of modernity and fashionableness, as well as assimilation. Nursing uniforms, for example, designated women's training and professionalism, while athletic uniforms denoted a modern woman's mobility and physical fitness. School uniforms were more syncretic, however, and choices of dress for other public occasions (such as weddings, graduations, and preaching tours) allowed for the most visible assertions of a distinct Filipina style. Filipina dress not only expressed agency and resistance to American acculturation by native women. At times, American women too adopted, or were invited to adopt, Filipina clothing. In wearing it, they too expressed a modern, cosmopolitan self and blurred the boundaries between colonialism and anticolonialism.[7]

Clothing and empire

Clothing provides a means of expressing identity, group identity as much as individual identity. Dress is also a representation of relationships of power, as especially evident in the context of imperialism and colonialism. Western styles of dress circulated around the world as part of Euro-American economic, political, and cultural expansion. Euro-Americans generally regarded (and thus encouraged) the adoption of Western clothing as a sign of civilization; though the wearing of trousers was not a substitute for conversion to Protestantism or for the pursuit of English-language-based education, styles of dress marked identities and allegiances, announcing one's inclination toward either colonial rule or resistance. Women's bodies served as especially important signifiers.[8] Too much constriction or concealment (as with veils) and too much exposure of the body both demanded 'Western sartorial intervention'.[9] The physical attributes, adornment, and presentation of female bodies marked the boundaries and distinctions between civilization and savagery under imperialism. Coincident with the 'golden age' of imperialism, the new technologies of visual culture gave these questions an ever more public stage through the nineteenth and twentieth centuries.

80 Laura R. Prieto

At the same time, clothing does not simply reflect political relationships between colonizer and colonized. Dress constitutes its own arena of negotiation and conflict. While asserting the superiority of Western forms of government and religion, colonizers sometimes discouraged the wholesale embrace of Western clothing by colonial subjects. Colonial powers sought to maintain distinctions between themselves and their 'charges', and sartorial imitation, when executed too well, threatened colonial hierarchy.[10] Often colonized men adopted Western clothing to facilitate, and later to signify, their access to education and civil service, while colonized women retained native dress as representatives of traditional culture. White, middle-class Euro-American women adopted elements of non-Western attire in turn, from turbans in the late eighteenth century to kimonos in the 1920s, as a form of exotic spectacle, meant to put their cosmopolitanism on public display. As costume historian Verity Wilson explains, 'Clothes from elsewhere had the power to hold back the banality of everyday life.'[11]

Mission stations hold particular significance as settings to explore the imperial politics of dress. This is first of all because missions were more fluid spaces than most in the colonial context. Simply put, religious conversion needed to be voluntary to count as authentic in the eyes of Christian missionaries. They could not simply force the observance of a new religion but rather had to appeal to local populations. Potential converts had opportunities to demand cooperation and compromise, often leading to syncretic practices that would be unimaginable under coercive state power. These conditions made mission stations and mission schools especially rich sites of interaction.

The nature of missions also makes them important sites of interaction between colonizing and colonized *women*, in particular. Women remained largely excluded from civil service and political participation in the imperial metropole, as well as in many of the indigenous societies being colonized. Yet in order to succeed, religious congregations and mission schools had to include both women and men. In fact, according to nineteenth-century missiology, women had a special mission to minister to their sex; women missionaries were considered essential to reach female converts, mothers, and future mothers who would bring their children with them into the faith. The centrality of women to the mission project meant that dress became a self-conscious arena of significant surveillance, conflict, and exchange there.

Consumer culture, fashion, and clothing in particular might seem minor concerns within missionary enterprises. But as measures of civilization and Christianization, they constituted an important preoccupation. The equation of certain dress and bodily practices with 'civilization' also appears in the contemporary American-Indian boarding school movement, in which assimilating middle-class American dress, posture, and so forth, was seen as a crucial sign of success in overcoming savagery. Photographs taken at mission-based and government-funded Indian schools carefully documented students before and after the transformative effects of their acculturation.[12] In this tradition, Dean C. Worcester, Secretary of the Interior of the Philippine Islands, opened volume 2 of his opus, *The Philippines, Past and Present*, with a pair of photographs depicting 'The Metamorphosis of a Bontoc Igorot', a boy named Pit-a-pit. As he grew older under American tutelage, Pit-a-pit abandoned his *song-kit-an* bark-fiber girdle for a white Western-style suit, hat, and leather shoes.[13] American teachers in the Philippines regarded American styles of dress as an important part of their mission to transform Filipinos into modern American colonial subjects.[14] Clothing as a measure of status and progress took on additional significance as public contestation over American women's dress increased. At the turn of the twentieth century, new women were lampooned and sexualized in visual culture for their purportedly masculine appearance. By the 1920s, even more strident controversy erupted over flappers' daring, baring fashion choices.[15]

The visual economies of missionary projects relied particularly on images to connect domestic supporters to faraway outposts. Reports and letters from the field took the form not only of words but also of photographs and postcards, collected in albums, preserved in archives, and printed in missionary magazines such as *Life and Light* (American Board / Congregationalist) and *Woman's Work* (Presbyterian). 'Please write me just as often as you can and send all the pictures that you can,' the American Board's corresponding secretary Kate Lamson wrote to missionary Frank Laubach.[16] The global circulation of such images benefitted from the advent of the Kodak camera, on the one side, and a revolution in printing technology, on the other. Mission workers also collected local examples of clothing (almost invariably women's clothing) to enlighten American supporters. The photographs and material objects collapsed the distance between the New England home office (or parlor) and the mission. As historian Hyeaweol Choi writes,

> From the viewpoint of missionaries, photography was an indispensable tool for recording, categorizing, and publicizing 'the other' as it captured the presumed essence of the local people, the unique, unusual objects and exotic natural setting, as well as the triumphs and tribulations of the mission field.[17]

Occasionally, converts travelled to the United States to meet supporters and presented their dress in person. These narratives, performances, and images attest to the close observation of dress as an indicator of civilized, modern womanhood versus savagery.

Of course, readers would have encountered missionary literature alongside many other representations of exotic locales and savage places. Through the nineteenth century, Americans voraciously consumed stereograph views, postcards, trade cards, illustrated guides, fair exhibits, and published narratives of foreign climes and peoples. They construed both armchair and actual travel as a way of understanding the world and exploring connections among different cultures.[18] American companies capitalized on the discourse of civilization to sell products. These advertisements often elided promotion with education, as in Singer's 'nation cards,' distributed free of charge beginning in the 1890s. Each card depicted native people in native dress, grouped around a Singer sewing machine; the back of the card related information about the country or region being represented, concluding with a testimonial about how Singer had helped to 'civilize' that part of the world with its products.[19] The card for 'Manila', for instance, depicted a young man and woman stitching with their machines. The pair's facial features, brown skin, and markedly non-Western dress are meant to represent the local combination of 'Indians and Spaniards' noted in the caption (Figure 4.1). As tourism expanded in the early 1900s, it remained 'intimately intertwined' with visual media, as art historian Krista Thompson argues. Taking snapshots became a quintessential tourist pastime, and locally produced 'scenic views' became popular souvenirs. Leisure travel functioned as a quest for picturesque views.[20]

Commercial, educational, and personal photographs alike trained the eye on native women, especially. Photographers almost never identified them by name but rather offered them as iconic, interchangeable racial figures. They composed these portraits of women and girls, individually and in groups, in such a way as to include their clothing. They drew attention not only to physiognomy but also to culture and style of dress as signifiers of race. The other prevalent type of depiction of native women showed them working; there too clothing figured prominently as the product of female labor. Women's attire served as a visual marker of their difference and by inference of the degree of their savagery. In this regard, the Keystone View Company's stereographs of 'Igarotte women on the trail' and Luzon embroiderers[21] have much in common with the Negrito mother and the Tagalog girls washing clothes, photographed by zoologist and federal commissioner to the Philippines, Dean C. Worcester.[22]

Dress and the civilizing mission in the Philippines

American evangelization and imperialism began in tandem in the Philippines during the heart of what Eric Hobsbawm called 'The Age of Empire'. By 1898, when

FIGURE 4.1 Singer Manufacturing Company, 'Costumes of All Nations' series advertising card, J Ottmann Lithographing Co., 1892, from the collection of Laura Prieto.

the United States replaced Spain as the ruling colonial power in the Philippines, the mission field employed well-educated, professionally minded American women who thought about dress in new ways themselves. American women's invasion of the public sphere, especially since the 1890s, had led to dramatic transformations in dress. Women's increasing presence in higher education, wage work, and athletics drove a rethinking of the restrictive styles prescribed to middle-class women through the nineteenth century. New silhouettes and shorter skirts accommodated greater ease in movement while maintaining feminine modesty. Missionary women from the United States brought these new aesthetics, activities, and ideologies along with the gospel, as part of converting, civilizing, and Americanizing Filipinas.

Mission stations and schools were a cultural borderland, however, where no single style of dress prevailed. Women at missions wore many different types of clothing, from Malay sarongs to Edwardian sailor dresses. Under US occupation, school and athletic uniforms incorporated both American and Filipino elements. American imperialists at home and on the archipelago noted approvingly when Filipina women 'tr[ied] to get American cloth for their dresses' and proved 'anxious to be American in every way'.[23] They read such interest as a promising sign of enthusiastic assimilation. Still, not only Filipinas but American women sometimes wore indigenous dress, including both the *traje de mestiza* and the *terno*. And although American observers seemed unaware of it, those native styles already embodied complex, transnational interchanges.

Long before 1898, Filipina dress had integrated diverse foreign elements, from Chinese fabrics and fastenings to European embroidery. Spanish colonial influence began to displace the *patadyong* (or *patadlog*, a type of sarong) with a skirt in the seventeenth century, while Catholic statuary influenced the innovation of the Filipino *baro* or *camisa*. Centuries of colonization, intermarriage, and direct instruction had influenced the adoption of the *camisa*, *saya*, and *pañuelo*, the ensemble of blouse, skirt, and delicate shawl that had remained popular since the nineteenth century. The very names of the garments derived from Spanish words; but the *saya* remained sheer and was covered with a darker *tapis*, markedly different from Spanish styles. In this way Filipinas had adapted rather than adopted outside styles. They favored patterns with stripes and windowpane checks. Along with the more traditional *traje de mestiza* or *Maria Clara* style, a newer silhouette with a shorter sleeved *camisa*, narrower skirts, and stiff starching had taken hold in the mid-1890s. The expansion of local textile manufacturing had introduced more cost-effective fabrics such as *sinamay*, made from the indigenous *abacá*, or Manila hemp plant. French imports influenced fashion among the *ilustrado* elites.[24]

American missionaries conceded that Filipino culture was distinct from that of other Asian countries. 'When we consider the general position of Oriental women the Filipina is in a class by herself,' wrote Anna Rodgers Wright in 1918. 'Girls and young women are always carefully chaperoned but they do not veil the face in public. . . . In short, girls and women of the Islands have an unquestioned freedom and independence of action in daily business and social life not enjoyed by their Oriental sisters.'[25] 'The most hopeful thing to me is the exalted position that women occupy,

84 Laura R. Prieto

different from most oriental countries,' confessed Olive Rohrbaugh.[26] But the very existence of these statements indicates the popular perceptions Wright and Rohrbaugh were trying to dispel: readers of *Woman's Work* were inclined to regard Filipinas as 'Oriental'. And this classification, in turn, influenced their perceptions of native dress as problematic. For a century or more, Europeans had depicted Eastern women as spectacularly subjugated to Eastern men. 'Oriental' in the early twentieth century called up persistent images of veiled women in harems. Condemnation of the veil as oppressive was excelled only by denunciation of foot-binding – so that whether Filipinas were associated with the 'Middle' East of Islam or the 'Far' East of Asia, as non-Westerners they seemed (at first glance) in desperate need of emancipation.[27]

Clothing could thus be a measure of imperial power and a site of conflict. In one encounter, an American missionary reported saving a Filipina bride from a custom uncannily like the notorious *Western* practice of tight lacing:

> . . . the bride and her helpers were at last ready. The putting in of every pin was a matter of time and consultation. In fact the demand for pins was so incessant, especially when it came to arranging the gauzy Filipina waist, that I felt quite pin-plucked when the process was finished! The little bride thought that fifteen inches was the proper waist measure for a wedding. I earnestly assured her she was not in fashion. 'Look at me!' I said, and with all the swagger I could assume I displayed the looseness of my modern dress. So the cruel lacings were somewhat loosened and at least one poor girl was stopped from inuring herself. When I ran upstairs and brought a fashion book, in my effort to make the effect permanent, and showed the village followers of fashion the pictures of present-day waists, the bride looked as if she could stand it to have the strings loosened a little more. But now the top dressing had begun so it was too late.[28]

At this 'first Protestant wedding in Batangas' province, the anonymous bride dressed herself in what she thought proper for such an important event; for her, a tight waist denoted formality and beauty. Elizabeth White Jansen persuaded her that a looser waist was more *fashionable* and *modern*. It was on those terms – not because the constriction was cruel – that the Filipina bride acquiesced in changing her appearance. Notably, she did not rearrange her waist as loosely as her fashion mentor urged. For this individual, Protestant Christianity did not mandate complete acquiescence to American dictates in matters of dress.

Consumer culture set the standards of beauty against which Americans measured Filipinas. As historian Kristin Hoganson observes, they perceived the adoption of European fashion as a gauge of civilization.[29] The missionaries' shared preoccupation with clothing betrays the extent to which Christianization and cultural assimilation were intertwined in their minds also. In a letter to the home office, missionary Effa Laubach praised a recently baptized Filipina, 'one of our stars,' for 'reading my *Ladies Home Journal* and know[ing] what the girls in America are

American imperialism, Filipina nationalism **85**

doing'.[30] 'Home missionaries' – supporters in the US – often sent dolls for distribution to Filipino girls; alongside imported fashion magazines, these would have implicitly modeled Euro-American styles of dress.

As under Spanish rule, class evidently played a part in which Filipinos did – or could – adopt the assimilated clothing. 'Little high class girls dress in dainty dresses with all the frilly underwear very like her [sic] little American cousin,' missionary Isabel Fox observed. By contrast, the poorer 'little girls that play about the thatch houses and in the market wear a single colored slip.'[31] The adoption of Christianity seemed to bring an expectation of more elaborate if not Americanized dress. Missionaries noted proudly how six-month-old Luz Dia, at her christening, 'was dressed in a wonderful costume of lace, red ribbon and big cap, holding a tiny doll to amuse herself'.[32] Similarly, mothers tried to dress up their small children for the *fiesta* to dedicate the new chapel at Dumaguete, marking the importance of the occasion with the fanciest outfits they could muster. 'The poor things who had been used to wearing only nature's smile were most uncomfortable in the new, gay dresses they had to endure on this occasion,' noted Laura Hibbard with some condescension. 'If mothers could not get red, pink or lavender dresses, their babies were wrapped in gayly bordered bath towels.'[33]

Missionary women associated modern American aesthetics in dress with comfort, cleanliness, and rationality. 'My girls are sensible children and prefer simple American clothes as a rule,' wrote Isabel Fox.[34] When faced with indigenous styles, they attempted to reform them. Isabel's sister Florence, a nurse at the mission, judged that, 'Filipino clothes are not very practicable,' and tried to encourage the use of wraps.[35] Meanwhile, Isabel confessed to a longing, 'to do something to their hair. It does look so untidy and uncomfortable'.[36] The missionaries proudly measured the declining Moro practice, in the southern Philippines, of darkening one's teeth with betel: 'They are fast learning the ways of civilization, and are all proud of their white teeth now.'[37]

Missionaries thought American clothing superior even for the local climate. As Ruth Swanson and her students prepared to travel to the mountains of Baguio for a women's conference, she reported, 'For many previous weeks missionary trunks and boxes had been ransacked for sweaters, coats, heavy dresses, etc., that the girls might be made comfortable in their first cold weather experience.' The preparations engaged the women in wholesome labor as well: 'At our own dormitory for a long time we had spent all our spare moments knitting sweaters, so all the Ellinwood girls were well supplied. . . . ' The missionaries knew best, according to this story: 'The girls wondered if they would ever need all those heavy wraps which they had brought along. Most of them had been donned, however, before the mountain ride had ended.'[38] In addition to providing warmth, the knitted garments Americanized the girls' appearance. The photograph 'Under the Pines' shows girls in sailor suits in the second row without wraps, whereas most of the others wear coats and sweaters (Figure 4.2). Whether inadvertently or by design, the assembly closely mirrors a girls' camp in the contemporary United States.

FIGURE 4.2 'Under the Pines' at the Third Annual Woman's Conference at Baguio, December 27–31, 1920. Photo sent by Miss Swanson. *Woman's Work* 36, June 1921, 125.

Uniforms and professional dress for 'modern' Filipinas

As the wedding incident and the sartorial preparations for the Baguio conference demonstrate, missionaries presented American styles not only as a sign of civilization but as a marker of modernity in certain contexts. They were most successful in introducing such modern clothing to Filipinas as most appropriate for modern activities: practicing professions (most notably, nursing) and engaging in athletic competition.

Nurse training schools first advocated uniforms in the 1830s, when their work was often regarded as menial and morally suspect, involving as it did intimate contact with the bodies of strangers, including men. Advocates 'saw standard uniform attire as fundamental to the new, modern nursing occupation because the nurse had to have a respectable and competent outward appearance, both as an individual and as a respected member of an occupational group'. Her modest, dignified dress distinguished the professional nurse from both the untrained attendants and the family members who also cared for the sick at hospitals. By adapting middle-class matrons' attire for themselves, nurses projected refinement, while the lack of ornamentation suggested seriousness and industry.[39] With its widespread adoption, by the turn of the twentieth century the nurse's dress, apron, and cap denoted professional credentials. That is why Florence Fox wore her uniform in some formal photographs; it identified her as the 'superintendent of nursing'.

For the same reasons – to visually signal their respectability, competence, and professionalism, counter to presumptions of their ignorance, savagery, and immorality – Filipinas wore nursing uniforms too, as students and while working in hospitals.[40] The US touted professional, modern medicine as one of the gifts its 'benevolent' empire brought to its subjects. Whether or not they agreed with that view, nursing also connoted being modern for Filipinas. Women had served as healers within indigenous traditions and under Spanish rule, and they had been able to train as midwives. In fact, the only higher education available to Filipinas under Spanish colonization was in the School of Midwifery at the University of Santo Tomas. The practices and responsibilities of healers and midwives differed substantially from those of nurses. From the Filipina perspective, nursing brought expanded opportunities: for education, for employment and economic self-sufficiency, and for mobility.[41]

Religious missions pioneered nursing education in the Philippines with the establishment of the Presbyterian Foreign Mission Society's Mission Hospital School of Nursing in Iloilo City in 1906.[42] Missionary literature trumpeted the production of Filipina nurses by featuring photographs of graduates in uniform, beginning with the very first class. In 1910, *Woman's Work* proudly introduced Felipa [de la Peña], Nicasia, and Dorotea as the 'First Nurses Ever Trained in Philippine Islands'. At 19, 17, and 22 years old, respectively, when they graduated in August 1909, the three women resembled their American counterparts in age. Notably, theirs is a studio portrait. Yet the moment being commemorated was not their graduation ceremony. In the photograph, the three women carry their diplomas, tied with ribbons; but instead of the white dresses they wore at graduation, they appear in striped dresses and nurses' white aprons and caps. This uniform distinguished them as nurses – and as Americanized, in a way their white dresses probably would not have, for Filipinas typically wore *ternos*, not American style dress, for formal occasions.[43]

Perhaps because of its modern connotations, some Filipinos resisted this very same nursing uniform for their daughters. Nurse and educator Lavinia Dock recounted that elite families objected to breaking with the tradition of 'three hundred years' of women wearing 'a long train which carries with it class distinction'.[44] The apron too may have connoted servility; the *tapis* had become less popular in this same period for that reason.[45] Yet Americans' desire to appeal to *ilustrados* did not overcome the requirement of a practical nursing uniform. The struggle ended with 'the student nurses look[ing] most attractive in their striped, gingham uniforms, with white caps and aprons'.[46]

Subsequent published group photographs of Filipinas in nurses' uniforms signified a transformation in women's opportunities. Their preparation in nursing attracted more attention than their actual practice of the profession. The published images favor studio backdrops over hospital settings, the fresh graduate over the working woman. An anonymous photograph of seven Filipinas in aprons and eight Filipinas in white uniforms seemingly spoke for itself, unaccompanied by any article on the employment they found or the medical care they now provided. Another group portrait of five nurses in uniform named only one of the women (Teodora, no last name given).[47] The composition and captioning of the photographs suggest that nursing uniforms mattered most in the aggregate, as visual evidence that missionaries were bringing Filipinas to modern medicine and modern hygiene as well as to Christ.

88 Laura R. Prieto

American dress eased the adoption not only of new professions and education for Filipinas but of women's athletics, especially baseball and basketball. 'Muscular Christianity,' as championed by the Young Men's Christian Association and others during this period, served not only as a prescription for men but also influenced greater encouragement of physical health for women and girls. The Young Women's Christian Association, and the newly formed Camp Fire Girls and Girl Scouts, strove to strengthen women through 'rugged outdoor experiences'.[48] In the US, the advent of basketball and other sports for college women had led to the innovation of the skirted gymnastics suit, 'the first widely accepted garment not only to encourage but to insist on no inner support in the form of corsetry for the female body'.[49] Ironically, 'Oriental' clothing – Turkish trousers in particular – also influenced the form; it was favored by European elites in the eighteenth century as comfortable and exotic.[50]

Within four years of its introduction in 1891, basketball became part of the physical education program for women at most coeducational schools and women's colleges. The demands of the game rendered the gym dress impractical. Women replaced it with a two-piece outfit: a navy blue blouse and short bloomers, to be covered by a skirt when outdoors. Though made of scratchy wool serge, the modernized gym suit was durable and less bulky than its predecessor.[51] Such was the uniform worn by the women's basketball team of Manila's Mary J. Johnson Methodist Hospital in their 1910 team photo[52] (Figure 4.3). Athletic uniforms and sportswear were an important physical manifestation of what modern womanhood meant in the US: mobility and physical fitness that balanced intellectual development. Filipino observers likewise saw it as a modern attribute for women of the archipelago to 'go in for sports in a grand way', as Vicente Barranco put it.[53]

American missionary women to the Philippines thus offered and modeled a modern definition of womanhood through preparation for the professions, athletics, and participation in public life. Filipinas' embrace of this modern womanhood can be difficult to separate from assimilation. Yet dress and material culture most strongly suggest that in seeking and valuing a modern revision of femininity, they were not simply acquiescing to Americanization. Even the Filipinas most strongly associated with missions did not consistently choose American styles. Some modified or combined American articles with their customary dress. The girls' school uniforms at Harris Memorial Deaconess Training School, for example, comprised a blue cotton skirt and a white cotton *camisa*, which evangelist writer Norma Waterbury Thomas explained was 'the stiff transparent jacket the Filipina women wear'.[54] Filipina teachers in American mission and public schools 'practiced their newly learned profession in a modified *traje* skirt made of *sinamay* with stripes and windowpane checks, and a plain or unembroidered upper garment'.[55]

The mission documents do not directly record Filipinas' reaction to American clothing and almost never discuss dress as anything more complicated than cultural superiority and inferiority. 'Sometimes I wish we could see ourselves through the eyes of our so-called heathen sisters,' mused Isabel Fox in a rare exception. 'I wonder if we look as ugly to them as they do to us, if our white teeth and tight complex

American imperialism, Filipina nationalism 89

FIGURE 4.3   Mary J. Johnson Methodist Hospital nurses' basketball team, 1910. Photograph by George E. Carruthers, BL003763, Box 1, plate 7, George E. Carrothers Lantern Slide Series. Reproduced with permission from the Bentley Historical Library, University of Michigan.

clothing and pale skin, and hair of all shades of brown seem curious and homely to them.'[56] But it is clear that Filipinas did not necessarily read American fashion or bodily practices *as* American. For example, most young Filipina girls wore their hair bobbed with bangs, as did fashionable American women of the 1920s; choosing this style more likely seemed juvenile than assimilationist. Elements of the modern girl style emerged around the world in the 1920s and 1930s, a 'global phenomenon' whose many forms owed as much to local conditions as to international film and advertisements.[57] Furthermore, as Homi Bhabha, Verity Wilson, and others have argued, 'to be Westernised in the colonial context is to be emphatically *not* "Western."' These people are not fashion victims. They are players in the game of identities, a game which is not yet played out.'[58]

The *terno* and Filipina nationalism

In the 'game of identities', visual records speak to what the written documents omit. Even when it was under the missionaries' direct control, the camera could inadvertently be a means of expression for its subjects, through their poses or expressions.[59] For example, the Filipina students at the Carruth Bible School in Cagayan wore with pride either American or Filipina dress. In one formal photograph, probably of the first graduating class of Bible scholars, the youngest Filipina wears a dress clearly cut from the same pattern as that of her teacher, Isabel Fox. The other three Filipinas wear the beautiful, elaborate *terno* (or 'butterfly dress'), which had evolved in recent decades.[60] Judging from published photographs, Filipinas graduating from Ellinwood and other mission schools, as well as nurse training programs, also wore the *terno*.

The *terno* developed and became popular in the period of American colonization, and its basic silhouette followed European fashion of the day. But the *terno*'s 'butterfly sleeves' differed markedly from contemporary Euro-American evening wear.[61] Its fabric, locally produced *piña* (made from pineapple fiber), also marked it as indigenous. It did not derive its elements, even the Western ones, from American styles. Rather, the *terno* (sometimes also called *mestiza dress*) combined the Spanish-influenced *camisa* and *saya*.

The context of US imperialism imbued this garment with political meaning. Wearing the *terno* indicated support of Filipino autonomy. Its use made women into nationalist symbols and bearers of a sophisticated Filipino culture. The *terno* did not really position women as bearers of tradition, since it was a newly invented style. Unlike nationalist movements in other places that privileged folkloric dress for women, the *terno* signaled modernity along with sovereignty.

The *terno* accordingly became associated with Filipina 'new women' who sought advanced education, entered the professions, claimed a place in the public sphere, and engaged in social and political activism. Filipina new women wore the *terno* strategically as they laid claim to the public sphere; its nationalist meanings gave legitimacy to women's presence there, while its modernity associated women with progress. It became the favorite public attire of Filipina suffragists in the 1920s and 1930s. Suffragist (and beauty queen) Pura Villanueva Kalaw praised her contemporary, María Paz Mendoza-Guazon, for her accomplishments as the first Filipina woman physician, for her active participation in the women's suffrage movement, and – in the same breath – for 'her elegant crimson Filipino *terno*'.[62] The *terno* connected women professionals, clubwomen, beauty queens, and suffragists, making suffragists seem less radical and beauty queens more progressive.[63] Its use on ceremonial occasions was respectable and not uncommon. *Woman's Work* noted approvingly of 'a Filipina lady in the costume of ladies of the Islands', who spoke at the Opera House in Manila to encourage participation in the Fourth Liberty Loan.[64]

It is striking to see Bible women in training choose such subtly but undeniably politicized clothing, and missionary literature touting their choice. Alongside group portraits of Filipina nurses in uniform and other evidence of sartorial Americanization, women's missionary magazines regularly published photographs of Filipinas in indigenous dress. That is, they used illustrations of Filipina students, converts, and Bible women in *ternos* and the more conventional *Maria Clara* ensembles of *camisa*, *saya*, and *pañuelo* – clothing styles that denoted higher class and mestizo race within what was distinctly Filipino culture. They carefully excluded visual depictions of Igorot women or other 'wild tribes' that so strongly suggested savagery to American audiences.[65] The captions and articles that accompanied the published images framed Filipina women as 'promising' and hardworking and some as evangelists in their own right.

The indigenous dress in the photographs thus still connoted difference but it did not designate primitiveness. For example, Emilia Cavan chose to illustrate her article with a portrait of herself in butterfly sleeves, standing next to Miss Clyde Bartholomew (Figure 4.4). Cavan is at no disadvantage, having studied and lectured throughout the US, as the photo caption emphasizes. Cavan's own words invoke the success of other Filipina Bible women, like Agripina. 'Only God can number the many, many souls she has led to Christ,' effused Cavan. 'She was useful too in straightening out the troubles that often arise in the churches, and Mr. Brown said of her that she was worth more to him than any three preachers he ever had. She is a woman whose faith and Christian life would put many of us to shame.'[66] Likewise, the thirty-two Sunday school teachers photographed in *María Claras* have already been transformed, no longer 'noisy and restless' but an orderly and 'pretty sight'. The students at Ellinwood exert a powerful influence against vice: singing a hymn 'as if by magic' halted the gambling and the boxing match attracting a crowd near the Sunday school.[67] In another photograph, rows of Ellinwood students, seated on the school's piazza, obscure the five American teachers and whatever they are wearing.[68] American women missionaries and their dress were not a visual standard of measure for the Filipinas.

The same American women who at times condemned Filipina dress, at other times admired it. Though she disapproved of their hairstyles, Isabel Fox praised Moro women's 'sorong' as 'very modest'.[69] At times, cultural distinctions blurred in the missionaries' eyes. When nine Bible women came to a meeting, Isabel noted 'their simple home dresses' without further description – reading neither savagery nor civility in their style.[70] Even as missionaries strove to 'modernize' Filipinas, they were attracted to traditional Filipino culture. Supporters back home urged them to send examples of native handicrafts, for use in building interest and raising funds among American audiences. Most commonly, the Board asked for locally made lace, piña fabric and examples of indigenous 'costumes'.[71] This keen interest from 'home' legitimized missionary women not only in collecting but wearing local

FIGURE 4.4 Emilia Cavan with Miss Clyde Bartholomew. *Woman's Work* 36, June 1921, 128.

dress (the butterfly dress, or *terno*), habits that would seem to be the antithesis of assimilation and Americanization.

Most intriguingly, some photographs show American missionary women in the Filipino *terno* as well. The newsletter of the American Baptist Foreign Mission Society published a photograph of the second graduating class of the Bible Training School at Jaro (1916). In it, the seven Filipina women and their American teacher, Anna V. Johnson, are all wearing 'long flowing gowns' and 'panuelo'.[72] It is difficult to imagine that American missionaries wore *ternos* as public advocacy of Filipino independence. Nevertheless, their sitting for photographs while wearing *ternos* suggests some sort of affinity or allegiance with local culture. In another series of such images from Cagayan, the Fox sisters wear *ternos* at an unnamed special occasion in 1924, likely a graduation ceremony. They pose with Isabel Maandig, a Bible woman, also in a *terno* (Figure 4.5). Contemporary instances abounded of American women commodifying 'the Orient', using dress and other forms of material culture to play with their gender identity and sexuality.[73] But Maandig's presence and the probable nature of the occasion suggest that the Foxes chose their attire not as costumes but

American imperialism, Filipina nationalism 93

Harvard University, Houghton Library, modbm_abc_78_1_fox_grace_0002

FIGURE 4.5   Florence L. Fox, Evelyn Fox, Isabel Maandig, 1925. American Board of Commissioners to Foreign Missions 78.1 (Photographs), box 15. Reproduced with permission of Wider Church Ministries, United Church of Christ and Houghton Library, Harvard University.

to honor their students. In an earlier letter, Isabel Fox had referred to 'a picture of *us* all in *our* native dress' (my emphasis), meaning herself with eight Filipina Bible scholars.[74] The resplendent silk *terno* that Evelyn Fox wears in a studio portrait from 1920 was a gift from her students.[75] Filipinas thus sought to share Filipino

94 Laura R. Prieto

symbology, including this part of modern womanhood so distinctively their own. And at times they were able to impose their own ideas about appropriate dress on those who had come to Americanize them.

This consideration of the politics of dress demonstrates two important, yet overlooked, facets of the effects of imperialism on culture. First, Filipina womanhood was not a wholesale American import. Filipinas defined modern womanhood in their own ways. Accordingly, they selected their attire according to their own criteria, not as simple compliance with assimilation. They adopted certain elements of American dress because of their broader meanings and connotations: education and respectability as in the case of nursing uniforms or mobility and practicality in the case of athletic uniforms. By wearing those clothes, Filipinas claimed a part in global communities of women professionals as well as among 'modern', cosmopolitan women. Their concurrent assertion of a distinct Filipina identity, most prominently in the *terno*, reveals how anticolonialism could accompany the selective appropriation of colonial elements.[76] Butterfly sleeves rejected American interference in symbolic and highly visible terms. Through dress, Filipinas championed local autonomy *and* accessed transnational ideas about femininity.

Second, American women missionaries themselves were susceptible to influence from the culture surrounding them and the individuals with whom they had personal relationships. This fascination, however irregular and unequal, unsettled the very definitions of gender roles, savagery, and civilization that the missionaries had brought with them. Perhaps the *terno* constituted a subtle and sophisticated combination of accommodation and resistance to imperialism, not only by Filipinas but by American women in the Philippines who also chose to wear it. Whatever their political consciousness, it is clear that American women were not the static bearers of modernity to the Philippines. They too adopted new modes of expression in response to imperialism. The intricacies of dress – its meanings, its history, its politics – allowed for different sorts of cultural exchange, and more complex expressions of identity, than we are accustomed to expect.

Notes

1 The Woman's Home Missionary Society of the Methodist Episcopal Church, *Fifty-Sixth Annual Report, for the Year 1936–1937*, Cincinnati, OH, 1937, p. 67.

2 S. Miller, *Benevolent Assimilation: The American Conquest of the Philippines, 1899–1903*, New Haven: Yale University Press, 1982, p. 27.

3 D. Silbey, *A War of Frontier and Empire: The Philippine-American War, 1899–1902*, New York: Macmillan, 2008.

4 See P. Kramer, *The Blood of Government: Race, Empire, the United States, and the Philippines*, Chapel Hill: University of North Caroline Press, 2006.

5 S. Steinbock-Pratt argues that the US educational system put particular pressure on Filipinas to adopt American dress, and that in response, Filipinas negotiated gender roles and nationalist identities through their clothing. Steinbock-Pratt, '"It Gave Us Our Nationality": U.S. Education, the Politics of Dress and Transnational Filipino Student Networks, 1901–45', *Gender & History*, 26:3, November 2014, 565–588.

6 See E. Edwards and J. Hart, eds., *Photographs Objects Histories: On the Materiality of Images*, New York: Routledge, 2004; P. Tinkler, *Using Photographs in Social and Historical Research*, London: Sage, 2013.

7 On cosmopolitanism, see K. Hoganson, 'The Fashionable World: Imagined Communities of Dress', in A. Burton ed., *After the Imperial Turn: Thinking with and through the Nation*, Durham, NC: Duke University Press, 2003, pp. 260–278.

8 Scholarship on this concept includes M. Roces and L. Edwards, eds., *The Politics of Dress in Asia and the Americas*, Eastbourne: Sussex Academy Press, 2008; K. Canning, 'The body as method? Reflections on the place of the body in gender history', *Gender & History*, 11:3, Nov 1999, 499–513; and T. Ballantyne and A. Burton, eds., *Bodies in Contact: Rethinking Colonial Encounters in World* History, Durham: Duke University Press, 2005.

9 Hoganson, p. 273. Also see M. Roces, 'Gender, nation and the politics of dress in twentieth-century Philippines', *Gender and History*, 17, 2005, 354–377.

10 E. Tarlo, 'British Attitudes to Indian and European Dress', in G. Riello and P. McNeil, eds., *The Fashion History Reader: Global Perspectives*, New York: Routledge, 2010, pp. 391–392. For other comparative cases and frameworks, see Roces and Edwards 2008, and J. Allman, ed., *Fashioning Africa: Power and the Politics of Dress*, Bloomington: Indiana University Press, 2004.

11 V. Wilson, 'Western Modes and Asian Clothing: Reflections on Borrowing Other People's Dress', in Riello and McNeil, eds., *The Fashion History Reader: Global Perspectives*, New York: Routledge, 2010, p. 428.

12 L. Malmsheimer, 'Imitation White Man: Images of Transformation at the Carlisle Indian School', *Studies in Visual Communication*, 11:4, 1985, 54–75.

13 D. C. Worcester, frontispiece, *The Philippines, Past and Present*, NY: Macmillan Company, 1914; A. E. Jenks, 'Bontoc Igorot Clothing', *American Anthropologist*, 6:5, 1904, 695–704. Cruz points out that other photographs in Worcester's volume implicitly contrast the savagery of "Bontoc Igorot Women in Banana-Leaf Costume" with the Spanish-inflected dress of "A Typical Spanish Mestiza." D. Cruz, *Transpacific Femininities: The Making of the Modern Filipina*, Durham, NC: Duke University Press, 2012, p. 40.

14 Steinbock-Pratt, 'It Gave Us Our Nationality', p. 569.

15 See M. Davis, 'The New Woman in American Stereoviews, 1871–1905', in E. Otto and V. Rocco, eds., *The New Woman International: Representations in Photography and Film from the 1870s through the 1960s*, Ann Arbor: University of Michigan Press, 2012, pp. 21–38.

16 K. Lamson to F. Laubach, 14 March 1917. Records of the American Board of Commissioners to Foreign Missions, Houghton Library, Harvard University, Cambridge MA (hereafter ABC), 17.9.1.

17 H. Choi, 'The visual embodiment of women in the Korea mission field', *Korean Studies*, 34, 2010, 91.

18 K. Hoganson, *Consumers' Imperium: The Global Production of American Domesticity, 1865–1920*, Durham: University of North Carolina Press, 2007, p. 155.

19 M. Domash, *American Commodities in an Age of Empire*, New York: Routledge, 2013, p. 64.

20 K. A. Thompson, *An Eye for the Tropics: Tourism, Photography, and Framing the Caribbean Picturesque*, Durham: Duke University Press, 2006, p. 8.

21 'Two Igarotte [sic] Women on the Trail, Philippines', and 'Native Women Embroidering, Islands of Luzon, Philippines', Keystone Mast Collection, University of California Riverside, California Museum of Photography.

22 'Philippine Photographs Digital Archive', University of Michigan, Special Collections Library. Thanks to Erin Faulder for leading me to the digitized photographic collections at the University of Michigan, California Digital Library, and California Museum of Photography.

23 L. W. Schwichtenberg, 'Tells of the Busy Filipino Woman', *Chicago Tribune* 1901, quoted Cruz, p. 47.

24 S. F. Bernal and G. R. Encanto, *Patterns for the Filipino Dress: From the Traje de Mestiza to the Terno*, Manila: Cultural Center of the Philippines, 1992, pp. 2–8.

25 Mrs. G. Wright, 'What Christian Women are Doing in the Philippines', *Woman's Work*, June 1918, p. 133.

26 O. Rohrbaugh, 'Turning the Reel', *Woman's Work,* 1934, p. 131.

27 On gender and orientalism, see the work of R. Lewis, especially *Rethinking Orientalism: Women, Travel and the Ottoman Harem*, New Brunswick, NJ: Rutgers University Press, 2004.

96 Laura R. Prieto

28 Mrs. F. Jansen, 'The First Protestant Church Wedding in Batangas', *Women's Work*, June 1918, pp. 128–129.
29 Hoganson, 'The Fashionable World', p. 268.
30 E. Laubach to K. Lamson, 28 May 1918, ABC 17.9.2.
31 A. I. Fox to K. Lamson, 7 June 1920, ABC 17.9.2.
32 N. Brown, 'Fresh Greetings from Albay, P. I.', *Woman's Work* 24, July 1909, 153.
33 L. Hibbard, 'Influence of Silliman Boys on Negros, P. I.', *Woman's Work* 24, July 1909, 151.
34 A. I. Fox, 'My Philippine Girls', *Life and Light* 51:1, Jan 1921, 22.
35 F. Fox to K. Lamson, 5 May 1921, ABC 17.9.2.
36 A. I. Fox, 'A Vacation among the Moros', *Life and Light,* Nov 1919, 496.
37 'On Tour and at Home in the Philippines', *Life and Light* 52, Feb 1922, 63.
38 R. Swanson, 'A Mountain Top Experience', *Woman's Work* 36, June 1921, 125.
39 I. Poplin, 'Nursing uniforms: Romantic idea, functional attire, or instrument of social change?' *Nursing History Review*, 2, 1994, 153.
40 All the personnel – nurses and attendants – who worked with Fox were Filipino and about half were women. F. Smith, 'Philippine Mission of the ABCFM Mission Hospital, Cagayan, Misamis', 1925, ABC 17.9.2.
41 C. C. Choy, *Empire of Care: Nursing and Migration in Filipino American History*, Durham NC: Duke University Press, 2003, chapter 1. Also see the section on the Philippines in L. Dock, *A History of Nursing*, vol. 4, New York: Putnam's, 1912.
42 A. Klein, 'The Union Mission Hospital at Iloilo, Philippine Islands', *The American Journal of Nursing*, 16:3, 1915, 227–229. Union Mission Hospital, Sabine Haines Memorial, was founded in 1900 and began its nurse training program in 1906. The first nursing school operated by the US colonial government did not open until 1907.
43 A. P. Klein, 'Nursing Experiences in the Philippines', *Woman's Work* 25, July 1910, 148. Mrs. J. A. Hall, 'Letters from Missionaries: Philippine Islands', later informed readers that two of the three nurses 'left to be married' however. *Woman's Work* 26, August 1911, 180. Dean C. Worcester's photograph of the first nurses to graduate from the government school depicts them wearing *ternos*; Worcester, p. 176.
44 Dock, p. 314.
45 Bernal and Encanto, p. 7.
46 Dock, p. 314.
47 'Graduates and Seniors of the Union Hospital, Iloilo. No. 1 is Dr. Hall; No. 2, Miss Benedict, a Baptist Worker; No. 3, Mrs. Hall. Photo. sent by Mrs. J. A. Hall', *Woman's Work* 31, Oct 1916, 228. 'Ready for Service. Photo. given by Miss A. P. Klein. The standing figure at right of the picture is Teodora, fiancée of Demetrio Plagata, who died of tuberculosis in California while studying medicine there; his letter is published alongside the photograph within the piece by A. Klein, 'A bit of life', *Woman's Work*, 32, 1917, 221.
48 C. Putney, *Muscular Christianity: Manhood and Sports in Protestant America, 1880–1920*, Cambridge, MA: Harvard University Press, 2001, p. 145. Also see T. Ladd and J. Mathisen, *Muscular Christianity: Evangelical Protestants and the Development of American Sport*, Grand Rapids, MI: Baker Books, 1999.
49 P. C. Warner, 'The Gym Suit: Freedom at Last', in P. A. Cunningham and S. V. Lab, eds., *Dress in American Culture*, Bowling Green, OH: Bowling Green State University Popular Press, 1993, pp. 140–141.
50 Warner, 'The Gym Suit: Freedom at Last', p. 143.
51 Ibid., pp. 154–155. Also see P. C. Warner, *When the Girls Came Out to Play: The Birth of American Sportswear,* Amherst: University of Massachusetts Press, 2006; and L. Antolihao, 'From Baseball Colony to Basketball Republic: Post-Colonial Transition and the Making of a National Sport in the Philippines', *Sport in Society*, 15:10, 2012, 1396–1412.
52 G. E. Carrothers, photographer. BL003763, Box 1, plate 7, George E. Carrothers Lantern Slide Series, Bentley Historical Library, University of Michigan, Ann Arbor.
53 V. E. Barranco, 'The Filipino Girl – Model 1939', *Herald Mid-Week Magazine*, 4 January, 1939, 8, 18; quoted in Cruz, p. 90.

American imperialism, Filipina nationalism **97**

54 N.W. Thomas, *Jack and Janet in the Philippines*, West Medford, MA: Central Committee on the United States Study of Foreign Missions, 1918.
55 Bernal and Encanto, p. 19.
56 I. Fox, 'A Vacation among the Moros', 469.
57 The Modern Girl around the World Research Group, *The Modern Girl around the World: Consumption, Modernity, and Globalization*, Durham, NC: Duke University Press, 2008.
58 Wilson, 'Western Modes and Asian Clothing', p. 434.
59 Choi, 'The visual embodiment of women in the Korea mission field', p. 91.
60 'Miss Anna Fox and Miss Florence Fox with girls, Cagayan, PI, 1924', box 15, folder 'Fox, Florence L.', ABCFM 78.1, Photos.
61 Rodell, *Culture and Customs of the Philippines*, p. 113.
62 Pura Villaneuva Kalaw, introduction to Maria Paz Mendoza-Guazon, *The Development and Progress of the Filipino Women*, Manila: Bureau of Printing, 1928.
63 See Roces.
64 'Editorial Notes: Great Awakening of National Spirit', *Woman's Work*, 34:3, March 1919, p. 50.
65 Filipinos also self-consciously distanced themselves from the 'wild tribes' of the archipelago. Steinbock-Pratt, p. 570.
66 Mrs. E. S. Cavan, 'Singing the Good News', *Woman's Work*, 36, 1921, 128.
67 T. M. Kalb, 'Ellinwood school-girls at work', *Woman's Work*, 26, 1911, 155. A. Rodgers Wright, 'Filling in the Chinks at Manila', *Woman's Work*, 26, 1911, 150. Curiously, Wright's article focused on the male seminary students, even though the accompanying photograph featured two female Sunday school students wearing *ternos*.
68 'Ellinwood School for Girls, Manila, December, 1912' and 'The three first graduates of the Ellinwood School', *Woman's Work*, 28, Oct 1913, 226–227.
69 A. I. Fox, 'A Vacation among the Moros', *Life and Light*, Nov 1919, 496.
70 A. I. Fox, 'Field correspondents . . .', *Life and Light*, 52:5, May 1922, 197.
71 Rodell, p. 113 mentions this economic dimension; American colonial officials tried to nurture the domestic production of local fabrics to cultivate self-sufficiency.
72 A. V. Johnson, 'Baptist missionary training school', *Pearl of the Orient*, January 1916, 33. P. D. Belo, 'Anna V. Johnson: Missionary pioneer, educator, and evangelist', *American Baptist Quarterly*, 12:3, 1993, 289, reproduces the photograph as an illustration.
73 M. Yoshihara, *Embracing the East: White Women and American Orientalism*, NY: Oxford University Press, 2003.
74 A. I. Fox to K. Lamson, 12 Oct 1920, ABC 17.9.2.
75 G. E. Fox, box 15, ABC 78.1.
76 Steinbock-Pratt likewise concludes that 'modern' Filipina identity was a 'hybrid', drawing from both Filipino and American elements. Steinbock-Pratt, p. 583.

5

THE WOMAN QUESTION AND THE NATIONAL QUESTION IN THE RUSSIAN EMPIRE

Interconnections between central and borderland women's suffrage organizations during the First Russian Revolution, 1905–1907

Olga Shnyrova

Over the last decades the history of the women's movement in Tsarist Russia during the second half of the nineteenth century and into the beginning of the twentieth century has attracted the attention of both Western and Russian researchers.[1] However, this existing scholarship concentrates on the events and activities at the centre of the Russian Empire, especially in the capital cities of Saint Petersburg and Moscow. We know much less about women's activity in the other parts of Russia or about the relationship between central women's organizations and national women's organizations located on the borderlands of the Russian Empire.[2] The only exception is the history of the women's movement in Finland. While a part of the Russian Empire, Finland became the first country in Europe where women got the parliamentary vote, so every researcher has to pay tribute to this fact.[3]

The concentration of existing scholarly studies on the heart of the Empire can be explained by several reasons. First, after the disintegration of the Russian Empire and then of the Soviet Union, women's histories of the former national borderlands became part of the national histories of newly independent states. National researchers usually wrote the histories of national women's movements as the history of independent movements, paying less attention to their connections with the Russian women's movement or to mutual influences. Second, the works of national historians, written in their native languages, are less known to the wider public in other countries. Language is a serious problem for every researcher who decides to study national women's movements in the Russian Empire as a complex whole, as the relevant documents were mostly written and published not in Russian but in native languages; thus you need to be a polyglot to study different national movements in their interrelations and interconnections. Besides, documents and archives of national women's organizations (Polish, Lithuanian, Georgian, Ukrainian, etc.)

The woman question in the Russian Empire **99**

are now located in different states, so a researcher has to cross state borders to work on them. This is why, in this chapter, I present the problem of interconnections between central and borderland women's organizations in the Russian Empire mostly through the eyes of Russian women's suffrage organizations and publications in the Russian women's press.

As the Russian Empire was a multinational state, the national and the supranational were often interconnected, intersecting in the Empire's political, economic, social and cultural processes. This was also true for social movements, including the women's movement. In this chapter I seek to analyze the relationships between the national and the transnational in terms of the complex historical interconnections between national and Russian women's movements. Here I follow Susan Zimmermann, who used these terms in her works devoted to the Habsburg Monarchy.[4] Drawing on her approach, I understand *transnational* in the context of a multinational empire as the realm of activity exceeding the limits of national, *supranational* as activities and dimensions uniting several nations within the frame of empire, and *subnational* as connected with components and actors operating within the frame of one national territory, which generally encompassed peoples of several different ethnic and national identities. To enable the non-specialist reader to better understand the state of the national and woman's questions in the Russian Empire, I begin this chapter with a short introduction to the national structure and national policy in the Russian Empire at the beginning of the twentieth century. I then set the scene for the emergence of the organized women's suffrage movement in Imperial Russia during the first Russian Revolution, moving on to show the interconnections between the central Russian women's suffrage organizations and the national women's organizations. Shifting my focus to the borderlands, I then explore a series of case studies of women's suffrage in Finland, Polish Partition and Lithuania, demonstrating both the interconnections of the national and the woman questions in different contexts and their different outcomes, and the complex relationships between the central Russian women's organizations and the independent national women's organizations. I also analyze the role of religious factors in shaping national women's movements, showing how these worked differently in different parts of the Empire depending on the dominant confessional group in each region. Finally, I conclude with a very brief outline of nationalism within the Russian women's movement, which can be considered as a reaction to the growing nationalism among women in the borderlands.

The Russian Empire at the beginning of the twentieth century was a highly stratified, multinational, multireligious and multicultural state occupying huge territories. National politics were fully subordinated to the state's interest in ensuring the integrity and security of this huge Empire. State authority sought to integrate different nations and ethnic groups within the framework of a policy of assimilation and Russification, as well as seeking to win the support of national elites by giving them social privileges in exchange for loyalty. Different parts of the Russian Empire had different names and juridical statuses, but these were determined mostly by political and historical, rather than national, factors. Poland and Finland, connected to the Russian Empire in the nineteenth century, had special status and were respectively entitled the Polish Kingdom (Tsarstvo Polskoe) and the Great Duchy of Finland. They initially enjoyed greater autonomy than other nations, but following national uprisings for independence, they became less autonomous by the end of the century.

The Empire's borderlands were inhabited by different nations and ethnic groups and represented a tangle of problems inherited from the nineteenth century. At that time nationality as an "ordering principle" became, for the first time, a significant factor in Russian imperial policy. However, religion remained strongly connected to ethnicity, and belonging to the title *Russian Nation* meant belonging to the Orthodox Church. That meant that Russians, Byelorussians and Ukrainians considered themselves as belonging to one nation divided into three peoples: Great Russians, White Russians and Little Russians. National identity often was equated to cultural identity and connected with mother tongue, education and religion. Religion could even be enough on its own, and different nations professing Islam also considered themselves belonging to a single large population group — that of Muslims, who were called *inorodtsy* (people of different origin).

The politics of Russification became more active and persistent at the turn of the nineteenth century. This was in reaction to the rise of national movements, especially on the Western borderlands, including the so-called South-Western Territory (Yugo-Zapadny Krai) and North-Western Territory (Severo-Zapadny Krai), organized into nine provinces. Revolutionary events gave a new impetus to the national movements in the Empire's borderlands. As Russia was a multinational empire and the Russian government's national policy was based on Russification and restrictions on other nations, the national question was sharp and became one of the main questions of the Revolution. The demands of national movements in different borderlands differed from cultural autonomy to full independence. The most active and persistent were Polish nationalists, who demanded full independence and supported the concept of the Great Poland restoration. National parties in Finland fought for the restoration of their autonomy, which had been destroyed in 1899. The question of cultural autonomy was the most significant for Little Russians (Ukrainians) and Lithuanians. In this context, national women's organizations became considered by nationalists as a resource for their movements, and they came under the strong influence of national ideals.

In the Russian Empire's context, the activity of all-Russian women's suffrage organizations, notably the Russian Women's Equality Union, can be considered supranational, as it determined programmes and activity not only among Russians but also among women's organizations in the other nations. A further complexity was that, as ethnic composition inside the national borderlands was not homogeneous, this led to the formation of specific relations and contradictions among different ethnic and national groups settled in these localities, which influenced relations among different national women's organizations and created a subnational level of development in the women's movement in the Russian Empire.

In the early periods of its formation during the middle of the nineteenth century, the women's movement in Russia was influenced by national questions, especially by Polish and Jewish ones. As famous Russian liberal publicist A. Amfiteatrov wrote in 1907, "non-Russian influence on women's question in Russia was determined by the intersection of Russian progress with Polish liberation movement and the problem of Jews' equality."[5] For Russian liberals in the nineteenth century, both men and women, the hope of freedom was linked to the freedom of Poland, as is evident from the slogan, "For our freedom and yours!" Large numbers of intelligent Russian women supported Polish insurrection in 1863: there were Russian nurses in Polish camps, and in Russia women collected funds in support of Polish rebels. All this facilitated the growth of civic activity among women. The cause of Jewish equality and the cause of women's liberation were also tightly connected. Large numbers of young Jewish women took part in the women's emancipation movement as well as in the radical revolutionary movement in Russia. This led A. Amfiteatrov to write in 1907: "There is no female anti-semitism – it is pure male phenomena."[6]

There is an important debate in the historiography on Russia as to whether the Russian women's movement of the second half of the nineteenth and beginning of the twentieth centuries can be characterized as feminist. The term "woman's suffrage" rather than "feminist" tends to be used in the works of foreign historians. Such caution is justifiable, since the women themselves who participated in the Russian women's movement opposed the term "feminist" being applied to them. Thus, the well-known activist N. Shakhmatova stated that "women of Russia had never been feminists and this fact in particular distinguishes them from their Western sisters."[7] For instance, the women delegates at the first two congresses of the Union of Women's Equality of Rights, which took place in Moscow in 1905 where a platform of the new organization was adopted, mentioned time and again that "a woman as a person may forget for a few minutes that she is a woman" and asserted that the question of women's equality of rights was second in comparison with the problem of the general democratic reform of society.[8] Linda Edmonson has stressed this typical characteristic of the women's movement in Russia and explained it by the fact that its activists were afraid that being marked out as feminists would lead to a distinction being made between the fight for women's rights and the wider social and political problems in Russia.[9] Instead, Russian women preferred to call themselves "*ravnopravki*" (fighters for women's rights), as that was a wider notion than "a suffragist," implying a fight for equality in all spheres of life.

Revolution and women's suffrage in central Russia

The women's suffrage movement in Russia appeared due to the revolutionary events from 1905 to 1907, known as the First Russian Revolution, and it was an integral part of this Revolution. The Tsarist *Rescript* (18 February) on People's Representatives, adopted in 1905 under the pressure of revolution, opened up a chance to speak about women's suffrage, and in May 1905 in Moscow, the inaugural meeting of *Soiuz Ravnopravia Zentshin* (Russian Union for Women's Equality – henceforth, RUWE), which was to become the most influential women's suffrage organization in Russia, was held. Its goal was to ensure the inclusion of the words "without distinction of sex" in election law. However, since in May 1905 the question of suffrage had not yet been settled, the new organization aimed to put special emphasis not on the political but on the civil rights of women, on the grounds that all Russian citizens were "politically disenfranchised, but woman has no human rights."[10] It was only after the passing of the election laws of 6 August, 17 October and 11 December 1905, which excluded women from the electorate and upset the gender "equality in illegality" (in other words, the earlier situation of a lack of political rights for both men and women), that the women's suffrage movement emerged in Russia. In 1906 the *Zenskaja Progressivnaja Partia* (Women's Progressive Party) was founded with the short-term aim of achieving full political equality between men and women. In the same year, the Department of Women's Suffrage was formed as a section of the Russian Women's Mutual Aid Society. Then in 1907, the *Liga Ravnopravia Zenshin* (League of Women's Equality) was constituted.

Immediately following their foundation, RUWE and the Russian Women's Mutual Aid Society presented petitions to party congresses, city councils and trade unions. These petitions demanded inclusion in the programmes of these organisations the demand for "universal, direct, equal and secret ballot without distinction of sex, nationality and creed."[11] Thus, as the revolutionary period saw a fight for universal suffrage, Russian women's suffragists, in contrast to those in Britain, immediately demanded political rights for *all* women (rather than for a particular section of the female population that was being discriminated against in comparison to its male equivalent). To lobby its interests from within the labour movement, RUWE became a member of the all-Russian organisation of trade unions, the Union of Unions. As a result of successful pressure, in summer 1905 the women's suffrage clause was included in the political programmes of the trade unions, the *zemstva* (local authorities in the county) and the *kadet* party (constitutional democrats). The same clause was included in the resolution adopted at the Congress of Cities' Councils. This allows us to state that on the revolutionary wave, the majority of the democratic community in Russia was in favour of women's suffrage, and public opinion was favourable to that question. It can be explained by the fact that in Russia, the demand for woman's suffrage was put forward jointly with the demand for universal suffrage backed by almost all Russian political parties.

The programmes of Russian political parties articulated clear positions concerning the issue of women's suffrage in particular and universal suffrage in general. The left wing of the Russian political spectrum – the Russian Social-Democratic Party, the socialist revolutionaries, the *trydoviki* (labours) and the *kadets* (constitutional democrats) – demanded universal suffrage and, as an intrinsic part of this, recognized women's suffrage. The political centre – *Oktyabrists* – was more cautious: they also demanded a universal, equal and secret ballot, but they believed that before this could be introduced, it would take a long time to perfect the Russian Civil Code. That is why, while not denying the principle of woman's suffrage, the political centre considered it to be a matter for the distant future. The right wing monarchist parties and groups vigorously rejected not only women's suffrage but all democratic

The woman question in the Russian Empire **103**

changes; however, these parties were in the minority in the first State Duma and had no decisive influence.

Thus, women's suffrage supporters had a really good chance to make a women's enfranchisement bill pass through the first State Duma, since the majority of the Duma's members were representatives of the left wing.[12] To convince deputies of the necessity to grant women the right to vote, suffragists collected signatures for the petitions demanding political equality for women. To the first State Duma, RUWE presented a petition with 5,000 signatures, and the Russian Women's Mutual Aid Society presented its own petition with 4,500 signatures. The latter inspired the famous lawyer and deputy from the *kadet* party, L. Petrazhitsky, to make an ardent speech in favour of women's rights. In 1907, during the second State Duma, women's organizations jointly presented to the Russian parliament a larger petition, with 19,984 signatures.[13]

From the very beginning the Russian women's suffrage movement was closely connected with political parties in the centre and to the left of the political spectrum. During the elections to the First State Duma local branches of RUWE canvassed in favour of the constitutional democrats (Cadets, left centre), the first party to include female suffrage in its programme. Later RUWE was associated with left parties. Since the women's suffrage movement in Russia emerged on the revolutionary wave, this led to its self-representation as a movement of women workers and peasant women. Without resorting to the militant tactics of civil disobedience, Russian suffragists nevertheless adhered to a radical platform, sometimes directly participating in revolutionary events. Members of RUWE helped Moscow workers during the armed revolt in December 1905: they organized canteens and first-aid posts and raised money for strikers. As a result RUWE established close contacts with trade unions and workers, who supported their activities. To promote its ideas, RUWE's members worked in a range of different organizations: the Red Cross, the Union of Unions, the Unemployment Commission and the Moscow Strike Committee. It should also be noted that the demand for women's enfranchisement was supported by almost all women's professional organizations and mutual aid societies. As a result, in 1907 a petition, mentioned above, was presented to the State Duma by twenty-one different women's organisations.

Reaction following the revolutionary peak of 1907, however, scuppered the chances of a women's enfranchisement bill being passed through the State Duma. As a result, between 1908 and 1917 suffragists confined themselves to the aim of achieving the principle of equality by promoting other laws that would improve the position of women, including municipal law, education law and property rights laws.

Russian Union of Women's Equality as a transnational organization

All the large Russian women's organizations – the Russian Union of Women's Equality, the Women's Progressive Party, the Women's Mutual Aid Society and the League of Women's Equality – were advocates of the right of nations to self-determination. The close connections of the Russian women's suffrage organizations with the political left were significant here, as it was only the left parties and organizations that supported the idea of cultural autonomy or self-determination for the nations in the Russian Empire.

Before 1905 the Tsarist regime had only encouraged the activities of charitable organizations, not political ones, and as a result a large number of different national women's clubs and mutual aid societies had been set up within the Empire, especially in large cities. But the Revolution stimulated the rise of women's self-consciousness throughout the Empire and facilitated the development of independent women's national movements. It led to the creation of women's suffrage organizations not only in Moscow but also all over Russia. During the Revolution a large number of new women's organizations were created on the Empire's borderlands. Like RUWE, they demanded political rights for women, but they combined this demand with the demand for national autonomy. Representatives of the Moscow group, together with delegates from national borderlands, came together at the First Congress of the Russian Union for Women's Equality in Moscow.[14]

This is why the most influential and active women's suffrage organization, RUWE, was multinational. Just after its formation, national branches of RUWE were formed. Programmes of these organizations connected the aim of achieving gender political equality with the aim of achieving national equality. Nevertheless, the means of, and mechanisms for, achieving gender and national equality in different national women's organizations were distinctive and were influenced by the level of sharpness of the national question in different parts of the Russian Empire. The democratic structure of RUWE enabled its branches to act as independent organizations and their strategies and ideologies varied. RUWE's branches in Lithuania, Byelorussia, Georgia and Ukraine demanded not only the political equality of women but also the recognition of cultural and national autonomy for its population, and the branches closely collaborated with local organizations aimed at national liberation. The Georgian delegate reported at the RUWE congress in 1906: "Solution of women's question in Georgia is very simple: women's liberation is strongly connected with liberation of men. That is why Georgian Union for Women's Equality considers that women's question will be solved just after the achievement of Georgian autonomy."[15] Such a position determined the membership of the Georgian Union for Women's Equality: it united members from different parties, both women and men, struggling for Georgian autonomy. So in national women's suffrage organizations, members mostly did not separate their struggle from the struggle of national autonomy or independence.

As mentioned above, the level of nationalism was different in different parts of the Russian Empire's borderlands: it was the strongest in Poland and in Finland. It was in these regions that there were the most active national women's organizations, as is now discussed.

National movement and victory of women's suffrage in the Grand Duchy of Finland

As Rachelle Rutchild notes, "the Russian Empire was the site of two of the earliest, quickest, and most complete female suffrage breakthroughs."[16] The first one happened in 1906 in Finland. Ceded from Sweden to Russia in 1809, Finland was a semi-autonomous Grand Duchy. But Tsar Nikolai II, who ascended to the throne in 1896, enforced a Russification policy and took steps to restrict Finnish autonomy. In 1899 the Tsar signed a decree that gave him the right to impose laws without agreement with the Finnish Seim (parliament). Such actions provoked a rise in national resistance, and in 1904 Finnish nationalist Eugen Schauman killed Nikolai Bobrikov, the General-Governor of Finland.

The Russian Revolution gave Finnish nationalists the opportunity to return to self-government on the basis of wide democratic representation. As Irma Sulkunen mentions,[17] the suffrage question in Finland was not the only political question, but it was a matter of national identity. Society in Finland was not homogeneous. A large proportion of population, mostly part of the elite, were of Swedish nationality, and the Swedish language was the first administrative language in the Grand Duchy.

While Swedish liberals were mostly against women's suffrage, Finnish parties supported universal and equal suffrage. As Sulkunen notes,

> This meant binding the ordinary people to a common patriotic cause, and it allowed no distinction to be made between women and men. On the contrary, the contribution of women to the construction of national unity was strongly emphasized, as was their crucial significance in bearing and raising a vigorous Finnish nation.[18]

This gave a good opportunity for women's organizations that joined the national movement to combine demands for self-government with demands for the enfranchisement of women. As a result, on 29 May 1906, soon after Finland regained its autonomy, the Finnish parliament granted the right to vote to both women and men over the age of 24. Finland became the first European country where women got the vote and the first country in the world where women also got the right to be elected to parliament. In March 1907 nineteen women were elected to the new parliament of Finland.

The enfranchisement of Finnish women was met with great enthusiasm by Russian women's suffrage supporters. One of RUWE's leaders, Zinaida Mirovitch, wrote:

> We are happy at the victory of our sisters in Finland, as if it is our victory. Let their example inspire us, breathe into us energy and courage, let their experience be for us a guiding star. Women of Finland obtained the vote

106 Olga Shnyrova

not only due to the happy combination of the historical circumstances. No, they gained the victory due to their determination, energy, concerted efforts. Fighting for freedom they forgot about party disagreements. I wish we also have unity, solidarity and refusal of personal and party interests as our mottos in our future struggle.[19]

As representatives of the imperial nation, leaders of the Russian women's movement had formerly been inclined to treat the members of national women's organizations as their "younger sisters," but the victory of Finnish women made Russian female suffragists consider them more experienced in political activity than they themselves were.

As Finland was part of the Russian Empire, the victory of Finnish women moved Russia as a whole from the periphery to the center of the international women's suffrage movement, and events in Russia began to attract close attention from the International Women's Suffrage Alliance and its leaders. Reports from Russia and about Russia were on the front pages of *Jus Suffragii*. Congratulating the women of Finland, women's suffrage supporters in other countries hoped that Russian women would also obtain the vote in the near future. In the end, however, Russia would need to survive another revolution before that happened.

Feminism and nationalism in Polish Partition

The other intense nationalist situation was in Russian Poland. There revolution stimulated mass demonstrations in favor of Polish autonomy in Polish Partition,[20] and in response to this unrest martial law was enforced. Depending on their position on the political spectrum, the demands of Polish parties varied from cultural autonomy to full independence for Poland.

Revolution stimulated the activism of women in Poland as well as those in Finland, and in 1905 several mass women's congresses were held in Galicia, Warsaw and other parts of Poland. But the attitude of most of the Polish nationalist parties to women's suffrage was negative. The largest and the most influential party of National Democrats did not include women's vote in its programme. Agitating for women to take part in the struggle for national autonomy, Polish parties from the National Democrats to the Social Democrats persuaded them not to organize separate women's organizations. For Polish nationalists, the idea of *polschizna* (Polish identity and interests) was much more important than other ideas and interests. As R. Blaubaum noted,

> The Polish nationalist movement (a coalition of organizations eventually grouped under the National Democratic Alliance or Endecja), whose response to the "woman question" would ultimately prove the most influential as it came to dominate the larger political discourse on the Polish "nation," viewed women as bearers and nurturers of peculiarly Polish values and equated patriotic duties with those of motherhood and child-rearing.[21]

Women were expected to subdue their gender interests for the sake of the primary purpose of achieving national independence. Nationalists often used Polish women's activity in their own interests. Activist women helped parties in their political agitation by transporting and disseminating political literature. For this activity women in Polish political parties received the nickname "dromedaries," as they ran the whole day with heavy bundles of illegal literature from one place to another, fulfilling the instructions of their party comrades.[22] That is why during these first congresses was discussed the same question, that was actual for Russian women: was it necessary to fight for women's equality by creating independent women's organizations, or do it in the ranks of those parties which included it the their platforms?[23] Polish writer and women's activist Romualde Baudouin de Courtenay noted that conditions for the development of an independent women's movement in Poland were worse than in Russia:

> Firstly, traditional and cultural frames are more strict than in Russia; secondly, women had to lead their activity in the country which is oppressed; thirdly, the most influential party, National Democrats, did not include the women's vote in its political programme.[24]

In spite of these negative factors, however, the Union of Equal Rights for Polish Women (UERPW) was organized in 1906 in Warsaw. It was organized due to the influence of RUWE's creation and was registered in 1907. Its charter declared its aim as the "achievement of equality and freedom for women of all classes." Proclaiming its non-party character, the Union nevertheless demanded from those of its members who participated in other organizations that they insist on the inclusion of the principle of women's equality in the programmes of those organizations.[25] Soon it expanded its activity not only in Russian Poland but also to the other towns in the Western part of the Empire: it had departments in Vilna (Vilnius), Kiev, Saint-Petersburg and Moscow. It was affiliated with RUWE and organized similar actions. Polish delegates were present at the RUWE's congresses in 1906. In 1906 UERPW members promoted a petition demanding political rights for women and managed to gain more than 30,000 signatures, which were presented to the Russian State Duma. When the Second Duma began to discuss the project of municipal reform, Polish women took part in the project's evaluation. When it became obvious that municipal reform for Poland meant exclusion of women from the voting process, the UERPW organized meetings of protest and sent petitions with its objections to the Duma. Like Russian women's suffrage supporters, UERPW members tried to give political education to women workers and peasant women, organizing meetings for them and distributing literature. Its founders and leaders, Jozefa Bojanowska and Paulina Kuczalska-Reinschmit, edited *Ster* – a popular journal published in Warsaw from 1907 to 1914.[26] This resource made the Union stronger and was widely used by its members for the propagation of their views. The Warsaw society marked itself as feminist and that sometimes disturbed some more moderate departments of

RUWE.[27] It was probably too feminist for some of its own members, as the Warsaw organization split during the first year of its existence and a group of its activists broke away and formed the Polish Women's Rights Association. Their demands for women's suffrage were often criticized as untimely, as they were put forward before the independence of the whole country had been attained.[28]

The other main trend of the UERPW's activity, especially outside of the Russian Partition area, was the promotion of Polish language and culture. This occupied a large place in the activity of its departments in Saint-Petersburg and Moscow. Saint-Petersburg's UERPW group tried to organize a Polish people's university, but the idea was blocked by the city mayor, who decided that such an educational organization could be opened only after the creation of a Russian people's university. All UERPW groups were also involved in temperance and antitrafficking activity, organized lectures on women's rights and publishing activities.

The majority of Polish women's organizations were less feminist and more nationalist than the UERPW. Their approach, as their spiritual leader – the famous writer Eliza Orzeszkowa – wrote, was as follows: "The programme of the women's movement can be summed up in two points: independent labour and earnings and women's aspiration to moral improvement by way of enlightenment and labour."[29] That is why the resolutions of the Congress of Polish Women, which was held in June 1906, timed to coincide with Eliza Orzeszkowa's 65th birthday, proclaimed the necessity of creating new professional women's unions and women's societies and promoting the equality of women in the professional sphere but did not pay much attention to women's political equality. However, great attention was paid to the problem of teaching the Polish language at school and to criticism of the Russification policy of the Russian government. Thus, for the large number of Polish women, national identity was prioritized over gender.

Feminism and nationalism at a subnational level: the Byelorussian case

It is important to note that within the Russian Empire there existed a complex system of collateral subordination of non-title nations. The role of Polish nationalism in Lithuania and Byelorussia reveals the complex and multilayered relationships of submission and domination among the nations forming part of the Russian Empire, the product of a kind of subimperialism within the Empire.

If the Polish considered themselves an oppressed nation, they were oppressors from the point of view of many Lithuanians and Byelorussians. In the Eastern part of the Polish territories (Kingdom), Polish people belonged mostly to the upper class of landowners, while Lithuanians and Byelorussians were mostly peasants. This situation is evidenced in official papers, such as the report of the Minsk governor in 1895, when he claimed that Belarusian Catholics were not "independent" (*samostoiatel'nyi*) in their opinions and actions because of the strong influence of Polish–Catholic clergymen. From the least Polish (and least Catholic) province of the region, the Mogilev governor noted in 1900 that despite the scant 3 per cent of the population made up by Poles, their influence was great, in particular because of the jealously patriotic *Pol'ki* (Polish women).[30]

After 1905, calls to "save Belarusians from Polonism" became more frequent and strident. That is why the efforts of the UERPW in Vilna (Vilnius) to enlighten Byelorussian peasant women were met with harsh criticism from the Byelorussian side. Prominent Byelorussian publicist Lykian Solonevicth considered Polish woman as the embodiment of conservatism because she "was strongly devoted to church, *ksiądz*, *polschizna*, and all old Polish traditions."[31] That is why he interpreted all attempts of the UERPW in Vilna to organize Byelorussian peasant women as the desire to *Polonize* Byelorussian people. Nevertheless such criticism of Polish domination of the women's movement did not lead to the formation of independent Byelorussian organizations struggling for women's equality. The small Byelorussian educated female elite at that time was mostly involved in educational and charitable activity.

Thus feminist and gender solidarity in the multinational Empire could and often did contradict with national identities. Inevitably it influenced the national women's movements and caused contradictions among them.

Religion and suffrage in the women's movement: the Lithuanian case

Some tension also existed between Poles and Lithuanians in the Western provinces. Revolution increased the feeling of national and gender identity among Lithuanian women and led to the creation of the independent Lithuanian women's movement.

In the summer of 1905 a women's congress took place in Vilna where a resolution to prepare a new bill concerning election to the Duma was adopted. Women representatives from every national group living in Vilna prepared separate bills. Lithuanians claimed that they could not agree with the law on the Duma election and that the nation could be satisfied only if it had autonomy within Lithuania's ethnographic borders with Seimas, elected by general, secret, equal and direct vote in Vilnius.[32] The meeting participants did not come to a unanimous decision, and women from every national group prepared protests and collected signatures under each.

The next step was the creation of the Association of Lithuanian Women in September 1905. The Association's programme copied the RUWE's charter and included such demands as national autonomy and equal rights for women and men. The Association of Lithuanian Women created a number of women's chapters in the province and made contacts with associations and unions of Russian women.

In 1906 the Tsarist government suppressed the activities of various organizations and associations. The activity of the Association of Lithuanian Women was weakened, and women's organizations were gradually dissolved. The revival began in 1908 when a new women's congress gathered in Kovno (Kaunas). It united more than 300 delegates, mostly peasant women and women workers. The national

110 Olga Shnyrova

character of the event was stressed by the fact that it was held in the Lithuanian language. The congress adopted several resolutions:

- Women's trade unions should be created.
- For the promotion of teaching the Lithuanian language at schools, teachers should be Lithuanians.
- To send a petition to the State Duma with the demand to abolish the sale of vodka, vodka should be sold as a medicine at pharmacies.[33]

The main point was the decision "to organize a Lithuanian women's union, in order to strive for the juridical and political equality of women and unite with similar unions in other countries."[34] But the problem was that the new organization from the very beginning was divided into two wings: Catholic and progressive. Catholic clergy were among the Congress organizers and they tried to establish control over the Union and limit the organization's activity to traditional forms of charity. During the discussions Catholic priests tried to dictate to women what to do, and on the second day of the congress debates became so hot that they led to confrontation. A correspondent reported: "during his speech *ksiądz*-speaker lost his temper and forgot about decencies. . . . When the chairwoman ruled him out of order, he cried to her: 'It is you who have no right to speak!'"[35] The negative attitude of Catholic priests to women's political activity and their aspiration to control the Lithuanian Women's Union soon caused its split into the Catholic Lithuanian Women's Union and the Union of Lithuanian Women, which was based in Vilna. So multiethnic and multiconfessional Vilna became the centre of the independent women's suffrage organization, whereas mono-ethnic Kovno became the center of the Catholic women's movement. The charity-focused Catholic Lithuanian Women's Union soon got registration permission from the province's authorities, but the Union of Lithuanian Women did not. Of course such a situation weakened the position of the women's suffrage organization in Lithuania.

The Catholic Church was strongly against women's emancipation. Appealing to Polish women *ksiądz* Karl Nedzialovsky wrote: "emancipation declared by feminists is the regress to Paganism," indicating that an emancipated woman could not be a good Christian.[36] The Catholic Church also tried to control and mobilize Polish women by stirring up their national feelings. In Warsaw the Catholic Polish Women's Union concentrated on charity and the promotion of Catholicism, although the Church did not manage to influence the activity of the UERPW in Poland as it was able to do in Lithuania. The religiousness of Polish and Lithuanian women was thus used as an argument against their enfranchisement, as it was in France, where the Catholic Church also had a big influence on the majority of French women.

Religious factors played an important role in the process of the institutionalization of national women's movements. The Russian Empire was multiconfessional and the attitude of different churches to women's emancipation varied. Evidence shows that the Catholic Church in Lithuania and in Poland was a consistent opponent of women's liberation. As for the Russian Orthodox Church, it also supported traditional gender roles in society and family, but it did not have a large influence on Russian women's organizations. Indeed, ideas of women's equality even influenced several Orthodox priests. In 1909 two Orthodox bishops, of Smolensk and of Eniseisk, appealed to the Synod with the suggestion to elect women as the Church wardens. As discussed below, the religious leaders most tolerant to the idea of women's political equality appeared to be Muslim clergy.

Women's emancipation, religion and multicultural interconnections in Eastern and Southern Borderlands of the Russian Empire

Revolution also facilitated the development of the women's movement in the Eastern and Southern provinces of the Russian Empire, which contained the majority of the Muslim population. In common with women of other nations and confessions, Muslims demanded emancipation and equality in petitions to the State Duma. The petition of the Muslim women from Orenburg declared:

> Muslim deputies, you ought to demand all rights for Muslim women, you ought to promote the Bill, which will secure us against the despotism of our husbands, and from oppression and suffering. We are mothers of the nation, we are the comrades of men, the upbringing and progress of the people are in our hands![37]

This petition vividly demonstrates the growth of the self-consciousness and self-valuing of Muslim women. The Muslim fraction in the State Duma also supported the idea of women's suffrage. However, the deputies had first consulted with Muslim religious leaders as to whether or not this idea was in violation of Islamic laws and the Koran. They got the answer:

> Allah created all people equal, there are no indications in the Koran that women should be deprived from political participation. If the Koran does not deny women's right to elect, she can be elected. This does not contradict with shariah.[38]

Representatives of the Muslim religious leaders also signed petitions in favor of women's political equality.

As the result of Muslim women's civil activity, several women's organizations were organized in the Southern and Western borderlands: the Society for the Promotion of Education among Muslim Women (Elizavetopol, Transcaucasia), Societies of Muslim Women (in Ganja, Azerbaijan, and Ufa), the Club of Muslim women in Baku, etc. Their aims included promotion of female education and emancipation and the development of national culture. Perhaps the most feminist was the Society for the Promotion of Education among Muslim Women, with its motto, "Veil

112 Olga Shnyrova

off! More light! More freedom!" These organizations were rather small in number and were organized mostly by well-educated women from the upper classes. The founder of the Society for the Promotion of Education among Muslim Women, for example, was Shafiga Usubbəyova, the wife of Azerbaijani aristocrat Nəsib bəy Usubbəyov, who later became an eminent national leader, and the daughter of İsmail Mustafa oğlu Gasprinskiy, one of the founders of Jadidism, the movement aimed at the secularization of Muslim education. But Muslim women's organizations only involved small numbers of women, and the Revolution did not promote the creation of any organizations campaigning for Muslim women's equal political rights. As the Muslim deputy from Baku, E. Beknazar-Uzbasheva, mentioned in her report at the First All-Russian Women's Congress (1908): "Muslim women still live in isolation and are deprived of rights."[39]

In multiethnic, multicultural and multiconfessional regions, women's organizations tended to be cosmopolitan, progressive and tolerant. The most typical were women's organizations in the large multinational cities of Tiflis and Kiev. In both cities women's organizations worked with women of different nationalities and their governing bodies were also multinational. As an example, I can mention Tiflis in Georgia. The most active here was the Society of Caucasian Women, created in 1909. The Society united Georgian, Armenian, Polish, Russian and Ukrainian women and maintained close contacts with the main Russian organizations: the Russian Mutual Aid Society, the Russian League for Women Equality and the Women's Progressive Party. Its Georgian section, which tried to only involve Georgian women, was less successful and was criticized by the Society's leaders for its separatism.

Nationalism and Russian women during the Revolution

The Revolution evoked nationalist feelings not only in the borderlands but also among Russians at the heart of the Empire. At the end of 1905 the Union of Russian People was created in Saint-Petersburg. It was a right-wing nationalist pro-monarchy mass organization, which had sixty branches in the cities and towns of Russia. It also tried to mobilize women, and it was under its influence that the Union of Russia Women was created in 1907. It was an ambitious project, as its charter declared that the Union was created forever and could be closed only by governmental decision.[40] Its aim was "the unification of Russian women independently from estate and wealth on the base of social and economic activity."[41] Nevertheless, from the national point of view this organization did not mean to be pure Russian. All female citizens of the Russian Empire except Jews could be members of the organization. Influenced by the Union of Russian People, it was anti-semitic. Its existence confirmed, rather than denied, Amfiteatrov's theses about the absence of female anti-semitism as, in spite of its ambitious founding aims, the Union remained small, acted mostly in Saint-Petersburg and was quickly transformed into a traditional charitable society. The organization closely collaborated with right-wing monarchic organizations but had no influence on the broader women's movement.

Conclusion

As Russia was a huge multinational, multicultural, multiconfessional Empire, achievements in the sphere of women's emancipation in its constituent parts varied both before and after the Revolution. The First Russian Revolution played an important role in the development of women's movements in both the centre of Empire and its borderlands. Their development was simultaneous with revolutionary events and most of them were created in 1906 and 1907. Their collective notions as well as the individual identities of members were shaped by a variety of norms and factors: gender, class, nationality and religion. Revolution mostly affected the European part of the Russian Empire, and within this area there were different histories of interaction between national and women's movements.

In Finland, as we have seen, women's organizations were included in the national movement for autonomy and were acknowledged by Finnish nationalists as equal partners. As a result Finnish woman got the active and passive vote in 1906. The victory of women in Finland was extremely important for Russian and other national women's suffrage organizations. It gave an example and model of successful strategy for the promotion of women's rights based on gender solidarity and active civil position. In contrast, in Catholic Poland, Polish nationalists treated women as a resource for national movement but did not recognize them as political subjects with specific interests. But proximity to Europe led to the spread of feminist ideas within the Polish Kingdom, especially in Warsaw, and to the appearance of feminist organizations, notably the Union of Equal Rights for Polish Women. In marking itself as feminist this organization disturbed some more moderate departments of the Russian Union of Women's Equality. Despite the fact that for women's suffrage organizations gender identity was dominant, explicit identification with feminism was a difficult point for both Russian and national women's suffrage organizations in the Empire. In Lithuania the women's movement was more influenced by the Catholic Church and it caused the split of the Lithuanian Women's Union into the Catholic Lithuanian Women's Union and the Union of Lithuanian Women. In multiethnic regions and cities of the Russian Empire, like Tiflis (Georgia), Kiev and Kharkov (Ukraine), women's organizations were cosmopolite, progressive and tolerant as they were multinational and worked with women of different nationalities.

Although the various national women's suffrage societies acted independently, their creation was mostly inspired by the activity of Russian women's suffrage organizations at the heart of the Empire, especially the RUWE. Many of the national societies were affiliated with the RUWE and took part in its congresses and campaigns. The RUWE was not only a Russian organization but also a transnational umbrella organization uniting women's organizations from different parts of the Empire. Its democratic structure allowed for cooperation among national women's organizations of different political orientations and levels of radicalism, though its central organization in Moscow was closely connected with political parties on the left of the political spectrum. As we can see from the publication in the RUWE's journal, *Souz zhenchin*, the successes of national women's organizations were important for the promotion of women's rights in the centre of the

114 Olga Shnyrova

Empire and were used by the RUWE, the Women's Progressive Party and the League for Women's Equality in lobbying women's interests in the State Duma and in propaganda work.

As in the Russian Empire, a complex system of collateral subordination of non-title nations existed, and relations among different national women's movements were not unclouded and were sometimes contradictory. But as all of them had common aims and strategies their contradictions, were not as sharp as the contradictions among nationalist organizations. National women's suffrage societies acted independently, but they felt that they belonged to one social movement. The concept of "sisterhood" was widely propagated in the Russian and national women's press and in the speeches of women's leaders. The multinational and multicultural composition of the Russian Empire gave national women's movements possibilities for cooperation on different levels: transnational, supranational and subnational, transferring mutual experiences and successes, using joint resources and organizing solidarity campaigns. While the First Russian Revolution did not provide a chance for women in other parts of the Russian Empire to repeat the success of their Finnish sisters, the Revolution did stimulate women's political and civil activity throughout the Empire. Large numbers of national women's organizations, created in the period after the revolutionary upheaval, became an integral part of developing national civil societies.

Notes

1 B. Clements, B. Engel, and C. Worobec, *Russia's Women: Accommodation, Resistance, Transformation?*, Berkeley: University of California Press, 1991; R. Stites, *The Women's Liberation Movement in Russia: Feminism, Nihilism and Bolshevism, 1860–1930,* Princeton, NJ: Princeton University Press, 1978; L. Edmondson, *Feminism in Russia, 1900–1917*, Stanford, CA: Stanford University Press, 1984; B. Engel, *Women in Russia, 1700–2000*, Cambridge, UK: Cambridge University Press, 2004; R. Rutchild, *Equality and Revolution. Women's Rights in the Russian Empire, 1905–1917*, Pittsburgh, PA: University of Pittsburgh Press, 2010; O. Khasbulatova, *Opyt I traditsii zhenskogo dvizhenia v Rossii* (Experience and Traditions of Women's Movement in Russia), Ivanovo: Ivanovo university Press, 1994; S. Aivazova, *Russkie Zhensciny v labirinte ravnopravia* (Russian Women in Equality Labyrinth), Moscow: RIK Rusanova, 1998; I. Yukina, *Russkii Feminism kak vyzov sovremennosty* (Russian Feminism as a Challenge to the Present), Aletheia, Saint Petersburg: 2007.
2 R. Blobaum, 'The woman's question in Russian Poland', *Journal of Social History*, 35:4, 2002; M. Bohachevsky-Chomiak, *Feminists Despite Themselves: Women in Ukrainian Community Life, 1884–1939*, Edmonton: Institute of Ukrainian Studies, University of Alberta, 1988.
3 See for example: R. Rutchild, *Women's Suffrage and Revolution in the Russian Empire, 1905–1917 Aspasia* (2007) vol. 1 having the part devoted to the struggle for the women's suffrage in Finland, New York: Berghahn Books; Irma Sulkunen Suffrage, 'Nation and Citizenship – The Finnish Case in an International Context Suffrage, Genrer and Citizenship: International Perspectives on Parliamentary Reforms', in Irma Sulkunen, Seija-Leena Nevala-Nurmi, and Pirjo Markkola, eds., Cambridge: Cambridge University Press, 2009.
4 S. Zimmermann, 'The Challenge of Multinational Empire for the International Women's Movement: The Habsburg Monarchy and the Development of Feminist Inter/national Politics', in K. Offen, eds., *Globalizing Feminisms 1789–1945*, New York: Routledge, 2010. Online: http://journals.berghahnbooks.com/aspasia/#sthash.agbMOdU4.dpuf.

The woman question in the Russian Empire **115**

5 A. Amfiteatrov, *Zhenschina v obtchestvennyh dvizheniah Rossii*, Saint-Petersburg: Zhivoe slovo, 1907, p. 62.
6 Ibid., p. 63.
7 N. A. Shakhmatova, *Chto takoe feminism?* (What Is Feminism?), Moscow: Liga ravnopravia zhenzhin 1912, p. 4.
8 Soiuz ravnopravia Zenshin, Bulleten #3 (The union of women's equality of rights), State Archive of Russian Federation, fund 516.
9 L. Edmondson, *Feminism in Russia, 1900–1917*.
10 Ibid.
11 A. Kalmanovitch, *Zhenskoe dvizhenie i ego zadachi,* Saint Petersburg: Tipografia Rabotnik, 1908, p. 15.
12 The First State Duma was ready to vote for giving women political equality. But it was dismissed ahead of time before the day, when the question of women's political rights was set for voting. The following State Dumas were "right"; moreover, the increasing political reaction did not provide an opportunity to add the topic of suffrage to voting. That is why the question about enfranchisement of women was raised only during the February Revolution of 1917.
13 *Soyuz zhenschin* (The women's union), 1, 1907, p. 6.
14 V. Jurėnienė Women's movement at the end of the nineteenth and at the beginning of the twentieth centuries, in Women's Movement and Feminism(s) in Central, Eastern, and Lithuanian Southeastern Europe (19th and 20th Centuries). Vienna, 2006, pp. 457–475.
15 Ravnopravie zchenchin, *Otchety i protokoly* (Equality of women. reports and minutes), Saint-Petersburg: Publishing house of J. Trey, 1906, p. 13.
16 R. Rutchild, *Women's Suffrage and Revolution in the Russian Empire, 1905–1917,* New York: Berghahn Books, 2007, vol. 1.
17 I. Sulkunen, Suffrage, 'Nation and Citizenship – The Finnish Case in an International Context', in I. Sulkunen, S.-L. Nevala–Nurmi and P. Markkola, eds., *Suffrage, Gender and Citizenship – International Perspectives on Parliamentary Reforms*, Newcastle upon Tyne, UK: Cambridge Scholars Publishing, 2009, p. 96.
18 Ibid.
19 N. Mirovitch, *Pobeda Zhenskogo Dvizenija v Finljandii* (Victory of women's movement in Finland). Moscow: Publishing house of I. Kushnerev, 1907, p. 18.
20 Polish Partition is a geographical notion defining Poland, divided between three empires: Russian, Austro-Hungarian and German.
21 R. Blobaum, The Woman's Question in Russian Poland, p. 802.
22 Dromaderki (Dromedaries) From Polish Journal 'Ster', *Souz zhenchin*, 5, 1907.
23 R. Baudouin de Courtenay, 'Iz zhizni polskih zhenchin' (From the life of Polish women), *Souz zhenchin*, 1, 1907, p. 17.
24 Ibid.
25 *Ustav Obtchestva Ravnopravija Polskih Zhenchin* (Charter of Union of Equal Rights for Polish Women), Warsaw, 1907, p. 3.
26 Their biographies can be found in Biographical Dictionary of Women's Movements and Feminisms in Central, Eastern, and Southeastern Europe, 19th and 20th Centuries. Budapest, 2006.
27 Ravnopravie zchenchin, *Otchety i protokoly* (Equality of women. Reports and minutes), Saint-Petersburg: Publishing house of J. Trey, 1906 p. 25.
28 Krzywiec G. Kuczalska–Reinschmit P. in F. de Haan, K. Daakalova, A. Laufti., eds., *Biographical Dictionary of Women's Movements and Feminisms. Central, Eastern and South Eastern Europe, 19th and 20th Centuries*, Budapest: Central European University Press, 2006, p. 276.
29 E. Orzeszkowa, 'Frantsuzam o polke' (French people about Polish women), in E. Orzeszkowa ed., Otkrytoe pismo nemetskim zhenchinam I frantsuzam o polke, Moscow: D. P. Ephimov, 1901, p. 112.
30 RGIA, *Chital'nyi zal*, op. 1, d. 54, Mogilev 1900, p. 5.
31 L. M. Solonevitch, *Novaja rol polskoi zhenchiny v Beloryssii I Litve* (New role of polish woman in Byelorussia and Litva), Vilna: Russkii Pochin, 1910, p. 2.

116 Olga Shnyrova

32 V. Jūrėnienė Formation of the Lithuanian Women's movement and Its Emergence in an International Arena in the First Half of the 20th Century // Gender maters in the Baltics, Ryga, 2008, pp. 269–294.

33 *Souz zhenchin*, 3, 1907, p. 15.

34 Ibid.

35 Ibid.

36 K. Nedzjialovsky, *Ne tuda doroga, milostivye gosydaryni* (It is a wrong way, ladies), Saint-Petersburg: 1901.

37 *Souz zhenchin*, 4, 1908, p. 15.

38 Ibid., 1 1907, p. 19.

39 E. G. Beknazar-Uzbasheva, 'Kratkie statisticheskie dannye o dejatelnosti I ekonomicheskom polozenii zhenshin v Baku' (Short statistical data about activity and economical status of women in Baku), in *Trydy Pervogo Vserossiskogo Zhenskogo s'ezda*, Saint-Petersburg: 1908, p. 94.

40 *Ustav Souza Russkih Zhenshin* (Union of Russian Women's Charter), Saint-Petersburg: 1907 p. 3.

41 Ibid., p .5.

6

THE ITALIAN EMPIRE 'AT HOME'

Fascist girls, imperial propaganda and the racialized memory of Italy, 1937–2007

Barbara Spadaro

The pictures illustrating this chapter emerged from uncatalogued boxes of the Italian colonial archives, fascist magazines and family collections of holiday snapshots and newspapers cuttings. From such disparate locations, they document a hitherto somewhat neglected, yet extraordinarily ambitious, fascist propaganda campaign that in the mid-1930s shaped the life trajectories and imagination of hundreds of thousands of women in Italy: the *Preparazione della donna alla vita coloniale* (Colonial life training for women). Run as a series of courses and training camps implemented around the country, this was a form of propaganda which staged the life that Italian women would be expected to live across the Italian Empire, as modern pioneers and genitors of a new dominant Latin race. At the height of this campaign, three training camps were also mounted on the outskirts of Tripoli in Italy's North African colony of Libya. These transported several thousand teenagers from the main Italian cities as *Giovani Fasciste Coloniali* ('Fascist Colonial Girls') into a stunning setting of sand dunes, Roman ruins, indigenous subjects and modern tourist facilities.

This chapter focuses on this fascist colonial propaganda campaign directed at young women and seeks to illuminate the intersecting national, colonial and transimperial circuits of representation that have been involved in shaping gendered and racialized memories in Italy since the 1930s. It juxtaposes visual and written propaganda material sources with the personal trajectories and self-narratives of two women propagandists to illuminate the nature of racial identifications and feelings of Italian belonging which took root in the fascist era. In taking female subjectivity as a site of interaction between the local and the global, my aim is to contribute to integrating the exploration of gendered identity formation, subjectivities and cultural memory into the study of transnational and global history.

Over the past decade, a body of international scholarship has investigated colonial fantasies and the racialized and gendered discourses of difference, modernity and

118 Barbara Spadaro

citizenship developed in Italy throughout the process of national unification and colonial expansion toward Africa and the Mediterranean. By adopting postcolonial tools for reading the Italian past and Italian national identity, this scholarship has demonstrated how, despite the limited duration and size of the Italian Empire, forms of colonial desire have shaped the imaginations, ideas of national belonging and forms of citizenship developed by Italians up to the present day.[1] Historians of Italian migration, in their turn, have shown how the meaning of Italian belonging has been constructed both inside and outside Italy by exploring the transnational trajectories of migrants from the peninsula.[2] These lines of research have opened new exciting perspectives for the study of historical actors from Italy and for examining the shaping of their subjectivities at times when 'nation', 'empire' and 'modernity' were central categories for the imagining of both individual and collective identities. It has become clear that, during the nineteenth and twentieth centuries, Italians inside and outside Italy experimented with multiple ideas of national belonging, modernity and colonial prestige. These have been manifested in material and cultural practices, forms of memories and self-narration that we have only just begun to investigate.[3]

This chapter considers both official and private sources associated with a propaganda campaign implemented in Italy by the Fascist National Party and its colonial and female organizations in the second half of the 1930s. I read these materials in a wide transnational framework, highlighting the micro-processes of individual appropriation of discourses of gender and whiteness circulating across imperial formations at times of accelerated transformation regarding gender roles, ideas of citizenship and their representation. In so doing, I take this example of fascist propaganda, and the subjectivities of women involved, as a local and historically situated manifestation of the manifold interactions between transimperial discourses of gender and whiteness, the ultranationalistic aims of the fascist empire and modern circuits of consumption and cultural imagination.

The chapter begins with an outline of the wider historical context of implementation of the colonial training for women in Italy, which considers the history of Italian emigration and settlement, earlier mobilizations of women linked to Italian imperial expansion, the development of fascist women's organizations and the transnational models of European colonial and Nazi propaganda. The chapter then introduces the vision of fascist colonial training for women and its relationship to fascist ideas of modernity as well as to the realities of colonial settlement and of women's own aspirations. I start by outlining the development of the two organizations in charge of the colonial training for women in Italy, stressing their correspondences with other networks of colonialists and the related attempts at developing a distinctive fascist Italian model of modern imperial womanhood. Subsequently, I show the class and gender tensions manifested in such an endeavor, which are apparent in the strategies of representations of the young women propagandists that circulated across new media, cultural industries and emerging circuits of mobility and consumption.

In examining the actual implementation of colonial training for Italian women, my reading stresses its nature as a propaganda campaign aimed at urban middle-class women in Italy rather than a practical training programme for female colonial settlement. My analysis considers the contents of the colonial training handbooks and the representation of the training camps, moving to examine how the Italian tourist industry and fascist propaganda technologies mobilized this campaign to stir the imperial desire of the urban middle classes. Overall, this section seeks to clarify the ways in which the training sought to create new types of modern and racialized Italians who would manifest a mature 'colonial consciousness'. Most of all, my aim is to shed light on the multiple voices embedded in fascist colonial propaganda, so as to unravel women's agency, concurrent projects of political, economic and cultural development and different understandings of gender and imperial modernity.

The final section of the chapter examines the memories of two women propagandists in the light of their life trajectories, stretching the time framework of this study up to 2007, the time of my interviews with two former propagandists. Here I build on Charles Burdett's work on Italian travel writing and fascism in the 1930s as forms of self-narration ensnared in a wider web of cultural images.[4] My analysis examines the discursive construction of the writing of these women propagandists and their memories. In highlighting the individual, micro-processes of negotiation of cultural memory operated by my interviewees, and in reading their acts of transmission as acts of self-narration, my aim is to point out how these women, while constituting themselves as social and historical subjects, have navigated different streams of identity narratives of their times. In so doing, my analysis is also indebted to feminist readings of memory as a human activity performed in a sociohistorical dimension.[5] Specifically, drawing from Marianne Hirsch and Leo Spitzer's work, I take the personal records and self-narratives of these women as 'points of memory that traverse temporal, spatial and experiential divides', that reveal the complexity and persistence of racialized cultural memories of empire.[6]

Colonial emigration, transnational contexts and the vision of fascist 'colonial training for women'

Both the projects and the narratives of Italian imperialism are woven into long-standing histories and representations of Italy as a nation of emigrants. One of these narratives claimed Italy's right to expansion on the basis of its image as a young, poor and prolific 'emigrant nation',[7] distinguished from other European empires built on military conquest and unequal exchange. In other words, Italian exceptionalism, central to the narrative of Italy's ethical mission as a nation and as an imperial formation, rested on an enduring representation of Italians as humble and virtuous families of hard-working emigrants-settlers, which would cultivate Italian home life, traditions and virtues anywhere in the world. Since national unification in 1861, images of Italians living below the proper standards of European civilizations were seen as signs of national shame, and these people became a major target for state projects of modernization both inside and outside Italy. Political elites took these masses as resources for either colonial settlement or commercial and cultural expansionism through informal transnational networks. Such imperialist top-down

120 Barbara Spadaro

politics had to be negotiated with the actual experiences of Italian migrants and their fluid and diverse feelings of belonging.[8] Nevertheless, romanticized representations of Italian emigrants thrived in the decades following unification, naturalizing women's attachment to allegedly Italian features and traditions and presenting feminine care as the key to preserving the moral integrity and material survival of Italian families around the world, something that would guarantee Italy's imperialist achievements.

During the fascist decades (1922–1945), this romanticized rhetoric and imagery surrounding Italian emigrant families was further developed in association with massive state-sponsored projects of land reclamation, settler colonialism and territorial expansion in Europe and Africa. These burgeoned in the years of the war against Ethiopia and the subsequent proclamation of the Italian Empire (1935–1941). In the space of a few years, propaganda in Italy intensified tremendously, with imperial fantasies shaping the efforts of the regime to define appropriate gender, class and racialized roles for an ideal fascist society. In decades of profound social and cultural transformation regarding gender roles and ideas of citizenship across the globe, fascist exponents were particularly concerned with the elaboration of feminine models, as they were facing the challenge of how to channel women's energies into a distinctive modern, ethical and totalitarian state-empire, the nature of which was a constant matter of contention. In 1935, this processes suddenly accelerated, as fascist organizations mobilized millions of Italian women into an unprecedented endeavor to resist the *inique sanzioni* (unfair sanctions) of the League of Nation against Italy's invasion of Ethiopia and the subsequent proclamation of the Italian Empire. Urban and rural women were mobilized as producers and consumers of goods to achieve *autarchia*, the economic self-sufficiency of Italy and its colonies.[9] To this end, female party organizations set up special training for women on how to optimize housework and minimize consumption by crafting clothes and small furniture, growing vegetables, rearing courtyard animals and so on. In short, the first mass mobilization of women in Italy marked a decisive moment for the country's imperial ambitions and for the definition of its politics of gender. This propaganda campaign spread a vision of the family, the household and their reproduction as the elected spaces and destinies for idealized Italian women actively participating in Italy's national community and its imperial projections.

Such propaganda had some precedent in Italy at the time of heightened national and imperialistic feeling during the Italo-Turkish War for the occupation of Libya (1911–1912).[10] It also resonated with earlier wider European attempts to define women's participation in the building of national and imperial communities.[11] However, compared to earlier initiatives, the campaign ran in Italy in the mid-1930s had unprecedented ambitions in terms of its scale and intensity of dissemination. This mirrors a stage of massive development in the technologies of totalitarian rule and propaganda of the regime, propelled by the implementation of fascist imperialistic aims.

In 1937, two fascist organizations became involved in the design and implementation of colonial training for women: the Fascist Colonial Institute (*Istituto*

Coloniale Fascista, ICF, later the Fascist Institute for Italian Africa, *Istituto Fascista dell'Africa Italiana,* IFAI) and the *Fasci Femminili,* the main Fascist Party organization for women. Since 1928 the ICF-IFAI had overseen a constellation of scattered formal and informal colonial circles, and from the early 1930s the *Fasci Femminili* had been developed as a mass organization for women of the urban middle classes. In the mid-1930s both institutions experienced a process of centralization and development directed by the Fascist Party, in line with its totalitarian ambitions and transformative mission toward Italian society. Besides the implementation of colonial courses for women, the Party established special units of *Giovani Fasciste Coloniali* ('Fascist Colonial Girls') within the Fascist Youth, so to secure the impact of the new campaign via the networks and structures of one of the most developed and pervasive fascist organizations.[12] As we will see, the establishment of cohorts of fascist colonial girls to put on display at public events would enhance the dissemination and visibility of the colonial training propaganda campaign.

The scheme of colonial training for women, which the two organizations developed, aimed to inculcate a 'colonial consciousness' into the Italian masses and was designed as a practical training in household management for the future mothers and educators of a new race of Italian colonizers[13] (Figure 6.1). Ultranationalist in its objectives, the scheme drew on both national experience and international examples. The newspapers and magazines of the colonial lobbies, such as *L'Azione Coloniale* and *Africa Italiana,* featured articles debating the role of women in the Italian Empire, which shed light on the way the scheme tapped into wider discourses circulating both inside and outside Europe concerning the condition and mission of white women in the colonies. As multiple studies analyzing ideas of gender and imperialism have illustrated, such discourses sought to deploy the energies and bodies of European women to reproduce whiteness across both empires and metropoles.[14] Italian fascist commentators drew on French scholarship on the condition of women in the colonies, evaluated training initiatives implemented in the Dutch and Belgian empires and criticized the inappropriate activism of defeminized 'English suffragettes' in relation to indigenous subjects in India.[15] Special attention was dedicated to German initiatives, mirroring the intensified exchange of visits and knowledge between sister fascist and Nazi colonial organizations. This occurred at a time of parallel processes of regimentation within party organizations: early sporadic correspondence between Italian and German colonial lobbies was intensified and formalized, and this also regimented the informal initiatives of women belonging to colonial circles.

In the name of a common goal of subverting an international order that had frustrated Italy's expansionist aspirations and deprived Germany of its colonies, the Italian fascist press featured articles celebrating pioneers of the German Empire, their colonial achievements and initiatives for training women pioneers. A number of these articles focused on the School of Rendsburg, an early initiative by ladies in German colonial circles to provide practical skills to young women destined for the German colonies and expatriate communities. Lora Wildenthal has illustrated how, under the Third Reich, the curriculum and scope of the school were adapted

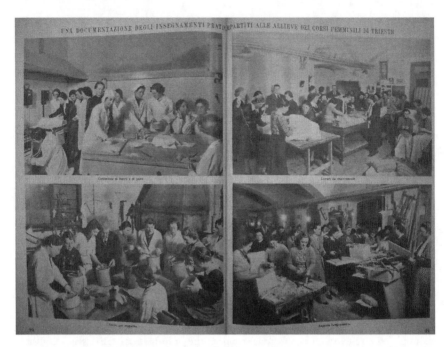

FIGURE 6.1 Photos of a colonial training course for women in Trieste. From the magazine *Africa Italiana*.

to better serve Nazi settlement plans, which included settlement of occupied territories in Europe.[16] Italian articles featuring the School of Rendsburg emphasize the thorough practical, theoretical and physical training imparted under a martial spirit and centralized control, to women selected according to strict physical and moral criteria. The school was praised as a formidable weapon for modern imperialist politics inspired by racist principles and aiming to spread and perpetuate Aryan communities around the world. Such a goal resonated with the rural and martial fantasies, and visions of utopias of regeneration, circulating within the Italian fascist hierarchy, which envisioned the Italian Empire as a space where new forms of Italian modernity, society and humanity would be forged.[17]

Most fascist exponents conceived the training of women destined for the Italian colonies within the framework of the massive state-funded and state-regulated settlement projects of the fascist regime. These aimed at the immediate transplantation of hundreds of thousands of peasants from Italy to its empire. A great deal of propaganda was mobilized in an effort to materialize such plans, including the organization of epic Mediterranean crossings to move contingents of *Ventimila* ('The Twenty-thousands') settlers from Italy to modern agricultural villages built in Libya. A flood of visual and textual representations trumpeted this venture as the first historical example of an organized mass settlement which conveyed only the 'best' – i.e. the most fertile, physically robust and motivated – men and women from the mother country to the *Quarta Sponda* ('Fourth Shore'), the North African land once colonized by the Romans. Such propaganda emphasized the transformative process that Italians would experience by populating and building the Fascist Empire.

In practice, however, colonial settlement was a complex, improvised and negotiated matter. In the first place, emigrants did not always match their idealized image in the fascist propaganda representations. Ideals of transformative fascist utopias and plans for mass colonial settlements had to be negotiated with the actual politics of labor and migration and practical assessments of the African terrain. Italian elites, like their European peers, tended to consider the colonies as dumping sites for the undesirables of the metropolitan society, and articles in the Italian colonial press speculated on how to optimize the discarding from Italy of human resources deemed of poor quality: for example, by transporting young women orphans from Italy to Africa so as to usefully employ their reproductive energies. Other commentators were keen to ease women workers' migration for the practical reason that their salaries were lower than men's, which would attract investors into the empire. At the same time most agreed on the necessity of strict monitoring of the circulation of single women, especially artists, singers, dancers and actresses – due to their alleged 'tendency to prostitution'. As they endlessly reiterated, colonial prestige required racial hierarchies to be upheld, necessitating the regulation of sexual relations and avoidance of the dangers of miscegenation.[18]

Another gap between fascist rhetoric and reality was that, despite official Party statements regarding specific colonial training for women workers and peasants to be implemented by female party organizations parallel to the *Fasci Femminili* – notably the *Massaie Rurali* 'Rural Householders' organization and the *Sezioni operaie e lavoranti a domicilio, SOLD*, for women of the urban working classes[19] – there are no signs of implementation of such initiatives. Similarly, there is no evidence of actual training for the women who applied with their families for land concessions in Libya and in Italian East Africa. According to Party statements, a certificate of attendance of the colonial course was mandatory for moving to the colonies, but this did not apply in practice.[20]

Third, the Italian and colonial press reflected not only official propaganda but also the hopes manifested among Italian women themselves for professional opportunities in the Empire. Urban women workers such as young secretaries, salesgirls, telephone operators and teachers requested information about the regulation of the job market in Italian Africa and called for courses providing professional skills and language teaching. Such hopes for new opportunities were unsurprising, given the severe limitations to women's careers imposed in the national job market to protect men's work.

Such expressions of interest from women in emigrating for professional opportunity and autonomous projects were dismissed as 'African fever' by male fascists concerned with retaining their power to define the scope and agenda of women's training for colonial life.[21] In 1937, just before launching the colonial training program, the Minister of the Colonies, Alessandro Lessona, made it clear that the Italian

Empire was not to be an arena for ladies in search of extravagant opportunities: Italian Africa was open for careers as wives and mothers only.[22] He defined two iconic categories of women useful to the empire: virtuous and adaptable spouses for travelling civil servants, and fertile hard-working companions for the settlers, stereotyped as humble emigrants adept at reconstructing the Italian home anywhere in the world. Minister Lessona also mentioned single, educated and professionally qualified women interested in the empire, but only to dismiss their ambitions as premature and as embarrassing to the current collective endeavor: the Fascist Empire would develop appropriate schemes to direct such excess female energies in the future, he said. This discourse left no space to autonomous women's initiative regarding the empire, especially any activities targeting African subjects. Italian women were to be trained as caregivers for fellow Italians, under the supervision of fascist organizations, and kept away from indigenous subjects, who were to be left under missionary care. Such directives expressed the imperialist plans and masculinist politics of a state-centered, racist and totalitarian regime.

Implementing colonial training for women of the urban middle classes, shaping gendered and racialized Italian selves

Nevertheless, when training for colonial women was implemented in practice, its scope exceeded the limits that Lessona had sought to impose, as Fascist Party organizations sought to appeal to Italian women of the middle classes by offering something that was closer to meeting their own expectations about their futures, whether in Italy or in Africa. Mirroring old and new social and cultural tensions in Italian society, and acting as a magnet for a wide range of energies mobilized by ideas of Africa as a frontier of Italian modernity, the training for colonial women in Italy would be negotiated, understood and appropriated in many different ways.

The implementers of fascist 'colonial training' drew inspiration not only from the set of discourses outlined above concerning the role of women in the empire, but also from recent experience of mobilizing women in the 1935 campaign to resist the League of Nations' sanctions on fascist Italy. The latter had involved the developing of a gendered discourse validating women's participation in an ultranationalist and imperialist endeavor. The continuity between the two campaigns is apparent in the archival materials shared among party organizations, colonial circles and other institutions that developed an interest in the scheme. The circulation of the same materials – frequently the same photographs – within multiple media and circuits of dissemination exposes various streams within which representations of the colonial training program were produced and remediated, for different audiences and purposes and by different authors. This sheds new light on the condition of Italian women of the urban élites and the middle classes in the mid-1930s, notably on the opportunities they would seek in colonial and political careers. It also illuminates the mechanisms of production of knowledge about Africa and of representations of women, whiteness and modernity in the Fascist Empire.

The experimental nature and massive ambitions of the new campaign, and the dearth of qualified figures for designing and teaching such a new type of training for women, required a great deal of flexibility and creative efforts from its organizers. This created space for women's involvement, although individual contribution would hardly be acknowledged. The national scale of the initiative, and its focus on women and Italian Africa, went well beyond the previous scope of the activities of the two fascist organizations involved. Both the Italian Colonial Institute-IFAI and the *Fasci Femminili* drew on the expertise of their members from the educated urban bourgeoisie and the aristocracy. Men and women holding social kudos as travellers and adventurers, or professional authority as doctors or scholars, provided 'colonial expertise' for the first round of conferences, lectures and events on colonial training for women, which were organized across the country by local branches of the two organizations. Texts of these conferences and lectures would then be gathered in official handbooks published under the auspices of the ICF-IFAI.[23]

No credit was given to individual authors in these handbooks; however, by comparing these texts with printed conference proceedings, archival records and press articles, it is possible to identify some of the writers, notably women, and thus to shed new light on Italian women's careers and motivations as propagandists for the empire.[24] This analysis reveals that, despite official statements to the contrary, the Italian Empire did provide professional opportunities to a handful of women who, while constantly swaying between informal and official involvement, contributed to developing and disseminating gendered and racialized ideas of Italianness and colonial otherness. Yet the life trajectories, personal experiences, imaginaries and expectations of these women – who could hardly be identified as a coherent group – exhibit a range of attitudes toward the regime and its politics of gender, which in turn reflect varied understandings of their brief careers as propagandists. At least one of these female figures is already well known: Countess Onorina Bargagli Petrucci, an aristocratic socialite who built a career as an expert on colonial matters, a propagandist, a travel writer and an overseas correspondent of scientific institutions.[25] Less well known are the women doctors, professionals, teachers and writers who enrolled in female fascist and colonial organizations, not to mention women missionaries, a subject crying for research.[26]

Before focusing on individual trajectories, however, it is important to explore the nature of the official propaganda, both in the form of the colonial training handbooks and in the parallel training courses and camps. All these initiatives targeted women of the urbanizing middle classes in Italy, since no training programme was implemented for women who were actually to become colonial settlers, as we have seen. The colonial training publications were intended to disseminate information about the Italian Empire and awareness of its potential for development and productivity. The handbooks adapted teaching materials from the 1935 autarky campaign's courses, which had promulgated stereotyped images of fertile, caring and self-sacrificing women joining the Italian imperialist endeavor in a disciplined way.[27] However, the new colonial training scheme aimed first and foremost to appeal to the women of the urban middle classes, whose position in a modern

126 Barbara Spadaro

imperial fascist society, as we have seen, was a constant matter of anxieties and contention. It thus attempted to elaborate and disseminate a new image of pioneer and modern colonial domesticity, prefiguring modern, gendered and racialized types of Italians as white Europeans, masters and consumers of a colonial empire. This resulted in clumsy forms of writing about the colonies and colonial domesticity in the handbooks, which expose the fantasies of the bourgeois women authors of the texts about African, colonial, pioneer, military and rural life.

The handbooks contained chapters on colonial fashion and home decoration that mirrored articles featured in magazines for bourgeois Italian readers. These practical sections combined expositions of modernist principles of home design with, for example, practical instructions on how to recycle petrol tanks as small furniture in adventurous settings. They illustrated how colonial outfits of modern Italian design could be fashioned out of robust white African cotton and featured cooking recipes for products of the Italian colonies that would substitute for scarce imported goods susceptible to rationing. More notional sections envisioned the future of Italians in the empire: chapters on the history and geography of Italian colonies trumpeted fascist conquests and state-sponsored projects of agricultural settlement and anticipated subsequent industrial and infrastructural development in both the metropole and the colonies.[28] Other chapters covered issues of colonial hygiene by praising the modern, state-implemented programs for mass maternal and childcare in Italy, which actually had no equivalent in the empire. Reflecting the limited reach of scholarship on tropical medicine within Italy, Africa was sketched out as a hostile environment in need of disinfection and domestication, where women were expected to provide care in looking after husbands and children – elder family members not being contemplated in the textbooks and hardly in the overall narrative of fascist imperial modernity.

In contrast to these lengthy sections on Italian colonial domesticity, the handbooks contained only a few short descriptions of different African populations, ranked according to their perceived level of civilization. African women were portrayed as submissive creatures to which Italian men would be tempted to turn to satisfy their physiological sexual instincts, and the handbooks stressed the important mission of support and companionship entrusted to Italian women in order to preserve and reproduce the Latin race. Physical and emotional separation among 'races' would be best achieved, they argued, by limiting the hiring of African servants and nurses and avoiding forms of familiarity with them. Women were constantly urged to leave all matters relating to indigenous subjects in the hands of missionaries – who were implicitly presented as male experts.

As we will learn from the notebook of a women propagandist presented in the last section of this chapter, the handbooks described above were used as teaching materials for courses organized by local branches of the *Fasci Femminili* and ICF/IFAI that spread all over Italy in the few years between the proclamation of the Italian Empire (1936) and the chaotic times of the Civil War in occupied Italy (1942–1945). Archival documentation is extremely fragmented, which makes it impossible to estimate the overall impact of the campaign, which was organized through multiple and ephemeral local branches. Scattered press and official party accounts indicate that the courses and training camps were organized mostly in Northern and Central Italy, targeting women and girls of the bourgeois élites and the middle classes.[29] Similarly, we have no reliable data on the attendance of the training courses: the magazine *Africa Italiana* claimed a massive 500,000 registrations the first year, whereas ICF records estimated only 10,000.

The prime aim of the camps and courses was as propaganda inducting upper middle-class Italian women and teenagers into fascist imperialist ideals. In addition to its impact on the trainees, the campaign aimed to reach a wider audience through the widespread publicity received within Italy, in which visual imagery played a key role. In different towns where the courses were organized, local news featured photographs of women exponents of local social and fascist hierarchies experimenting with this new form of public engagement involving open-air and sporting lifestyles.[30] This evoked modern forms of leisure and social gentility for young women, aimed to stir desires of emulation in middle-class families and triumph over the parental and marital controls that fascist directives still had to negotiate to access the bodies and energies of women for propaganda purposes. The more martial representations of young women training at the camps in colonial uniforms mirrored crucial aspects of fascist ideology – notably militarism, the ambition of a totalitarian rule over perfected bodies and minds and the construction of the foundational myth of such transformation: the Roman Empire. These themes are conveyed in images of cohorts of fascist colonial girls parading as modern women legionaries in imperial displays, such as the spectacular parade for the 1938 visit of Hitler or the opening of the excavated *Ara Pacis Augustae* at the heart of the fascist urban planning of Rome[31] (Figure 6.2). At the same time, and rather self-contradictorily, the training courses spread romanticized ideas of modern patriarchal families of small landowners as quintessential to society both within Italy and within its empire. Such representations also created a distorted perception of Italian Africa, which was in fact an urban society mostly populated by lower middle-class migrants and military forces engaged in committing ferocious human and environmental abuses.

To girls born under fascism, colonial uniforms and outdoor life had the potential to appeal as new spaces of visibility, social activity and leisure, which held much more attractiveness than the competing imagery of self-sacrificing family life conveyed by representations of migrants and settlers. Propaganda tried to find ways of combining these different elements in describing the colonial training camps: published photos stress the pioneering and energetic spirit of the fascist youth by picturing girls exercising in the wilderness or washing their tins in small streams. One article accompanying such images in a magazine for fascist women explicitly referred to the spirit of the pioneering blonde heroines of the Wild West Hollywood films that populated the Italian imagination during this period.[32] Press accounts, and a short film shoot of a camp in Northern Italy,[33] portrayed cheerful, healthy and diligent young women, profoundly committed to the mission of colonizing Africa and sincerely devoted to the authorities: God, the King, the Duce and their parents. Such ideal fascist-pioneer girls of Catholic modesty would spend their spare time after martial exercises and classes decorating camping tents and writing letters home. The articles stressed the girls 'natural' aptitude for domestic

128 Barbara Spadaro

FIGURE 6.2 Fascist colonial girls parading as Roman legionaries on the Via dei Trionfi in Rome. From the magazine *Africa Italiana*.

life, as manifested in their gentility in confronting the hardest aspects of outdoor life (Figure 6.3).

Awareness of the seductive potential of the fascist colonial girls is apparent in the development of the advertising strategies of the colonial tourist industry in Libya. Under the governorship of Italo Balbo (1934–1940), this industry was centralized and reorganized according to the latest international standards. An articulated system linked archaeological and tourist sites with new infrastructure and facilities to showcase the modernity of this Italian industry and its ability to compete with the more established French and international services, notably in the circuits of Mediterranean cruising populated by American tourists. The success of this tourist industry was intended to be a driving force for the economic and symbolic development of a modern Italian fascist Mediterranean empire.[34] The new central authority for tourism in Libya (*Ente Turistico e Alberghiero per la Libia*, ETAL) and the Italian Touring Club experimented with commercial culture and modern media in producing representations of women, demonstrating 'the interaction between soft and hard power, between cultural influences and political forces in the context of the evolving world of interwar (Italian) . . . commercial culture' recently described by Bianca Gaudenzi[35] (Figure 6.4). Italian tourist advertising campaigns in magazines for the urban middle classes featured photographs of slender and glamorous young white women in tourist outfits visiting archaeological sites and desert and coastal landscapes or on luxury cruises. Although filtered through rigorous fascist

FIGURE 6.3 Illustrated article on the colonial camps, 'Bella e fiera gioventù femminile fascista in Africa'. From *L'Italia Coloniale. Rivista dell'espansione Imperiale*.

and Catholic censorship, the photographs documenting the colonial training camps for girls in Libya echoed these registers.[36] They staged the girls in the camps as romantic pioneers, energetic comrades or sophisticated tourists disembarking from Mediterranean cruises (Figure 6.5).

The colonial training camps in Libya enrolled several hundred teenagers from wealthy families belonging to the bourgeois elite and to fascist and colonial circles

FIGURE 6.4 Cruise advertisements. From *L'Illustrazione Italiana*.

FIGURE 6.5 Fascist colonial girls disembarking to attend a training camp in Libya. From the IsIAO Photographic Collection, Rome.

of Rome, Milan, Padua and other cities of Northern Italy. Three fortnight-long camps were organized annually between 1938 and 1940. Parents saw the colonial camps as opportunities to display their cosmopolitan modernity, show their fascist enthusiasm and bolster their feelings of belonging to an emerging white European fascist elite. Press accounts of these camps contributed to the visibility of the new Italian colonial industry – and of its idealized protagonists: white Italians of the upper and middle classes – while echoing the latest repertoires of commercial representation featured in magazines for urban readers.

While fascist rhetoric stressed the importance of future reproducers of the Latin race experiencing Italian Africa, these camps were obviously conceived as a taste of modern tourist experience rather than as an exposure to the actual lives of Italian settlers in Libya, though the settlers featured as part of the tourist display, as much as the indigenous subjects. The visiting program of the fascist colonial girls replicated those of many international political, royal and sporting personalities, whose visits to Libya were covered in the press and by tourist agencies. The girls were shown around archaeological sites, monuments to fallen Italian soldiers and modern Italian colonial settlements and plantations. They were also taken to desert oases and remote African villages, where they attended 'indigenous fantasies' – choreographies performed as spectacular displays for visitors.

The young women themselves were given the opportunity to write news items and publish snapshots showing them riding on camels (Figure 6.6). Their articles

FIGURE 6.6 Report and photo from a training camp for women in Libya. From *Colonizzazione Demografica*, 1 Nov 1938, p. IX.

expressed energetic youthful enthusiasm for the empire and drew on the tropes of fascist propaganda in emphasizing feminine virtue, patriotic and filial devotion and fascist commitment. Gianna Sibaud for example, an ICF-IFAI participant who published at least two accounts of training camps in Italy and Libya, wrote mostly about the program excursions.[37] Her articles drew on images recurrent in travel writing, novels and fascist imperialist rhetoric of her times, revealing how her experience of the sites in Libya was mediated by the complex web of literary, historical and religious associations within her cultural repertoire.[38] Yet in appropriating themes and images of the Italian colonial discourse, Sibaud's writing materialized new images for the fascist cultural archive: namely, figures of young Italian women excited by the immensity of the desert and the promise of newly cultivated land, amused by the colorful spectacle of indigenous dances in local villages and pampered in the elegant premises of the Garian Hotel, where they would stop for photographs on a camel. Sibaud voiced the feeling, on visiting the remains of the Roman city of Leptis Magna, that she had been transported through time to wander among valiant Romans and their fine women. And she immortalized her group of fellow fascist girls standing modestly before the monument to fallen Italian soldiers, where Italian women would transform the glorious aura of their Latin ancestors into prayers for the Duce.

Memories of women propagandists: grand metaphors, everyday experience and individual acts of transmission

The powerful impact of fascist propaganda on the 'colonial girls', and the impact of their own active participation in this propaganda, did not die with the end of the fascist regime in Italy, as the self-narratives and memories of two female propagandists reveal.

When I interviewed Orsola Rossi (pseudonym) about the 1938 camp in Libya and her career as a young columnist on the colonial press, she repeatedly stressed that she was confident in her mastering of the language of fascist propaganda, as she had lived the first decades of her life in Rome, on the central stage of the Italian Empire. Orsola was a student at the prestigious *Liceo Giulio Cesare* in Rome, whose stunning modernist building was frequently showcased as an example of the design of a modern fascist educational institution. She was from a wealthy, cultured and cosmopolitan family 'in a flurry of books, guests, and extravagant expenses', as she put it in her privately published memoir.[39] The enrollment of Orsola and her little sister as fascist colonial girls, along with their participation in the 1938 camp in Libya and other spectacular parades and imperial displays of those years, stemmed from their father's background as a diplomat and retired officer of the ICF-IFAI. When Italy entered the Second World War and the family's economic situation deteriorated, Orsola started earning some money and gaining professional skills by editing a new two-page section entitled 'The Woman and Africa' for the magazine *Africa Italiana*. For these pages she invented short stories, recipes for using food rations, emotive articles commemorating 'The Day of Faith', in which Italian women donated their wedding rings to the empire, resolute incitements to victory, friendly salutations to girls enrolled in the German sister colonial organization and eventually she printed letters from readers.[40]

At our interview, Orsola brought out a photo of herself and a friend on a camel, a newspaper cutting of one of her propaganda articles, and her more recent manuscript of memories that had served to preserve in family legend stories of the camp in Libya, along with other episodes in the cosmopolitan childhood of the daughter of a

134 Barbara Spadaro

diplomat. Our conversation explored this memory framework, revealing the collapse of different spaces and times in her narrative. Comparing the personal geographies of her propaganda writing of the 1930s and 1940s with her more recent memories, I was struck by the similarities between episodes described in the recent memoir and two short stories that she published in the 1940s: tales of Italians in Tunisia and vignettes of the Mediterranean as the imperial *Mare nostrum* of Italians.[41] These latter texts illuminate the creative process behind her 'African' articles, showing how she drew from episodes of her childhood in Albania (where her father was appointed as a diplomat and she used to play with Albanian children in the streets) and of seaside life in Dalmatia (where she spent all her holidays in the family's summerhouse) to fashion literary images for fascist imperial and war propaganda about Africa. After the fall of fascism, moving on in her professional and personal life, she discarded that rhetoric; yet our encounter in 2007 revealed that memories from the 1940s continued to inform her perceptions of otherness. This was apparent when we talked about the figure of a Muslim boy named Safet featured in one of her 'Tunisian' tales. It became evident that her various encounters with street kids in different locations and contexts had been confused and amalgamated in the literary, racialized figure of indigenous type in the article and that this confusion persisted to the present day:

OR: Yes, he was Libyan. He was always around with a sack on his head, we loved each other so much . . . but he was Libyan, and I was grown up.
BS: And how did you meet him?
OR: Oh, that, I don't know. It was in Albania, wasn't it? In Albania I had a little friend, or two, I used to play with them, and this Albanese boy . . . he wasn't Tunisian, I'm mistaken. But I met a Libyan boy that year (at the camp in Libya).

Similarly, Orsola's limited recollections of the colonial training camp in Libya intertwined with memories of her life in Rome, in a family of colonial officers and diplomats under the spotlight of the fascist imperial spectacle. During our interview, the colonial uniform and outdoor activities at the camp overlapped with her memories of exercises at school, while the indigenous choreographies she had seen in Libya were confused with her memories of the imperial parades and African displays attended at Piazza di Siena in Rome. In these memories, the spatial distinction between imperial Italy and colonial Libya had collapsed.

In the years of her career as propagandist, Orsola's understanding of her role was filtered through the world of her affects and self-perceptions: she navigated fascist propaganda and ideology skillfully, while developing and voicing its discourse in articles published under various pseudonyms and even under her father's name, as she would occasionally 'help him out'. Her brothers and sisters would tease her for voicing such a *persona*: 'They would say, "Here she comes, Orsola Rossi!", meaning arrogant or pedantic. They thought I was showing off, and I would understand them, but that was the spirit of the time, that was it.'[42] In fact, she had mixed feelings toward such visibility: she didn't show off her published writing to her friends, but she eagerly searched for herself in newsreels and photographs, with a hint of envy for her tall, younger sister, who got systematically displayed as standard-bearer in parades and ceremonies. This interplay of emotions, affects and images of the past manifest the shaping of Orsola's self-narration and memory.

The private archive and memories of another woman propagandist, Angela Maria Guerra (1897–1978), further illuminate the shaping and persistence of a sense of white Italian identity and belonging which stretched beyond the physical borders of Italy and its colonies. Guerra's life began and ended in a small town of 3,000 inhabitants in Northern Italy, Viguzzolo.[43] Yet some of its crucial years were spent in Buenos Aires, where Guerra was brought by her family as a child and uprooted as a young lady so to avoid an inopportune engagement. Back in Italy, she spent the rest of her life as a daughter whose expressions of filial devotion enhanced those for God, the *Patria* (fatherland, in her case Italy) and the Duce. Her writings are filled with quotations from Mussolini's sentences through to the last years of her life, which she spent in isolation writing letters in Spanish and Italian to imaginary correspondents linked both to her past, such as General Franco and the Queen Jolanda, and to her present: contemporary exponents of the Italian neofascist party, journalists, political and religious leaders. The archive of Guerra's papers, which she bequeathed to her hometown, constitutes a self-narrative of its creator, and its existence shows her efforts to preserve and transmit a personal heritage to the community of her hometown. Beyond the records' value as factual evidence of the context and contents of the colonial training, they provide fascinating insights into her subjectivity.

The training course for colonial life that Guerra attended in Genoa from 1936 to 1937 was, it seems, the first form of public commitment and active engagement that she undertook beyond parental control. It inaugurated a rapid and intense career as leader of the *Fasci Femminili* in her hometown of Viguzzolo. This culminated in the years of German occupation and civil war in Italy, when she managed to rally about 350 women of different social and familial backgrounds to assist a flood of refugees and soldiers from disparate fronts, including local partisans. After the war, when she was charged with collaborating with the enemy and taken to trial as a notorious propagandist and fascist, the acknowledgment of her aid work would protect her from conviction. Yet her self-defense on that occasion was a profession of faith in fascism, stressing how it inspired her actions, sense of duty toward her community and her personal trajectory. The period of the trial saw the beginnings of her autobiographical writing through which, in notebooks and letters, she recalled episodes in her life and revealed the high emotional charge of her fascist vocation.[44]

Guerra's autobiographical writings begin with memories of dramatic episodes of pro-communist and anti-Catholic protest experienced by her family and their friends, both in Argentina and in Italy in the early 1920s. The latter were marked in Guerra's life as capital moments, and capital threats, to her 'home': a small and cherished world of middle-class families that performed their social identity and white belonging within local and transatlantic networks of the Catholic Church, Italian educational institutions and familial circles. Growing up in such context, Guerra took Mussolini and the rise of fascism as divine interventions rescuing her world from catastrophe and extinction, and she embraced fascist statements as vital principles.

136 Barbara Spadaro

Her direct political engagement began in the climate of the autarkic campaign and women's imperial mobilization outlined in the first half of this chapter. She enrolled in a colonial course organized in Genoa in January 1937, and from the notebook and teaching materials that she kept until her death, we know that she attended evening classes organized twice a week in a girls' school by the local female fascist federation. Her notebook reports on lectures in colonial geography, colonial economy, domestic hygiene, home decoration, food preparation and preservation, child-rearing, race and empire. With a frequent misspelling betraying her mixed linguistic background, she laboriously noted, word-by-word, the sentences pronounced by the teachers – the barristers, doctors and professors listed in her course materials. She recorded the names of Abyssinian heights, Libyan plains and the grand fascist routes traced by the imaginary offspring of Roman legionaries. She meticulously noted data on the traffic in Somali ports, the mineral resources of Eritrea and sponge fishing in the Gulf of Sirte. She drew patterns for tailoring colonial uniforms and nappies from African cotton and detailed recipes for making candied fruit and chocolate and lists of medical treatments.

Guerra's lecture notes replicated the structure and content of the course handbook, one of the official publications of the Fascist Colonial Institute of Rome, which she also preserved among her papers.[45] Chapter 3 of the handbook, entitled 'Defense of the White Race', described the law of January 1937 against mixed unions of white men and indigenous women and pointed to the virtuous examples of German and Belgian colonizers in Africa. Fascist women are urged to stop the decay of miscegenation, presented as a failed utopia of the liberal empires. It read as follows:

> This issue is not limited to the satisfaction of the male sexual instincts.... Our colonization will not be achieved until in our overseas land the nucleus of the family, noble foundation and sustain of Latin societies, will faithfully reproduce the Italic family nucleus.[46]

Echoing these sentiments in her lecture notes, Guerra wrote:

> The extenuating climate, the struggle against the elements, the strains, responsibilities, thoughts about the family, in colonial setting make a man more irritable, and even more in need to find at home a cheerful wife, a spouse who would take care of everything, who wouldn't annoy him, avoiding petty grumbling, gossip, squabbles for a nothing that might seem important to her.[47]

This fascist ideal of love and marriage was one she would hold on to for the rest of her life, although she never left for Africa, and she never had children and a husband to honor, obey and keep away from African women. The ideal is also reflected in the quotations from Benito Mussolini, General Franco and Catholic personalities that she transcribed onto her personal belongings over decades, materializing her understanding of her position in the world. She composed from these quotations from her male idols a safe life map within which she could navigate human relations and perform her social identity as an individual and community member. This map tracks her subjectivity: her sense of hierarchy and obedience to authority, her understanding of the appropriate ways of showing respect and solidarity toward fellow Italians and co-religionists. Her personal records became something that she wanted to leave as a trace of her passage in the world, along with her properties, to her hometown. This was in fulfillment of her personal understanding of the duty of a single woman with no children toward her hometown community, which she felt compelled to honor despite the persistent feelings of mutual repulsion between her and many of the town's inhabitants, a repulsion rooted in deep differences in political belief and manifested in the divided memory of the small community.[48]

Guerra's archival records of colonial training give a sense of the deep lifelong impact that this fascist propaganda campaign could have on individual women, fostering a racist, sexist and hierarchical understanding of global human relationships. The creation and personalization of these records, and her act of conservation in a personal archive, were acts of self-narration which incorporated grand metaphors into everyday experience, filtered fascist fantasies of global power through personal gestures and attempted to secure positive memories of the fascist era through an individual woman's act of transmission to a local community.

Conclusion: racialized memory, women's agency and the politics of 'Italian' history

As previous scholarship has pointed out, Italian imperial discourse centered on Italians themselves rather than on colonized subjects, and the fascist empire as a frontier of modernity was meant to act as a transformative force on Italians' own consciousness.[49] The materials analyzed in this chapter have illustrated how, whether articulated in propaganda, commercial or cultural representations, or individual acts of memory and self-narration, the self-manifestation of Italians as white Europeans/ Westerners was performed against a backdrop of indistinct, hierarchical perceptions of Africa and difference. This manifests the internalization of a Eurocentric – and self-centered – colonial gaze by the authors and mediators of such representations. As a distinctively Southern European discourse of identity and whiteness, the discourse elaborated by Italian élites constructed a racial hierarchy in which a new Italian Latin race stood at the apex, driving the other white European, Anglo-Saxon, Aryan and Latin races toward a New World Order. In this discursive – both political and cultural – fascist project, the forging of new historical narratives and cultural memories of the Roman Empire played a pivotal role as an endless source of creative inspiration, rather than as a nostalgic leitmotiv. Overall, Italian imperial discourse stemmed from the intersection of the global circuits of Italian migration and colonial settlement, with the fascists striving to build a modern, nationalistic imperial formation which would demonstrate the global preeminence of Italy's political,

138 Barbara Spadaro

economic and cultural influence. My attempt has been to illuminate further levels and circuits of this process, notably its transimperial cultural dimension, Italian women's historical contribution to such dynamics and the gendered representations of identity and power which emerged within interconnected discourses and media.

I have approached this by focusing on a propaganda campaign which was run at the heart of the Italian Empire in the 1930s and which was woven into a complex web of political and cultural discourses shaping ideas of Europe and its internal and external 'others', discourses in which ideas of gender, class, 'race' and culture intersected. As we have seen, colonial training for women sprang out of an intense historical moment: the mid-1930s, when the mobilization of new actors, media and technologies reconfigured the global circuits of imperial and commercial culture and challenged the existing global political order. This wider context is mirrored in the fascist hierarchies' attempts to convey the human, political and economic resources of Italians across the world in a distinctive new model of imperial modernity.

Such a project was a matter of contention and micro-negotiation, and a key aim of this essay has been to stress the multiple voices, forces and processes embedded in the fascist attempt at developing a distinctive gendered ultranationalist ideology around empire. As I have shown in revealing the different strategies involved in the representation of fascist colonial girls, this was never articulated as a single coherent narrative, partly because of the limited development and rapid collapse of the fascist empire. Most of all, the coalescing strategies of representation of these 'girls' – the potential vanguards of white women in fascist imperial modernity – mirror issues at stake in the representation of women and modernity in Italy. The urban nature of fascist imperial society remained a problematic – and unresolved – challenge in developing a distinctive and coherent discourse on Italian modernity. This was because the Italian urban middle classes, treasured by the fascist regime as the bulwark of political consensus, would not identify with the sturdy peasant protagonists of the massive settlement projects implemented across the Italian peninsula and the empire. Thus this campaign illuminates some of the tensions within which different sectors of the Italian society negotiated their national, political and social identities in decades of intensified social and cultural changes across the transforming circuits of imperial power and global inequalities.

This chapter has further explored gendered intersections of national and imperial histories by illuminating the imaginaries and ambitions of middle-class Italian women beyond local and national circuits. While professional opportunities and chances of personal development for women were drastically limited in Italy by the gendered politics of the fascist regime, the wider horizon of Italian imperial modernity, and its experimental nature, opened new spaces for women's energies, albeit under new forms of censorship and social constraints to women's careers, stemming from the dictatorship's imperialist ambitions. Such uneven power dynamics casted long shadows: as the glimpses offered in this chapter suggest, both the agency and the contribution of women to the Italian Empire – whether as propagandists, missionaries, professionals or housewives – need to be dug out both from the contemporary gendered politics of representation and from historical memory, with its own politics of gender and representation. In recent years, feminist and postcolonial scholarship has been dismantling the epistemological bias in earlier writings on the history of Europe and its empires, pointing out material and discursive aspects of their interdependence.[50] This study of memories and subjectivities stemming from the Italian Empire aims to take such approaches further, toward a more inclusive and plural understanding of the shaping of racialized memories and cultures within Europe. I have highlighted the emotional, cultural and material practices performed by women constituting themselves as social and historical subjects through forms of self-narration. My analysis of the memories of women propagandists has focused on the micro-processes of appropriation and remediation of fascist gendered and racialized representations, and on their creative memory processes. I believe that by collapsing time and space, the narratives and acts of transmission explored here link the fascist imperial past and its configuration to present self-perceptions and geographies. Both the memories and the representations of these women propagandists show how Italian gendered and racialized identities, while powerfully shaped by feelings of local and national belonging, and indeed materialized in individual gestures and micro-negotiations, are historically rooted and continuously reimagined within wider imperial, global and transnational circuits of contacts and cultural memory.

Notes

1 Key studies in English include P. Palumbo, ed., *A Place in the Sun : Africa in Italian Colonial Culture from Post-Unification to the Present*, Berkeley: University of California Press, 2003; J. Andall and Derek Duncan, eds., *Italian Colonialism: Legacy and Memory*, Bern: Peter Lang, 2005; R. Ben-Ghiat and Mia Fuller, eds., *Italian Colonialism*, New York and Basingstoke: Palgrave Macmillan, 2005; D. Duncan and J. Andall, eds., *National Belongings: Hybridity in Italian Colonial and Postcolonial Culture*, Oxford: Peter Lang, 2010; Ruth Ben-Ghiat, *Italian Fascism's Empire Cinema*, Bloomington: Indiana University Press, 2015. Recent works on the discursive construction of whiteness in Italy are: L. Re, 'Italians and the Invention of Race: The Poetics and Politics of Difference in the Struggle over Libya, 1890–1913', *California Italian Studies Journal*, 1:1, 2010. Online: http://escholarship.org/uc/item/96k3w5kn; C. Lombardi-Diop and C. Romeo, eds., *Postcolonial Italy: Challenging National Homogeneity*, New York: Palgrave Macmillan, 2012, and *Ead.*, 'The Italian postcolonial: A manifesto', *Italian Studies*, 69:3, 2014, 425–433; D. Baratieri, *Memories and Silences Haunted by Fascism: Italian Colonialism, MCMXXX-MCMLX*, Bern, New York: Peter Lang, 2010. Scholarship in Italian is burgeoning: see N. Labanca, 'Post-Colonial Italy. The Case of a Small and Belated Empire', in D. Rothermund, ed., *Memories of Post-Imperial Nations: The Aftermath of Decolonization, 1945–2013*, Daryaganj, Delhi, India: Cambridge University Press, 2015; C. Lombardi-Diop and G. Giuliani, *Bianco e nero: Storia dell'identità razziale degli Italiani*, Firenze: Le Monnier, 2013. See also important work of S. Patriarca, *Italian Vices: Nation and Character from the Risorgimento to the Republic*, Cambridge, UK: Cambridge University Press, 2010, chapters 3–5; D. Forgacs, *Italy's Margins: Social Exclusion and Nation Formation Since 1861*, Cambridge: Cambridge University Press, 2014.
2 See D. Gabaccia, *Italy's Many Diasporas*, London: UCL Press, 2000; D. Gabaccia and Franca Iacovetta, eds., *Women, Gender, and Transnational Lives: Italian Workers of the World*, Toronto: University of Toronto Press, 2002 L. Baldassar and D. Gabaccia, eds., *Intimacy and Italian Migration: Gender and Domestic Lives in a Mobile World*, New York: Fordham University Press, 2011; M. Choate, *Emigrant Nation: The Making of Italy Abroad*, Cambridge, MA: Harvard University Press, 2008.

140 Barbara Spadaro

3 B. Spadaro, *Una colonia Italiana. Incontri, memorie e rappresentazioni tra Italia e Libia*, Milano : Le Monnier, 2013. The writing of this chapter, first conceived for the 2013 IFRWH Conference *Women's Histories: The Local and the Global*, has been developed under the umbrella of the AHRC-funded project *Transnationalizing Modern Languages: Mobility, Identity and Translation in Modern Italian Culture*. I would like to thank Clare Midgley and Charles Burdett for invaluable support and feedback throughout this writing process.

4 Charles Burdett, *Journeys through Fascism. Italian Travel Writing between the Wars*, New York and Oxford, Berghahn Books, 2007, p. 11.

5 M. Hirsch and V. Smith, eds., 'Feminism and cultural memory: An introduction', *Signs*. 'Gender and Cultural Memory', 28:1, 2002, 1–19; E. Apfelbaum, 'Halbwachs and the Social Properties of Memories', in S. Radstone and B. Schwarz, eds., *Memory: Histories, Theories, Debates*, New York: Fordham University, 2010, pp. 77–93.

6 M. Hirsch and L. Spitzer, 'Testimonial objects: Memory, gender and transmission', *Poetics Today*, 27:2, 2006, 353–383.

7 Here I borrow the title of Mark Choate's study, *Emigrant Nation. The Making of Italy Abroad*.

8 Gabaccia and Iacovetta, *Women, Gender and Transnational Lives*; Gabaccia and Baldassar, *Intimacy and Italian Migration*. For the impact of such myths on Italians settlers in Libya, see R. Pergher, 'Borderlines in the Borderlands: Defining Difference through History, "Race", and Citizenship in Fascist Italy', *EUI Working Paper*, MWP 2009/08, European University Institute 2009; *Ead.*, 'A Tale of Two Borders: Settlement and National Transformation in Libya and South Tyrol under Fascism', PhD dissertation, University of Michigan, 2007.

9 P. Willson, 'Empire, gender and the "Home Front" in Fascist Italy', *Women's History Review*, 16:4, 2007, 487–500; P. Terhoeven, *Oro alla Patria. Donne, guerra e propaganda nella giornata della fede fascista*, Bologna: Il Mulino, 2006; M. Castellani, *Donne italiane di ieri e di oggi*, Florence: Bemporad, 1937.

10 C. Papa, *Sotto altri cieli. L'Oltremare nel movimento femminile Italiano (1870–1915)*, Roma: Viella, 2009.

11 For early conceptualization of 'Imperial Motherhood', see Anna Davin, 'Imperialism and Motherhood', in F. Cooper and A. Stoler, eds., *Tensions of Empire. Colonial Cultures in a Bourgeois World*, Berkeley, Los Angeles: University of California Press, 1997, 87–152. For the application of the concept in the study of different imperial context see, for example: L. Wildenthal, *German Women for Empire, 1884–1945*, Durham & London: Duke University Press, 2001; C. Jacques and V. Piette, 'L'Union Des Femmes Coloniales (1923–1940) : une association au service de la Colonisation', in A. Hugon, ed., *Histoire des Femmes en situation coloniale*, Paris: Karthala, 2004   E. Locher-Scholten, *Women and the Colonial State. Essays on Gender and Modernity in the Netherlands Indies (1900–1942)*, Amsterdam: Amsterdam University Press, 2000   B. Bush, 'Britain's Conscience on Africa: White Women, Race, and Imperial Politics in Inter-War Britain', in Clare Midgley, ed., *Gender and Imperialism*, Manchester, New York: Manchester University Press, 1998, 200–222; N. R. Hunt, 'Le Bébé En Brousse': European Women, African Birth Spacing, and Colonial Intervention in Breast Feeding in the Belgian Congo', in F. Cooper and A. Stoler, eds., *Tensions of Empire: Colonial Cultures in a Bourgeois World*, op cit., pp. 287–321.

12 For the 'totalitarian turn' from the mid-1930s see E. Gentile, *La via italiana al totalitarismo. Il partito e lo Stato nel regime fascista*, Rome: NIS, 1995 for the issue of consensus in fascist Italy see R. Pergher and G. Albanese, eds., *In the Society of Fascists: Acclamation, Acquiescence, and Agency in Mussolini's Italy*, New York: Palgrave Macmillan, 2012.

13 Foglio Disposizioni (hereafter FD) n. 853, 9/8/1937, in Archivio Centrale dello Stato (ACS, Rome), PNF, Direttorio Nazionale – Servizi Vari, serie I, b. 207. See also B. Spadaro, 'Intrepide massaie. Genere, imperialismo e totalitarismo nella preparazione coloniale femminile durante il fascismo (1937–1943)', *Contemporanea*, 13, 1, 2010: 27–52.

14 See references cited in note 11 of this chapter, and A. Stoler, *Carnal Knowledge and Imperial Power. Race and the Intimate in Colonial Rule*, Berkeley, Los Angeles, London: University of California Press, 2002.

15 As an overview of European initiatives of colonial training for white women consider Nemo (pseudonym), 'La preparazione della donna alla vita coloniale com'è intesa all'estero', in *Africa Italiana* (Special Issue: 'The Italian Woman and the Empire') 16–17, 2–3, Feb–March 1940. On inopportune English suffragettes, see for example the article of the Governor of Italian Somalia, Maurizio Rava, in 'L'Azione Coloniale', 18/2/1937. Italian references to French scholarship point to Clothilde Chivas-Baron, Georges Hardy, and the well-known *Fédération nationale de l'enseignement ménager*, on which consider Ann Stoler, *Carnal Knowledge*, and Marie-Paule Ha, *French Women and the Empire: The Case of Indochina*, Oxford: Oxford University Press, 2014, chapters 3 and 4.

16 L. Wildenthal, *German Women for the Empire*. As for Italian reportage on the school, see Nemo, 'La preparazione della donna alla vita coloniale com'è intesa all'estero'.

17 See R. Ben-Ghiat, 'Modernity is Just Over There: Colonialism and National Identity in Italy', *Interventions. International Journal of Postcolonial Studies*, 8:3, 2006, 380–393; M. Fuller, *Moderns Abroad: Architecture, Cities and Italian Imperialism,* London, New York: Routledge, 2007.

18 On the orphanages see A. M. Galli, 'La donna Italiana in colonia', in *L'Azione Coloniale*, 4/2/1937, p. 8 and the untitled article of M. Rava, in *L'Azione Coloniale*, 18/2/1937, p. 8. On the politics of labor see E. Massart, 'Funzione della femminilità nell'Impero: compattezza delle famiglie, economia e stabilità del lavoro', in *Africa Italiana*, March–April 1940, p. 18. For debates on prostitution and miscegenation in the Italian Empire see B. Spadaro *Una colonia Italiana*, pp. 30–40; G. Barrera, 'Sex, Citizenship and the State: The Construction of the Public and Private Spheres in Colonial Eritrea', in P. Willson, ed., *Gender, Family and Sexuality: The Private Sphere in Italy, 1860–1945*, Houndmills: Palgrave Macmillan, 2004, pp. 157–172; B. Sorgoni, *Parole e corpi: Antropologia, discorso giuridico e politiche interrazziali nella colonia Eritrea (1890–1941)*, Napoli: Liguori, 1988, pp. 229–248; Richard Pankhurst, 'The History of Prostitution in Ethiopia', *Journal of Ethiopian Studies*, 1974, 2, 159–178.

19 On women's organization in fascist Italy see classic studies by Perry Willson, *Peasant Women and Politics in Fascist Italy: The Massaie Rurali*, London, New York: Routledge, 2002; Victoria De Grazia, *How Fascism Ruled Women*.

20 For an overview of regulation see 'Norme per il disciplinamento del personale femminile in AOI', *Africa Italiana*, March–April 1940, pp. 61–62.

21 On 'African fever' among young Italian women see M. Pomilio, 'Via libera alle donne', *L'Azione Coloniale*, 25/2/1937, p. 7; requests for courses in African languages and useful skills were made by women teachers and graduate students commenting on the training camps, for example E. Ferrari, 'A proposito di campi coloniali e precoloniali', *L'Italia d'Oltremare*, 20 March 1942, p. 5, and *L'Azione Coloniale*, 2 April 1942, p. 8; S. Ilardi, 'Orientamenti e tendenze', *L'Azione Coloniale*, 10 April 1940, p. 8; M. G. Crocetta, 'Coscienza coloniale e alcuni problemi del colonialismo', *L'Azione Coloniale*, 13 August 1942, p. 8.

22 A. Lessona, 'La donna coloniale', *L'Azione Coloniale*, 11 March 1937, p. 7.

23 See the 1937 report of the ICF, p. 5, in ACS. At least two editions of official handbooks were published, in 1937 and 1941, mostly in Rome: Istituto coloniale fascista Roma, *Nozioni Coloniali per le organizzazioni femminili del Partito Nazionale Fascista*, Roma: Soc. An. Tipografica Castaldi, 1937; *Nozioni Coloniali per le organizzazioni femminili del Pnf*, Trento: Tipografia Alighiera, 1939; Istituto fascista dell'Africa italiana, *Elementi pratici di vita coloniale per le organizzazioni femminili del Pnf e della Gil*, Roma: Scuola tipografica Pio X, 1941. Handbooks for male members of the party were published in parallel, for example *Nozioni Coloniali per gli iscritti alle organizzazioni del Pnf*, Trento, Tipografia Alighiera, 1939. As for an early French example, which was referred to in Italian sources, see C. Chivas-Baron, *La femme Française aux colonies*, Paris: Editions Larose, 1929.

24 Party records appointing individual women as contributors to handbooks or local courses provide some scattered information (f.e., Ernesta Durini di Monza in FD 915, ACS, Rome, PNF, Direttorio Nazionale – Servizi Vari, serie I, b. 207). For published lectures by women see E. Randi, *Corso di preparazione della donna alla vita coloniale : Economia domestica,* Firenze: Casa Ed. Poligr. Universitaria di C. Cya, 1938. Elisabetta Randi was established as an expert in professional household teaching.

142 Barbara Spadaro

25 On the career of Countess Onorina Bargagli Petrucci as propagandist see B. Spadaro, *Una colonia Italiana*, Chapter 3.
26 On women's writing on the Italian Empire see Rebecca Hopkins, 'Italian women writers and the fascist "Politica Islamica" in Colonial Libya', *California Italian Studies Journal*, 1, 2010, 1–22; Cristina Lombardi-Diop, 'Pioneering Female Modernity: Fascist Women in Colonial Africa', in R. Ben-Ghiat and M. Fuller eds., *Italian Colonialism*, New York: Palgrave Macmillan, 2005, pp. 145–154; C. Burdett and D. Duncan, eds., *Cultural Encounters: European Travel Writing in the 1930s*, New York: Berghahn Books, 2002.
27 See references cited in note 9 of this chapter
28 See handbooks cited in note 24.
29 See notably C. E. Gadda, 'Volontà e azione nell'Italia di oggi : la donna si prepara ai suoi compiti coloniali' *Le Vie d'Italia. Rivista mensile della consociazione turistica Italiana,* 44, 10, October 1938, pp. 1248–1251.
30 Consider Anonimo, 'Campi pre-coloniali', *L'Azione Coloniale*, 7/7/1938, p. 8 Angela Vella, 'I campi pre-coloniali delle Giovani Fasciste in Italia', *L'Azione Coloniale,* 1/9/1938, p. 7.
31 See the newsreel Giornale Luce B1383, 28 September 1938, Roma. *L'inaugurazione dell'Ara Pacis nel nuovo assetto urbanistico.* Online: www.archivioluce.com/archivio/
32 Wanda Gorjoux Bruschi, *Roma madre accoglie le compatte coorti*, in "La Donna fascista", May–June 1938, p. 13. On the pervasive impact of Hollywood icons in Italian society since the 1930s see D. Forgacs and S. Gundle, *Mass Culture and Italian Society from Fascism to the Cold War*, Bloomington and Indianapolis: Indiana University Press, 2007.
33 Giornale Luce B1371, *08/09/1938. Lago d'Iseo.Le attività al campeggio Pre-Coloniale per Giovani fasciste che si preparano alla "Vita Coloniale" in Africa.* Online: www.archivioluce. com/archivio/.
34 B. L. McLaren, *Architecture and Tourism in Italian Colonial Libya: An Ambivalent Modernism*, Seattle and London: University of Washington Press, 2006; B. Spadaro, *Una colonia Italiana,* Chapter 3; S. M. Hom, 'Empires of tourism: Travel and rhetoric in Italian colonial Libya and Albania, 1911–1943', *Journal of Tourism History* 4, 3, 2012, 281–300.
35 B. Gaudenzi, 'Press advertising and fascist dictates: Showcasing the female consumer in Fascist Italy and Nazi Germany', *Journalism Studies*, 14:5, 2013, 663–680.
36 Archives of the Istituto Italiano per l'Africa e l'Oriente (IsIAO, previously IFAI ICF and ICI), collection "Libia", uncatalogued materials and series 'Turismo and Attività Sportive'. For an overview of this photographic archive, S. Palma, *L'Africa nella collezione fotografica dell'Isiao: Il fondo Eritrea-Etiopia,* Rome: Istituto Italiano per l'Africa e l'Oriente, 2005. On the representation of women and ideas of female beauty in fascist Italy and mass culture see S. Gundle, *Bellissima. Feminine Beauty and the Idea of Italy*, New Haven and London, Yale University Press, 2007.
37 G. Sibaud, 'Ricordi del campo femminile in Libia', *L'Azione Coloniale*, 20 October 1938.
38 See C. Burdett, *Journeys through Fascism*, and note 4 above.
39 *Appunti di Famiglia*, Trieste, 2011, p. 85. This is a private edition of the interviewee's memories. To protect her privacy, I will be using the pseudonym Orsola Rossi, the one she chose for publishing in the colonial press in the 1930–1940s.
40 Interviews with Orsola Rossi (pseudonym) Trieste, 29 and 30 April 2007. Transcriptions deposited at La Sapienza University of Rome within the thesis B. Spadaro, « *L'intrepida massaia* ». *La preparazione della donna alla vita coloniale durante il fascismo,* July 2007. The two-paged section 'The woman and Africa' for the 'Bollettino IFAI' was published within the monthly magazine 'Africa Italiana' from October 1940 to July 1943
41 See 'Da un mare all'altro', in *Bollettino IFAI*, 9, September 1940, 11 'Una firma per il ricordo', *Africa Italiana*, 2, February–March–April 1943, 69.
42 Interview with Orsola Rossi, Trieste 29 April 2007.
43 Angela Maria Guerra Archive, Viguzzolo, Italy – hereafter AMGPA. See also the notes of the archivist, published in G. Gaballo, *Ero, sono e sarò fascista: un percorso attraverso il fondo archivistico di Angela Maria Guerra*, Recco, Genova and Alessandria : Isral, 2001. I would like to thank Giulia Barrera for directing me to this archive and other precious sources of this study.

44 For a detailed biography see the study of G. Gaballo, *Ero, sono e sarò fascista*.
45 Istituto Coloniale Fascista Roma, *Nozioni coloniali per le organizzazioni femminili del Partito nazionale fascista,* Roma:Tip. Castaldi, 1937.
46 Ibid., p. 155, my translation.
47 Notebook B2, AMGPA,Viguzzolo, my translation. Original fragment quoted also in G. Gaballo, *Ero, sono e sarò fascista*, p. 27.
48 John Foot, *Italy's Divided Memory*, New York: Palgrave Macmillan, 2009.
49 See works cited in note 1 and throughout the chapter.
50 See pioneering work in Catherine Hall (ed.) *Cultures of Empire. Colonizers in Britain and the Empire in Nineteenth and Twentieth Centuries*, New York: Routledge, 2000; Ead., *Civilising Subjects: Metropole and Colony in the English Imagination, 1830–1867*, Chicago and London: University of Chicago Press, 2002, notably the *Introduction*; C. Hall and S. O. Rose, eds., *At Home with the Empire: Metropolitan Culture and the Imperial World*, Cambridge: Cambridge University Press, 2006.

PART III

Localizing the global/ globalizing the local

7

TOTAL WAR, GLOBAL MARKET AND LOCAL IMPACT

British women's shifting food practices during the Second World War

Natacha Chevalier

By the dawn of the Second World War, British food practices and eating habits had been shaped by decades of imperial and global trade. All people, rich and poor, were accustomed to consuming commodities which originated from all around the world. The war radically changed this, as imports of food and other goods were drastically reduced. Many commodities were rationed, became scarce or simply disappeared, affecting the diet of the population and the day-to-day existence of British housewives. This exceptional wartime situation made visible the relationship between everyday life in Britain and the country's relationship with the world of global commodities. Drawing on testimonies found in the Mass Observation Archive, this chapter explores the gendered interconnections between global trade and local practices through the lens of the impact of the wartime reduction of food importation on the everyday lives of those traditionally in charge of food matters, namely women.[1]

The choice of food to study the connections among global, local and women is easily justified. Commodities and their travel from one place to another make them a valuable instrument to investigate the connection between the global and the local.[2] In addition, because societies give food cultural and social values, the study of eating habits gives insights into the shaping of national, regional and social identities.[3] Furthermore, due to the traditional gendered distribution of roles, food is also 'an excellent vehicle to contextualize women's lives', to quote Avakian and Haber.[4] Confirming the importance of studying the wartime food situation from a feminine perspective, Ina Zweiniger-Bargielowska stated the following: 'Housewives did the most of the queuing, contriving and making do in order to preserve, as much as possible, customary culinary traditions and domestic rituals.'[5] Indeed, because of their traditional role of primary caregivers that included the purchase and preparation of food for the family, women were at the front line in experiencing and discussing the impact of the war on their local market and their food practises. Their testimonies provide a history from below of the complex interconnection between the global and the local. They also provide significant insights into contemporary perception of such connections, particularly in relation to the impact of the Empire on the British metropolis.

This chapter begins by presenting the role of global and imperial trade in the development of British food habits, highlighting the omnipresence of imported commodities in British diets and the significance of this to national identity. It then establishes the wartime food context and its negative consequences on food imports before turning to an exploration of the consequences of this situation on the population by examining contemporary women's narratives of their wartime experiences. Certainly, the connections among food, identity and society in Britain have previously been explored by a number of scholars writing from colonial, post-colonial and transnational perspectives.[6] Indeed the specific question of the extent of the influence of the Empire on the British society has been hotly debated. For example, Bernard Porter, author of *The Absent-Minded Imperialist*, claims that the Empire and its consequences were of small interest for the 'domestic society', while, in contrast, Catherine Hall and Sonya Rose, in *At Home with the Empire*, argue that the 'everyday lives [of most Britons] were infused with an imperial presence'.[7] The last two decades have also seen an increasing interest in the connections between women and food.[8] Nevertheless, while the question of imperial food trade has been studied from a social, political or economic angle, the feminine dimension, essential to measure its real impact on everyday lives, is lacking. Regarding the period studied in this chapter, the day-to-day experiences of British housewives during the war has attracted some attention, and a few wartime testimonies written by women have been published, notably the diary kept by Nella Last for Mass Observation.[9] However, gendered approaches to the study of the war usually concern female work or citizenship rather than questions of housewifery. When wartime food issues are discussed, it is usually in relation to policies such as rationing or as part of general accounts of the Home Front experience.[10] As a consequence, the relationship among women, global war and food has been noticeably neglected in the historiography.[11] Aspiring to fill such gap and to throw new light on the relationship between local lives and global trade, this chapter gives a voice to women whose wartime testimonies have been waiting to be discovered in the archive of Mass Observation.

Set up in 1937 by two young men, Tom Harrisson and Charles Madge, Mass Observation aimed to collect data and analyse and comprehend British contemporary experiences.[12] During the war, the organisation, already using observation, interviews and monthly questionnaires for its researches, asked its volunteers to write a monthly war diary. These diaries were used in addition to fieldwork to produce wartime reports for the organisation as well as for the Ministry of Information.[13] Today, the material gathered in the Mass Observation Archive is one of the richest sources of information available about 1940s British society and the Home Front experience, with the diaries in particular giving access to individual intimate wartime lives and perspectives. Undoubtedly, these sources have limitations in their usefulness. First, the individuality of the diaries does not lend itself to a macro analysis. However, the personal experiences they reveal enable a better understanding of wartime daily life and help to nuance or even challenge established historical perspectives. Second, the recognition by the diarists that they were writing for an audience may have influenced the content of the diaries. Thus with reference to food, this awareness could have influenced the willingness to complain or the inclusion of information about illegal purchases. However, the diarists presented in this study give the impression of writing openly, candidly describing their wartime practices and expressing their emotions. A third issue concerns the appropriate methodology to deploy in working with a huge quantity of qualitative data. In this research, the questionnaires and diaries examined were analysed using mixed quantitative and qualitative methods. In addition to exploring women's opinions and feelings about food issues, elements extracted from the sources – accounts of food purchases, preparation and consumption, remarks or complaints about the wartime food situation, and so on – were grouped into categories to create quantifiable data that could be compared and used to measure the impact of the wartime food situation on the eating practices of the diarists. This mixed approach permitted the determination of the degree of importance of particular topics – such as the main kind of food missed or purchased. Finally, lack of social representativeness due to an over-representation of the middle class can be a problem when using the Mass Observation Archive.[14] Indeed, while the diarists selected here did come from varied familial and economic backgrounds, they actually all belong to the middle classes.[15] However, such predominance is an advantage concerning this study because the middle class was more affected by the disruptions in the global market and suffered more disturbances in its food practices than the working class.[16] The rationing, shortage or disappearance of their usual commodities coupled with a noticeable price increase were issues for better-off individuals, who were accustomed to a diet comprising a significant variety of imported products. As regards the feminine dimension of this issue, the wartime food situation was especially demanding for housewives who had to maintain higher standards of diet and provide decent meals for their family despite the lack of their usual ingredients.[17]

Global trade and local practices: contextualisation and circumstances

The construction of British food practices and tastes has been a long-term process. However, many British eating habits familiar in the 1940s were shaped during the Victorian period.[18] The development of a globalised trade network since the mid-nineteenth century had a crucial influence on the British food system and the diet of the population.[19] The consumption of sugar, coffee, tea and cocoa expanded during the eighteenth and nineteenth centuries as their price decreased.[20] The use of ice, then refrigeration, and the improvements in transportation revolutionised the preservation and retailing of food.[21] By 1914, most of the wheat and meat consumed in Britain was imported from overseas. In the interwar period, beef from

150 Natacha Chevalier

Argentina, lamb and butter from New Zealand and bacon, butter and eggs from Denmark were commonly found in British shops.[22]

The importance of global trade in shaping local food practices was manifest in the early twentieth-century British diet. While the lower class lived mainly on bread made with Canadian or American wheat and sugar and tea from the colonies, the wealthy ate imported exotic fruits, coffee and chocolate.[23] New attitudes and richer diet patterns and standards of living rose in the expanding middle classes, whose income allowed some latitude and choice in food purchases. As a result, middle-class women became both targets and actors in a globalised market.[24] A good example of the interaction among global trade, local practices and female consumers were the pro-imperial marketing movements organised during the interwar period.[25] Women's organisations such as the British Women's Patriotic League campaigned to encourage shops to offer imperial products and encouraged consumers to buy them. The promotion of the consumption of imperial goods was also supported by the government with the creation of the Empire Marketing Board in 1926.[26] Exhibitions, posters and advertisement encouraged imperial purchase habits and consumers' consciousness of their importance for the imperial economy. These campaigns were particularly aimed at women, referred to as 'empire builders' assisting the Empire by providing colonial food to its families.[27]

This focus on women made sense. After all, as stated by the husband of the head of the British Women's Patriotic League, women 'were the principal shoppers and they would create a demand for Empire goods'.[28] While such discourse indicates the empowerment of women as customers and their potential impact on the food system, it also emphasised and reinforced their social role as family caretakers in charge of the food supply. The emerging science of nutrition combined with the new concerns about low birth rate and high infant mortality – perceived as a threat for the country and the Empire – added the weight of patriotism to female family duties.[29] Educational campaigns and measures were implemented countrywide, while organisations promoting health flourished from the first decade of the new century.[30] The new knowledge about bacteria and vitamins led to the promotion of images of the 'professional housewife' and the 'scientific mother' through doctors, childcare manuals or women's magazines.[31] The health and well-being of the family were presented as women's responsibility, impacting their role as consumers.[32] Food and diet became a major part of infant care as mothers learned about the importance of nutrition and vitamins.

It is difficult to assess the impact of such campaigns on eating habits. Nonetheless, the significance of exotic fruits in the diet of the population is validated by investigations made about food and shopping by Mass Observation prior to the war. Two surveys conducted in November 1938 (with retailers) and during summer 1939 (with customers) demonstrate that imported commodities were a major part of the shopping basket.[33] Exotic products such as tea, coffee, cocoa and sugar were mentioned repetitively in the purchase lists provided by the interviewees. Danish or 'Empire' butter from New Zealand was also mentioned by many. The importance of fruit, especially bananas and apples but above all oranges, is also indisputable: in the fifty-seven questionnaires, fewer than a dozen interviewees had not bought oranges that week. In addition, reflecting the impact of the nutritional advice discussed above, two mothers specified that their purchases were for their children.[34]

The small scale of these two surveys prevents any generalisation. However, the impact of imported food on the eating habits of these customers is incontestable. Research into other sources suggests that imports represented nearly 70 per cent of the total calorie intake of the British population.[35] This global trade not only included exotic commodities but also foods that could easily have been produced locally.[36] As illustrated on the map below, in addition to the tropical products brought in from the Middle East, Africa, Asia and South America, dairy products, temperate climate fruits and vegetables, wheat, flour and meat were imported from North America, Argentina, Australia, New Zealand or Europe.[37]

Such a situation was not sustainable during the war. Shipping space had to be used for military material and the merchant navy was under threat from German U-boats. Therefore, restrictions had to be made on imported goods, including any food items not considered absolutely necessary. Lord Woolton, in charge of the Ministry of Food, was acutely aware of the transformation the war would bring to the country. In his memoirs, he recounted his decision making regarding the planning of the wartime food supply:

> In time of peace food was cheap and of wide variety: we were careless in its use and therefore wasteful. . . . As a nation, it was broadly true to say that we were indifferent to both our agriculture and horticulture. We could get cheap food abroad. . . . It was clear that it could not continue in war-time. . . . I came to the conclusion that the only safe way was to make home agriculture the basis of our food supplies, and to bring into this country only such foods as were necessary to supplement our food production and to give a balanced diet to the public. It was easier said than done.[38]

Despite difficulties, Woolton's plan to rebalance the food supply in favour of local production was successfully implemented with a decrease of about 50 per cent of food importations – from 22,500 tons from 1934 to 1938 to 11,000 tons in 1945.[39] This reduction varied from one commodity to another, as can be seen in the following table (Fig. 7.2).

The distribution of these resources was regulated through rationing and controlled prices by a government seeking to avoid inflation, food shortages and social tensions. Rationing started in January 1940 with sugar, butter, ham and bacon. Commodities were gradually added to the primary ones and by July 1942, meat, fats, eggs, milk and cheese as well as sweets and chocolate were under control.[40] The rations fluctuated during the war, due to the rise and fall of imports and/or war events. The invasion of Denmark and France, for instance, had a severe impact on the importation of butter and sugar beet crops. Cheese rations underwent numerous variations, from 1 oz at worst (May 1941) to 8 oz at best (July 1942), depending on American supplies.[41] To facilitate the fairest distribution of unrationed goods, a point scheme was introduced in December 1941. In addition to the fixed rations, customers received sixteen points every four weeks to spend on canned foods, dried

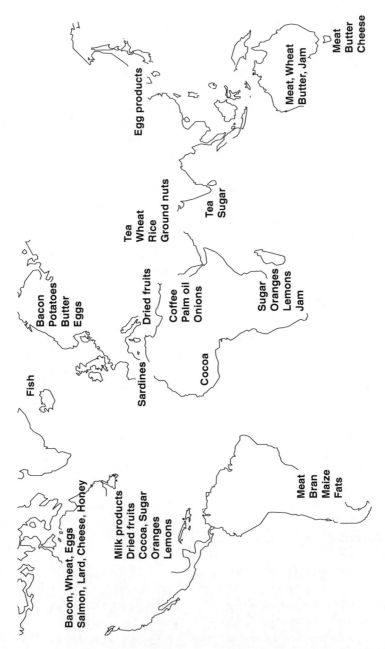

FIGURE 7.1 Map of prewar commodities' provenance. Sources: F. Marquis, *The Memoirs of the Rt. Hon. the Earl of Woolton,* London: Cassell & Company LTD, 1959, pp. 210–211; R. Hammond, *Food.* London: H. M. Stationery Office, 1951, p. 395.

Commodity	1934–38 Average	1940	1941	1942	1943	1944	1945
Wheat	5031	5754	5393	3487	3256	2824	3552
Meat (including carcasses)	1096	1128	1073	1047	1051	1182	832
Bacon and ham	387	241	281	362	387	408	244
Canned meat	63	122	226	249	246	206	97
Sugar	2168	1526	1652	768	1425	1155	1066
Butter	480	264	218	134	152	153	190
Cheese	142	156	203	315	207	252	191
Processed milk	104	87	167	261	223	177	96
Eggs in shell	159	99	59	23	15	23	48
Fresh fruits (including nuts)	1502	839	115	131	58	213	398
Canned fruit, pulp and juices	257	202	112	114	72	125	87
Vegetables (including preserved)	705	392	105	67	23	58	79
Tea, coffee, cocoa	346	370	371	344	422	381	321

FIGURE 7.2   Imports of food into the United Kingdom (in thousands of tons).

Source: R. Hammond, *Food*. London: H. M. Stationery Office, 1951, p. 392.

fruits, cereals, condensed milk or biscuits.[42] Commodities such as poultry, fish, offal and sausages were not rationed but became scarce, if not disappearing altogether. The same situation prevailed for vegetables and fruits. In addition to the limitation of quantities and availability, the increase in price was another issue for housewives, as was the deterioration of the quality of most products.[43]

A comparison of prewar consumption patterns shows the impact of rationing on the everyday life of civilians. The rationing of sugar, for instance, meant a decrease of 25 per cent, then 50 per cent, compared to prewar average household purchases.[44] Middle-class consumption of fresh eggs was reduced by nearly 80 per cent (5.6 eggs per week from 1937–1938; went down to 1.2 in 1944) and a similar significant diminution occurred for butter, fats and meat.[45]

This wartime food situation, together with its influence on the opinion and food practices of the population, was of interest to Mass Observation, as demonstrated by the surveys and reports on food tensions, rationing, shopping and communal feeding in the archives.[46] However, the comments about the commodities they missed and the food difficulties they faced recounted by the diarists offer perhaps the greatest insight into the intimate relationship between the global market and everyday lives of the Home Front.

Total war, global trade and local impact: contemporary narratives

The impact of wartime restrictions on eating habits is clearly established in the female testimonies analysed. The population had 'to do without many things', to quote a female respondent.[47] These 'many things' included products such as sugar, tea, butter, milk, eggs, meat or fruit. Regarding sugar, for instance, its rationing often meant having to drink unsweetened coffee or tea (sometimes despite profoundly disliking it).[48] Prewar recipes were modified and the quantity of sugar was reduced when making jam or baking – as presented with humour by a diarist writing about 'sugar-less griddle scones'.[49] Behaviours and priorities were also influenced. Despite being illegal or publicly condemned as immoral, use of the black market and hoarding were common, at least for those with enough financial means, according to the testimony of an upper class diarist reporting the important stock of sugar made by her friends and herself.[50] The possibility of exchanging the jam ration for more sugar offered by the government during fruit season was said to be looked for by women with no intention of making jam at all, but rather keen on making cakes or custard instead.[51] The limitation of sugar altered attitudes to hospitality as well. While one diarist suggested that visitors should have saccharine to spare the family sugar ration, another deliberately offered drinks other than tea to her guests for the same reason.[52] In public spaces, practices could also be adapted to the new circumstances, transforming the relationship with clients, like the waitresses at Cooper's who would themselves add sugar to tea or coffee to prevent exaggerated consumption or stop customers from taking it from the café.[53] Regarding other imported commodities, the lack of fruit, particularly oranges and bananas, was the main focus of remarks in questionnaire replies of April 1943 and was a major topic in the diaries as well.[54] These numerous observations indicate the importance of imported fruit in the diet of the respondents, as already evident in the analysis of the prewar Mass Observation surveys about shopping. Oranges were especially significant, as demonstrated by the time spent queuing at the grocers and the price people were willing to pay to get some.[55] The prewar omnipresence of imported fruit, its importance in the eating habits of the diarists and the consequences of the limitation of the global and imperial trade were vividly expressed by the writer and Mass Observation diarist Naomi Mitchison:

> V. [daughter] had brought a small orange back from school; She and R. [secretary] and I ate it, feeling frightfully nostalgic and talking about fruit we had eaten, . . . about fruits in London, always cases of oranges, big bunches of bananas and all the foreign fruits, the plums and apricots and passion fruits and lichees. . . . I can still smell orange on my fingers.[56]

In a similar vein, a middle-aged teacher recounted the reaction of her colleagues in June 1943 at the sight of a banana:

> A boy brought a banana wrapped in a handkerchief. A sailor had come home with a bunch, and had given one to all the children in the street. I took it round to all the staff and said 'Prepare for a shock!', and was rewarded with gasps of amazement, and almost unbelief. The 'head' held it up, and showed the whole school, like a curiosity.[57]

Another diarist, comparing her household's peace-time habits with the current situation, noted: '[Before the war] we did have a lot of fruit – both tinned and fresh – and how I miss it now. There is little in the shop and the prices are prohibitive.'[58]

In this single sentence she reflected the general feeling expressed in the diaries about fruits and their scarcity. The drastic cut of fruit importations (fresh as well as canned) was felt and discussed, indicating a substantial prewar consumption of foreign fruit. The complaints about the scarcity of lemons and oranges are especially revelatory of the place taken by South African and American fruit in the British diet. The question of price is also revealed in the sources. While prior to the war lower middle-class housewives could afford to buy a dozen oranges weekly, their wartime costs were a deterrent – and an illustration of the interconnection between the global situation and local food practices.

All the diarists complained about fruit shortages and prices. The complaints could be linked to the lack of vitamins in the wartime diet but were also related to the difficulties in providing sweet pudding and dessert or making jam and marmalade. The combination of fruit shortage and sugar rationing was a major issue for housewives, as it made the preparation of the usual sweet dishes difficult, if not impossible. The problem was made worse by the limitation of the fat, eggs and milk supply. To some extent, imported products from the US. eased these difficulties, as housewives adapted their cooking habits to the dried eggs, evaporated milk or SPAM (canned meat) that entered the British market.[59]

The reception of this American tinned food was observed by Mass Observation. The products were said to be usually appreciated, even if some interviewees found them too expensive and said they would have chosen the Australian varieties if possible, indicating a prewar use of such commodities and dissatisfaction with the shift of supplier induced by the war.[60] The eating habits of the diarists were affected by these new American products. Imported tinned meat, for example, became a regular part of their diet. It was often due to necessity rather than preference, but it helped housewives manage the family meals.[61] Dried eggs appeared on the diarists' tables as well, substituted for fresh eggs in omelettes, cakes, puddings or custard.[62] As for condensed milk, it was especially helpful for mothers, as it could replace fresh milk for young children or be used to make pudding.

The gendered role of married women as housewives and caregivers, their responsibility to provide meals for the whole family and the effort this demanded in the conditions of global war are manifest in the sources. While the narratives establish that commodities from abroad were a major part of the eating habits of the diarists, they also show that the impact of the reduction of their importation especially affected women, as they found it much harder to fulfil their prescribed household duties and roles. As one young woman expressed it in 1943:

> Before the war I was not married and lived, in the main, on snacks – eggs, bacon, kippers, lots of fruit and tomatoes etc.... Now of course I spend quite a lot of time cooking.... In the ordinary way, I might somewhat resent all the thought and ingenuity necessary to produce nice meals.[63]

This testimony echoes the concerns expressed by a young bride-to-be, who was also well aware of her new responsibilities. 'Another cut in the meat ration', she wrote in January 1941. 'I don't mind having no meat, but I'm going to find [it] difficult to provide adequate meals for James when we're married.'[64] After their wedding, she regularly referred to her struggle with rationing and shortages. The meat ration was too small to manage when compared to what she would normally have. It was a problem, as it occasionally left her husband hungry after their dinner.[65] Her own health suffered from the situation. Feeling exhausted, she blamed the food restrictions. 'Wartime diet has a lot to do with it, I'm sure,' she stated in October 1941. 'I can't satisfy my husband and get adequate fat and proteins myself as well.'[66]

While the sacrifice of housewives' rations for the benefit of their husbands and children is not emphasised in the testimonies, it is evidenced by such quotes. One of the traditional roles of women, as Ina Zweiniger-Bargielowska has pointed out, was to moderate the effects of crisis on the family. The consequences were that many housewives not only took on the increased wartime burden of purchasing and preparing food for their families, but they also could suffer the greatest impact from wartime food scarcity as they gave up certain commodities for the benefit of other family members.[67] Such dietary self-sacrifice could be considered a mark of motherhood, though, as can be seen in the diary of a young mother of two in August 1941:

> In my opinion, such vital food as oranges should be reserved for children and invalids. In my experience, mothers who are at all conscientious go without such things as fruit, tomatoes and eggs altogether to let the children have them.[68]

The use of the term 'mother' and not 'parent' is noticeable in her discourse. However, this is not to say that fathers did not sacrifice their rations. While the husband of the quoted diarist gave up his share of fruit and sweets in favour of their children, other diarists mentioned children getting the main part of the family milk or sweets rations. Nonetheless, the female role as principal food manager as well as the weight of good motherhood and housewifery promoted in the interwar period is manifest in these women's narratives. In addition, the diarist's use of the term 'vital food' with regard to oranges indicates the influences of interwar discourses of scientific motherhood.

While the quotes above demonstrate the connection between imported commodities and British eating habits, the diarists themselves did not associate local food availability with the disruption of the global food system. This lack of awareness or interest in the provenance of their usual goods is a feature of all the diaries. Such disinterest or ignorance is disconcerting. The interwar imperial propaganda that related imperial goods with patriotism and exotic pleasure was expected to have left some traces.[69] This is even more surprising as the diarists were from the middle and upper classes, the social groups most involved in women's imperialist organisations and the targeted public for advertising.[70] Even if we assume that these particular women did not participate in such movements, their prewar food practices could not have been exempt of imported products. Besides, all the diarists reported receiving parcels of food sent by family or friends from Canada, the US, South Africa, India or Bermuda and consequently were using commodities from the colonies and dominions.[71] Interestingly, though, despite receiving tea from Canada or chocolate from America, none conceptualised the provenance of the product received in relation to the imperial commercial system: instead all located the origin of the parcel with its specific sender, not with the product itself.

Such silence may confirm the significant British lack of knowledge about the Empire reported by Uma Kothari in her study of the Empire Marketing Board campaigns.[72] This interpretation is supported by the results of a survey conducted on the subject by Mass Observation in 1940: only a third of the fifty people asked knew the difference between a colony and a dominion, with a significant gendered difference: 54 per cent of men compared to only 12 per cent of women.[73] The testimonies examined indicate that, during wartime, the link between the local situation and the global conditions was not made by consumers either. The correlation between reduced imports and food shortages did not incite a reflection on the connections between global market and local supply. Moreover, the shifting from a situation in which interwar British customers were urged to help the Empire through their purchasing power to a situation where the consumers of wartime Britain were being supported by the colonies and dominions did not inspire comment. Such disinterest and unawareness is corroborated by another research study conducted by Mass Observation on behalf of the Colonial Office in 1948.[74] The findings stressed that, 'Even the best educated sections of the population are ignorant of matters that seem self-evident to the expert . . . the population as a whole lacks fundamental geographical knowledge about the commonwealth.'[75] This deficiency of knowledge was particularly perceptible among housewives, no matter what their class or degree of education.[76]

Regarding imported food and raw material, 63 per cent of nearly 2,000 interviewees were unable to name a single colonial product, and only 5 per cent could name three or more items and their correct provenance. The writer concluded that, 'an educational programme, giving basic information about the extent of our dependence on the Colonies for food and raw materials', was seriously needed, as 'people's knowledge of the Colonies, and our relations with them, is sketchy and inadequate in the extreme'.[77]

It is not to say that all housewives were ignorant of the provenance of their ingredients. Oranges from South Africa were mentioned by one diarist, for instance, and Nella Last, while savouring a piece of cake, took some time to think about its ingredients 'from so many different far-off places'.[78] Nevertheless, she did not specify the places in question and her comment was a nostalgic one rather than a practical reflection on the exigencies of imperial trade. Indeed, nothing in the diaries indicates that these women were interested in the colonies, paralleling the lack of interest shown by nearly half of the people interviewed in the 1948 survey.[79]

Conclusion

As this chapter has discussed, British eating habits have been shaped by the global and imperial food systems; at the outbreak of the Second World War, imported commodities were widely present in the diet of the whole population. This study has demonstrated that the influence of the global commodity chains on local practices was a reality both in terms of markets for exotic commodities and in terms of food that could have been produced locally. It has also been shown that, because of their gendered roles, women were the most aware of the alteration in the food supply caused by the wartime emergency. Therefore, the responses and reactions of British housewives to the wartime reduction of imports provide important insights into the complex relationship between global trade and local markets, confirming the central role of the globalised food system in eating habits. On the one hand, the decrease in imports from the Empire and Europe greatly impacted the daily lives of these women, making the purchase of food and the preparation of meals extremely demanding in time, effort and creativity. On the other hand, substitute imported commodities from North America modified the content as well as the preparation of meals.

At the outset of this research, it was assumed that the challenge to the global trade system caused by the war and its impact on the availability of their usual ingredients would draw the diarists' attention to food provenance. The results of this study, however, reveal differently. While the concerns about food supply articulated by the women establish the reality of the impact of global trade on local practices, their silence about the origins of the commodities they bought and consumed calls into question their comprehension of the fundamental role played by global and imperial markets on their daily lives. This, as first sight, seems to go against Catherine Hall and Sonya Rose's vision of the Empire 'at home' – a nation infused with imperial culture – and to support Bernard Porter's opposing view that the Empire was of little interest to the average citizen. Indeed, the disinterest in the relationship between the global trade and the local market suggests that British housewives were rather absent-minded imperial customers, to paraphrase Porter. However, it is my opinion that these two apparently opposing interpretations can, in fact, be reconciled by taking into account the invisibility conferred by familiarity and the notion of individual priorities. While the imperial and global products were so integrated into everyday lives that they had become unnoticed, the wartime restrictions focused housewives' attention on their local difficulties in shopping and producing meals rather than encouraging them to look outward at the global situation that was causing the food shortages. In any case, the testimonies discussed in this chapter certainly suggest that the global and imperial sources of commodities were taken for granted, supporting Hall and Rose's argument that the Empire has become 'a natural aspect of Britain's place in the world': the diarists seem to have been unable to conceive of a different reality, as if this global market was so omnipresent in their environment that it simply merged with the local one.[80]

The contemporary material on British women's wartime diaries presented in this chapter provides an interesting new gendered perspective on the relationship between local consumption and global trade. However, study of this topic clearly needs further extension to include working-class housewives to provide a fuller global history from below; in this respect, the predominance of middle-class volunteers in Mass Observation is a limitation. Nevertheless, the act of viewing a period of global war from the intimacy of local British homes and kitchens not only offers new insights into the everyday lives and concerns of women over the wartime period but also contributes to bringing the day-to-day reality of local lives into the 'grand narrative' of global war.

Notes

1 Extracts from the Mass Observation Archive [henceforth MOA] are reproduced with permission of Curtis Brown Group Ltd, London on behalf of The Trustees of the Mass Observation Archive. Copyright © The Trustees of the Mass Observation Archive.
2 S. Hazareesingh and J. Curry-Machado, 'Editorial – Commodities, empires, and global history', *Journal of Global History*, 4:1, 2009, 2.
3 See P. Caplan, *Food, Health, and Identity*, London, New York: Routledge, 1997, pp. 9–12; G. Valentine, 'Eating in: Home, consumption and identity', *Sociological Review*, 47:3, 1999, p. 493; A. Nützenadel and F. Trentmann, 'Introduction, Mapping Food and Globalization', in A. Nützenadel and F. Trentmann, eds., *Food and Globalization: Consumption, Markets and Politics in the Modern World*, Berg. Oxford; New York, 2008, p. 1.
4 A. Avakian and B. Haber, *From Betty Crocker to Feminist Food Studies: Critical Perspectives on Women and Food*, Amherst: University of Massachusetts Press, 2005, p. 7.
5 I. Zweiniger-Bargielowska, ed., 'Housewifery', in *Women in Twentieth-Century Britain*, 149–64. Harlow: Longman, 2001, p. 154.
6 For instance: A. Murcott, W. J. Belasco and P. Jackson, *The Handbook of Food Research*, 2013; J. Burnett, *Plenty and Want : A Social History of Diet in England from 1815 to the Present Day*, London: Scholar Press, 1979; D. Oddy, *From Plain Fare to Fusion Food : British Diet from the 1890s to the 1990s*, Rochester, NY: Boydell Press, 2003; S. Mennell, *All Manners of Food: Eating and Taste in England and France from the Middle Ages to the Present*, Oxford, New York: B. Blackwell, 1985; F. Trentmann, *The Oxford Handbook of the History of Consumption*, Oxford, New York: Oxford University Press, 2012; A. Nützenadel, F. Trentmann, *Food and Globalization: Consumption, Markets and Politics in the Modern World*, Oxford, New York: Berg, 2008.
7 B. Porter, Bernard. *The Absent-Minded Imperialists: Empire, Society, and Culture in Britain.* Oxford, New York: Oxford University Press, 2004, pp. 306–310: C. Hall and S. O. Rose, *At Home with the Empire: Metropolitan Culture and the Imperial World*, Cambridge, UK; New York: Cambridge University Press, 2006, p. 2.
8 For an extensive review on the subject, see A. Avakian Voski and B. Haber, *From Betty Crocker to Feminist Food Studies: Critical Perspectives on Women and Food*, Amherst: University of Massachusetts Press, 2005.
9 J. Purcell, *Domestic Soldiers*, London: Constable, 2011; J. Purcell, 'The Domestic Soldier: British Housewives and the Nation in the Second World War', *History Compass*, 4:1, 2006, 153–160; L. Stanley, 'Women have servants and men never eat: Issues in reading gender, using the case study of mass-observation's 1937 day-diaries', *Women's History Review*, 4:1, 1995, 85–102; V. Hodgson, *Few Eggs and No Oranges : A Diary Showing How Unimportant People in London and Birmingham Lived throughout the War Years 1940–1945*, London: Persephone Books, 1999; C. Milburn, *Mrs Milburn's Diaries : An Englishwoman's Day-to-Day Reflections 1939–1945*, London: Futura, 1989; N. Last, *Nella Last's War : The Second World War Diaries of "Housewife, 49"*, London: Profile Books, 2006.
10 Zweiniger-Bargielowska, *Austerity in Britain*; Calder, *The People's War*; Purcell, *Domestic Soldiers*. N. Longmate, *How We Lived Then : A History of Everyday Life during the Second*

160 Natacha Chevalier

World War, London: Pimlico, 2002. F. Trentmann, Frank and F. Just, *Food and Conflict in Europe in the Age of the Two World Wars*. Houndmills, Basingstoke, Hampshire, New York: Palgrave Macmillan, 2006;

11 An exception would be the work of anthropologist Sydney Mintz, who examined the multiple factors and consequences related to sugar production and consumption. Historian Joanna de Groot also focused on one commodity, tea, to explore the impact of the imperial market on British women as well as the evolution, or domestication, of exotic products. S. Mintz, *Sweetness and Power*, New York: Viking, 1985; J. De Groot, 'Metropolitan Desires and Colonial Connections: Reflections on Consumption and Empire', in C. Hall and S. Rose, eds., *At Home with the Empire: Metropolitan Culture and the Imperial World*, Cambridge, UK; New York: Cambridge University Press, 2006, pp. 166–190.

12 M. Pickering, 'Democracy and communication: Mass observation 1936–1943', *Journal of Communication*, 36:1, 1986, 41–56; D. Sheridan, 'Writing to the archive: Mass-observation as autobiography', *Sociology*, 27:1, 1993, 29; J. Hinton, *The Mass Observers: A History, 1937–1949*, Oxford: Oxford University Press, 2013, p. 1.

13 Pickering, 'Democracy and Communication', 53; T. Harrisson and Mass-Observation Archive, D. Sheridan and C. Dixon, *The Mass-Observation Archive, a Guide for Researchers*, University of Sussex Library, 1987, pp. 2; 6. For an extended discussion of the work of Mass Observation, see N. Hubble, *Mass-Observation and Everyday Life Culture, History, Theory*, Houndmills, Basingstoke, Hampshire, New York: Palgrave Macmillan, 2006. For the history of the organisation, see Hinton, *The Mass Observers*.

14 Courage, 'The National Panel Responds: Mass-Observation Directives 1939–1945' quoting Stanley Nick, 1981. The extra dimension: a study and assessment of the method employed by Mass-Observation in its first period, 1937–1940. Non-published PhD; Savage, 'Changing Social Class Identities in Post-War Britain', 459–465.

15 Two diarists were single, five were married and one was a widow. Five of them had children and three did not. In regard to their social class, according to their income, education, standard of living and occupation for those working (a teacher, a secretary, a writer and a mathematician), one diarist came from a Scottish aristocratic family, one was upper middle class, three belonged to the middle middle class and two to the lower middle class. The male diarist (married, two children) was a skilled manual worker (electrician).

16 Quoting PRO, INF 1/292 27 Aug – 3 Sept 1941, from a report by the Cambridge Regional Information Officer (emphasis in original) Zweiniger-Bargielowska, *Austerity in Britain*, 2000, 71.

17 Zweiniger-Bargielowska, *Austerity in Britain*, 2000, 71; 99 See Chapter 4: Women.; MOA D 5239, January 1941

18 E. Rappaport, 'Packaging China', in F. Trentmann, ed., *The Making of the Consumer Knowledge, Power and Identity in the Modern World*, Oxford, New York, 2006, p. 125.

19 Nützenadel and Trentmann, 'Introduction', p. 4; A. Bryant, L. Bush and R. Wilk. 'The History of Globalization and the Food Supply', in A. Murcott, W. J. Belasco and P. Jackson, eds., *The Handbook of Food Research*, Bloomsbury, London: Murcott, Anne, 2013, p. 74.

20 De Groot, 'Metropolitan Desires and Colonial Connections', pp. 170–171.

21 Bryant, Bush and Wilk, 'The History of Globalization and the Food Supply', pp. 41–43; Warde, 'Eating' p. 381.

22 Burnett, *Plenty and Want*, pp. 286–287.

23 A, C, E and Calcium in particular, see Table 9, I. Gazeley and A. Newell, 'The First World War and Working-class food consumption in Britain', *Economic Department Working Papers* 14 (2010), p. 22; Burnett, *Plenty and Want*, pp. 207–209, 238–239, 285.

24 See for instance: M. Nava, "Modernity Tamed? Women Shoppers and the Rationalisation of Consumption in the Inter-War Period", in Andrews Margaret R. and Mary M. Talbot, eds., *All the World and Her Husband: Women in Twentieth-Century Consumer Culture*, London; New York: Cassell, 2000; M. Hilton, "The Female Consumer and the Politics of Consumption in Twentieth-Century Britain," *The Historical Journal* 45:1, 2002, 103–128.

25 In the 1920s and 1930s, the postwar financial situation and the de-globalization incited a new protectionism and the promotion of products from the Empire and the

Total war, global market, local impact **161**

Commonwealth. Burnett, *Plenty and Want*, p. 287; Nützenadel and Trentmann, 'Introduction', p. 11.

26 O'Connor K, "The King's Christmas Pudding," 139–140.

27 U. Kothari, 'Trade, consumption and development alliances: The historical legacy of the Empire Marketing Board poster campaign', *Third World Quarterly*, 35:1, 2014, 44–7; 54.

28 Quoted by O'Connor K, 'The King's Christmas Pudding', 140.

29 E. Yeo, 'The creation of "motherhood" and women's responses in Britain and France, 1750–1914', *Women's History Review*, 8:2, 1999, 201–202.

30 A. Davin, 'Imperialism and motherhood', *History Workshop*, no. 5, 1978, 10–13.

31 M. E. Brembeck, 'The Twenty-First-Century "Food Consumer": The Emergence of Consume Science', in A. Murcott, W. J. Belasco and P. Jackson, eds., *The Handbook of Food Research*, Bloomsbury, London: Anne, 2013, pp. 294–299.

32 E. Asquier, 'Domesticity and Beyond: Gender, Family, and Consumption in Modern Europe', in F. Trentmann, ed., *The Oxford Handbook of the History of Consumption*, Oxford; New York: Oxford University Press, 2012, p. 573.

33 MOA TC WorktownCollection Box 31 Christmas and January Sales.

34 MOA TC WorktownCollection Box 32 Food and Shopping.

35 A. Wilt, Alan. *Food for War: Agriculture and Rearmament in Britain before the Second World War*, Oxford, New York: Oxford University Press, 2001, p. 2

36 Zweiniger-Bargielowska, *Austerity in Britain*, p. 17.

37 R. Hammond, *Food*. London: H.M. Stationery Off, 1951, p. 395.

38 F. Marquis, *The Memoirs of the Rt. Hon. the Earl of Woolton*. London: Cassell & Company LTD, 1959, pp. 192–193.

39 Hammond, *Food*, 392.

40 In 1942, the average adult weekly ration would have been about 4 oz (113 gr) of bacon and ham, between two and three pints of milk, between 1 and 4 oz (28 and 113 gr) of cheese, 2 oz (56 gr) of butter and tea, 8 oz (226 gr) of sugar, 12 oz (340 gr) of sweets per month and one egg per week (if available, but often in the form of dried eggs). Meat was rationed by price (1 shilling and 10 pence and 11 days worth for children) equivalent to about a pound of meat for an adult. Calder, *The People's War Britain, 1939–1945*, p. 380–1; R. Minns, *Bombers and Mash : The Domestic Front 1939–45*. London: Virago, 1980, Chronology.

41 R. Minns, *Bombers and Mash*, Chronology; Hammond, *Food*, 114–115; 121; 283; 395

42 Zweiniger-Bargielowska, *Austerity in Britain*, pp. 19–22; Hammond, *Food*, pp. 202–203, 283.

43 Zweiniger-Bargielowska, *Austerity in Britain*, p. 36.

44 Fine, *The World of Consumption*, p. 103; Calder, *The People's War*, pp. 380–381.

45 See Table 1.3 Weekly per capita food consumption Zweiniger-Bargielowska, *Austerity in Britain*, pp. 40–41.

46 For a description of the material available on food in the Topic Collection, see: N. Chevalier, *The Magical Treasure Chest and the Endless Treasure Hunt: Mass Observation Topic Collections and Its Primary Sources on Food*. Available through: Adam Matthew, Marlborough, Mass Observation. Online: www.massobservation.amdigital.co.uk.ezproxy.sussex.ac.uk/FurtherResources/Essays/MassObservationTopicCollectionsAndItsPrimarySourcesOnFood

47 MOA DR April 1943, 3026.

48 MOA D 5378, September, December 1940; May 1943.

49 MOA D 5378, April, August 1941; May 1943.

50 MOA D 5427, July 1940; October 1940.

51 MOA DR 2903, February 1943.

52 MOA D 5240, April 1940; MOA D 5378, July 1941; August 1941.

53 MOA D 5390, September 1941

54 One-hundred fifty-three of 248 respondents wrote about a decrease of fruit consumption and/or missing fruit in their diet, sometimes repetitively in their replies. No other commodity, including the rationed ones, received more attention. The shortage and price of fruit were also key complaints in the diaries.

55 Such value was recognised by the government and the distribution of oranges was regulated. They should be reserved for children under eighteen with a double allocation for

those under five. Zweiniger-Bargielowska, *Austerity in Britain*, p. 134. MOA D 5240, January 1941; MOA D 5201, October 1941.

56 MOA D 5378, November 1941.
57 MOA D 5240, June 1943.
58 MOA D 5390, August 1940.
59 Zweiniger-Bargielowska, *Austerity in Britain*, pp. 37, 71; Hammond, *Food*, p. 369; Calder, *The People's War*, p. 231.
60 MOA FR 999 American Tinned Food, p. 3.
61 MOA D 5239, January 1941; MOA D 5201, May 1941; January 1942.
62 MOA DR 2500, October–November 1943; MOA D 5427, November 1942; MOA D 5239, July 1941.
63 MOA DR April 1943, 3002.
64 MOA D 5239, January 1941.
65 Ibid.
66 MOA D 5239, October 1941.
67 Zweiniger-Bargielowska, *Austerity in Britain*, 127–128.
68 MOA D 5318.1, August 1941.
69 De Groot, 'Metropolitan Desires and Colonial Connections', p. 170.
70 See: C. Midgley, 'Bringing the Empire at Home: Women Activists in Imperial Britain, 1790s-1930s', in C. Hall and S. Rose, eds., *At Home with the Empire: Metropolitan Culture and the Imperial World*, Cambridge, UK; New York: Cambridge University Press, 2006, pp. 230–250.
71 MOA D 5378, September 1942; MOA D 5240, December 1942; MOA D 5239, December 1943.
72 Kothari, 'Trade, Consumption and Development Alliances' p. 49.
73 MOA FR 514 Colonies Questionnaire, pp. 1–2.
74 1921 civilians, male and female of various social statuses, were interviewed about their knowledge of the Empire. The survey included questions about the food and raw material imported from colonies and dominions.
75 MOA FR 3010 Public Opinion on Colonial Affairs, p. iv.
76 Ibid., pp. 4, 8.
77 Ibid., pp. 10, 16.
78 Last, *Nella Last's War*, 22.
79 High degree of interest: 22 per cent; fair degree of interest: 31 per cent; little interest: 27 per cent; no interest at all: 20 per cent. "MOA FR 3010 Public Opinion on Colonial Affairs," 22.
80 Hall and Rose, *At Home with the Empire*, p. 2.

8

THE LOCAL AND THE GLOBAL IN WOMEN'S ORGANIZING IN THE PACIFIC REGION, 1950s–1990s[1]

Patricia Grimshaw and Hannah Loney

At the Pacific Women's Conference in Fiji in 1975, International Women's Year, a Maori delegate, Hana Jackson, paid tribute to the veteran indigenous rights advocate, Whina Cooper, for the crucial leadership role she played revitalizing the campaign for land rights in Aotearoa/New Zealand. At nearly eighty years of age, Cooper earlier that year had led a march from the northernmost tip of the North Island to the southern capital, Wellington, to protest Maori land alienation, gathering supporters as she went to present a petition to the Prime Minister. Cooper's initiative, Jackson said, illustrated 'the new involvement of women in a leadership role in the land issue' that had always in the past been 'left in the care of men'.[2] The march illustrated another step in Cooper's long activist career. Most notably, in 1951, Cooper played a pivotal role connecting Maori and Pacific women when, as inaugural President, she oversaw the birth of the Maori Women's Welfare League and the entry of the League into the international Pan-Pacific Women's Association. Also present at the Fiji conference to hear Cooper praised was Grace Mera (later Molisa), a 29-year-old delegate from the New Hebrides, the South Pacific island group that in 1980 became Vanuatu. A student at the University of the South Pacific in Suva, Molisa's participation in the conference heralded a new generation of Pacific women leaders. These younger women, Molisa prominent among them, would not only organize women in their region but would also enable the voices of Pacific women to be heard on a world stage through participation in the UN's sponsored conferences on women between 1975 and 1995. Their politics took shape within what Nellie Wong has termed 'multi-issue oppression – one that was not limited to gender issues alone – but in which colonialism, ethnicity, race and class were centrally informing and intersecting categories of importance'.[3]

Historians of international women's movements have focused primarily on studies of individual women and organizations based in Britain, Europe and North America that have tended to exclude non-Western women's activism on behalf of women.[4] Alternative perspectives have emerged from a minority of scholars, some from previously colonized countries, whose aim has been to 'deprovincialize' or 'decolonize' this history. Over twenty years ago the Indian historian, Chandra Talpade Mohanty, asserted the importance of 'feminist analysis within the framework of the intersecting histories of race, colonialism, and capitalism', noting women's experiences of broader structures of domination and their capacity to agitate against them.[5] In succession, such scholars as Kumari Jayawardena, Antoinette Burton and Clare Midgley have analyzed the impact of imperialism and colonialism on local Asian women's movements and their capacity to network internationally.[6] These scholars note that within analyses of women's activism are intersecting factors and broader power structures that shape women's lives and must be taken into account when studying women's organizing in any specific locale. Sylvanna Falcón and Jennifer Nash go further with their emphasis on the imperative for feminist scholars to engage with intersectionality and transnationalism as 'anti-subordination projects that seek to redress inequality and violence'.[7] Despite these and other scholars' interventions, the European historian Francesca de Haan recently deplored what she considers a continuing focus on white, Western, liberal, 'gender-only' feminism within writing on transnational feminisms and women's movements. She calls for studies that counter the 'invisibilization' of Second and Third World individuals, organizations and countries.[8]

In this chapter we engage with de Haan's aim that such women's organizing should be acknowledged for its significance within transnational studies of the international women's movement, while paying heed to the specificity of local women's struggles. The shift of emphasis in women's activism, from local or national struggles in countries where the women were also integral components of anti-colonial struggles, to broader spheres of women's organizing, extends the scope of their agendas in crucial directions. At times these developments were concomitant with a critique of white, Western feminism for perceived race-blindness, yet they could also open for examination men's gender discrimination within indigenous rights movements themselves. Scholars of Pacific island societies, such as Margaret Jolly, Martha Macintyre and Caroline Ralston, have recommended flexibility in assessing the intersections of feminism, nationalism and globalization in the Pacific region.[9] Theories generated in Eurocentric feminist models, such as gender binary oppositions and dichotomies, Ralston cautions, may be irrelevant to the 'cultural presuppositions, and to the structures and living patterns of the small-scale, pre-industrial kinship societies' of the Pacific Islands.[10] The Australian historians, Fiona Paisley, Angela Woollacott, and Marilyn Lake, have demonstrated to historians of ex-British settler colonies the utility of extending interpretations of women's twentieth-century organizing to their cross-cultural international networking through, for example, the Pan-Pacific Women's Association.[11]

We have adopted a biographical approach to this study of women's movements in the Pacific, in agreement with de Haan's advocacy for a focus on individual women's lives to uncover 'transnational connections, activism and agendas' that are often absent in the emerging field of transnational feminism.[12] Indigenous women in the Pacific region, however eminent, rarely left extensive archives; Cooper and Molisa were no exception. Both women gave extended interviews that have been retained, but this chapter relies primarily on public writings and speeches and the documentary archives of organizations to which they were affiliated.[13] The chapter begins with an examination of the intersections among gender, race and class in Cooper and Molisa's lives as they served apprenticeships in activism, prior to their emergence into national prominence as organizers. They did so in a context of reshaping traditional gender relations that colonization set in train that impacted men and women differently.[14] We consider how the women were situated within Maori and Vanuatuan communities: their circumstances of birth and lineage, religion and education, employment and family. Beginning with Cooper's activities from the 1950s followed by Molisa's from the 1970s, the chapter traces the intersectionality of gender, race and class in their capacities to relate to indigenous and non-indigenous women and men and to non-indigenous women, locally and beyond national borders. We view Cooper's work as a protagonist for Maori and Pacific women as couched in the assumptions of first-wave feminism while Molisa and her associates, who initially distanced themselves from women's liberation, nevertheless benefited from the revitalization of the international women's movement.

Apprenticeships in activism

An analysis of intersectionality within Cooper and Molisa's early lives involves an understanding of the interactions among gender, race and class within their specific cultures and of the ways in which their identities took shape amidst two distinctive structures of colonialism. The older of the activists, Whina Cooper, was born in 1895 in northeastern Aotearoa/New Zealand, an ex-British colony where, despite settler government protestations of racial equality, most Maori were impoverished and marginalized.[15] Grace Mera Molisa was born in 1946 in the southwestern Pacific Island group, then named the New Hebrides. The islands were renamed Vanuatu after the British and French departed in 1980, leaving the new nation in poverty and with sharp internal tensions.[16] The women's careers were part of the struggles of colonized peoples across the Pacific and Southeast Asian region. Their experiences as members of previously subjected, impoverished and oppressed peoples set Cooper and Molisa apart from the white women of their countries, even more so from the middle-class women of European and American origin with whom they eventually engaged in their advocacy for indigenous women.

To situate either Cooper or Molisa in terms of class, gender and race is a demanding assessment. Most settlers and their descendants in antipodean British colonies and ex-colonies viewed indigenous peoples as members of the lower classes unless their education, talent and capacity enabled them to acquire an advanced education and well-paid employment. But an assignation of 'class' for indigenous societies involved their status based on lineage and family that in missionized societies was also connected to religious affiliation. As Tony Ballantyne demonstrates in his recent study, *Entanglements of Empire: Missionaries, Maori and the Question of the*

Body, religion played a key role in facilitating complex political, cultural and economic encounters between the colonizer and the colonized.[17] In the first instance churches – Catholic and Anglican, respectively – facilitated Cooper and Molisa's generation of new 'entanglements' by conferring status on their fathers as office holders and by opening opportunities to their daughters for a sound Western education. Cooper and Molisa would sustain their early spirituality throughout their mature years. Though born into male-dominated cultures within Maori and New Hebridean societies, men, especially fathers and grandfathers, could single out particular girls endowed with unusual vitality and spirit for special attention. This was the fate of both Cooper and Molisa. Rather than serving years of apprenticeship within organizations, they emerged as charismatic leaders from their first entry into public life. As married women and mothers they performed feminine caring duties, but these did not negate their capacity to become activists for their communities. Race and racial issues dominated their sense of self and how others viewed them, particularly so for Cooper, who belonged to a minority group within a considerably larger settler population. Indigenous concerns drove their awakening in politics.

Though Whina Cooper's national prominence dates from the early 1950s, she had served a valuable apprenticeship in Maori concerns at the level of her *iwi* (tribal group) from her youth. While her early and later activism centred on land rights, her goals always encompassed the rights of Maori families and communities and, as part of this agenda, the rights of Maori women to occupy a central place within advocacy networks. Cooper was born Hohepine (Josephine) Te Waka at Te Karaka in northern New Zealand on 9 December 1895. Her father, Heremia Te Wake, a Ngati Manawa chief, was a community leader and a catechist in the Catholic Church who had a strong influence on his daughter's life. As a bright girl of a prominent family, she attended not only primary school, but through the intercession of her father's friend, Maori Minister of Native Affairs, (Sir) James Carroll, became a boarder at St Joseph's Maori Girls' College in Napier. Western markers of gender status in Maori society, like class, did not readily conform to accepted forms in this context. From a young age, Cooper was seen to have *ihi* (a quality of authority that inspires awe). This resulted in her selection as natural heir to her father as a local leader, even ahead of her brothers.[18] After finishing school, Cooper worked successively as a trainee teacher at Pawarenga Native School and at the Catholic presbytery in Rawene. Cooper's first act of protest came at eighteen years of age, when she became involved in a dispute over the leasing of mudflats to a Pakeha (a New Zealander of white descent) farmer, although Maori had traditionally used the land for gathering seafood. Cooper led a party of young adults, who filled in the drains as workers dug them; police were called, but the charge of trespassing was dropped.[19] Cooper married at a young age and remarried after her first husband's death; she bore and raised six children. A hard-working woman on the land, she established herself over several decades as the prominent Maori leader of the northern Hokianga region and a foremost supporter of the Minister for Maori Affairs, Sir Apirana Ngata's schemes for land development. Cooper stood out within her community as an energetic, charismatic and somewhat uncompromising woman.

Grace Molisa was similarly marked out as exceptional, both as an indigenous Vanuatuan and as a woman. Molisa's apprenticeship in activism some fifty years later differed from Cooper's, partly because it was nurtured within an active colonial struggle to get rid of British and French rule. Parallel with Cooper's background in New Zealand, Molisa was a member of a family of high standing in the New Hebridean community. She was born on 17 February 1946, the daughter of a well-respected Anglican clergyman, Father Basil Mera. From her childhood Molisa felt great pressure to become a leader. 'Everybody else had expectations of everything under the sun for me to do when I grew up,' she later wrote. 'They wanted to see somebody do all the sorts of things that my father stood for.'[20] In later years she attributed her values and achievements to her upbringing in a Church environment, writing in an autobiographical essay:

> I have been a groundbreaker in terms of my Island, women and Vanuatu, operating within the Vanuatu cultural context. Throughout my life it wasn't a case of I wanted to do this or that, or that I planned to do this or that or the other. I have been brought up to do the things I've done. I haven't had much choice. Maybe I chose my husband but everything else has been chosen for me by my society, upbringing and education, which have given me my attitudes and beliefs.[21]

This was a life statement that few white female activists would have made.

As a result of her family's position Molisa, like Cooper, had access to advanced levels of education that were unprecedented for a New Hebridean woman. After some years at the local village school and nearby boarding school (where she was the sole female student in attendance), she travelled to New Zealand to attend the Queen Victoria Maori Girls' School in Auckland. After training at the Auckland Teachers' College, she returned to the New Hebrides to teach on her island. Her next move was to Fiji, to undertake a bachelor of arts degree that saw her become the first female graduate of the New Hebrides. Molisa's varied educational experiences provided her with a sense of trans-Pacific mobility that gave her first-hand knowledge and enabled her to liaise with similarly educated Pacific Island women.[22]

As a student in Fiji, Molisa met outstanding Pacific anticolonial activists, including her future husband, Sera Molisa. Upon the completion of their degrees, they married and returned to Vanuatu to participate in the independence struggle. The Anglo-French Condominium that ruled in the New Hebrides had created serious divisions among the archipelago's multiple geographic, linguistic, social and cultural groups that had restricted the development of a unified independence movement. The struggle for independence was thus violent and sharply contested, significantly shaping the trajectory of postindependence politics. Grace Molisa was a member of the Vanuatu National Constitution Committee and one of the signatories to the new Constitution of the Republic of Vanuatu when it was promulgated in 1979. It was during these later years of the 1970s that Molisa would become immersed in efforts to initiate Pacific Islander-led organizations across the Pacific region.

168 Patricia Grimshaw and Hannah Loney

Just as the intersections of gender, race and class shaped the possibilities for Cooper and Molisa to position themselves as national leaders, these intersections continued to complicate their futures in regional and international organizing. Though their particular concerns were grounded in their respective peoples and communities, the tenor of their activism resonated across the Pacific world and highlights some of the ways in which the local concerns of indigenous groups in the Pacific intersected with broader movements for women's rights.

Whina Cooper and the Maori Women's Welfare League

Whina Cooper began her career as a pan-Maori leader when, in the early 1950s, she became involved in Maori women's concerns on a national level. In September 1951 she received an invitation to attend the conference of welfare committees in Wellington. This gathering was part of a recognition that Maori needed to prepare themselves for the rapidly changing economic and social conditions brought about by the increased number of Maori choosing to move to urban areas in the wake of World War II. For the first time, Maori women pushed for a place in discussion and action on these processes. Around ninety women delegates from welfare organizations across the country attended the conference. The most significant outcome was the establishment of the Maori Women's Welfare League: *Te Ropu Wahine Maori Toko I te Ora*, the first such Maori organization at a national level. Their standing as Maori women was central to their identity as a collective, and it informed their approach to welfare issues.[23] The government, as the historian Barbara Brookes pointed out, was also keen to see a grassroots group of Maori with whom it could confer.[24] According to Princess Te Puea Herangi, the first Patroness, the League 'arose out of a desire on the part of Maori women throughout New Zealand for an organization that would essentially be theirs – a potent force which could play an integral part in facilitating positive outcomes for Maori people through enabling and empowering Maori women a whanau [in the family]'.[25] Cooper played a dominant part in discussions from the onset, and it was perhaps no surprise that she was nominated for the post of Dominion president. Cooper accepted, though she later commented: 'Why? Why did they pick me? I didn't go to university. When they picked me I cried. . . . I thanked everybody that voted for me. . . . I was really overwhelmed – and humbled.'[26]

The aims of the League were underpinned by the women's desire for action on Maori disadvantage and discrimination and informed by a willingness to cooperate with Pakeha women in the pursuit of the well-being of women and children. It aimed to promote fellowship and understanding between Maori and European women and cooperation with other women's organizations, state departments and local bodies in the furtherance of core objects:

> . . . to take an active interest in all matters pertaining to the health and general wellbeing of women and children of the Maori race; to provide opportunities for discussion and instruction in the proper care and feeding of babies,

the preparation of meals, the care and maintenance of the home, and in the benefits to be derived from fresh air and sunshine; to encourage the making of vegetable and flower gardens, the growing of fruit trees, shrubs and plants, and the creation generally of attractive home conditions; to encourage young mothers to learn knitting and dressmaking, needlecraft and kindred arts and crafts, and to assist and instruct them in the proper clothing of their children.[27]

From a contemporary perspective, this reform agenda might seem rather modest. However, in light of the conditions of extreme poverty and ill-health faced by many Maori women in urban areas, leading Maori women viewed these objects as practical steps toward enhancing the well-being of Maori women and their families.[28]

The gender-specific character of the League required justification in the wider Maori community. One of Cooper's first responsibilities as League President was to travel around the country to publicize the League and to create a network of branches. She encountered criticism not only for speaking in districts where she lacked tribal ties but also for perceptions that she was 'taking a man's role' by speaking in public.[29] Cooper was able to transcend cultural assumptions by marshalling the force of her robust personality in face-to-face confrontations to challenge male Maori's assumptions of dominance. Merimeri Penfold, a Maori educator who was present at the first conference, noted Cooper's shrewdness in her decision to set up branches around the country and her eagerness to speak to men as well as women. The League's concerns were about Maori-based, rather than gender-based, social inequality. Cooper persuaded her audiences: 'This is a treasure I bring before you. Consider where our people are. We need an organization that will assist families.'[30]

The League's secretary, Mira Szaszy, remembered this time as 'a marvellous experience' and called Cooper herself 'dynamic'. 'She was so full of physical and mental energy, and she put it all into those early stages of the organization of the League,' Szaszy later recalled. 'She held back nothing in order to give the League her full attention.'[31] The early League member, Te Arahori Potaka, reflected:

> The most important part about the League, from the very beginning, was the way Whina Cooper got the housing going, organised herself up in Auckland to make a general survey of the way people lived. . . . That was the first time that nice houses came up for our people.[32]

The League, according to one Maori writer in 1954, became an organization that was 'well-known to Maori and European alike for its vigour in attacking the social welfare problems of Maori' but also teaching 'the secrets of certain arts and crafts works which would otherwise be lost to us with the passing of an older generation'.[33]

Beyond her capacity to unite Maori in a national objective, Cooper also oversaw the entry of the League and the introduction of Maori concerns into the regional organization, the Pan-Pacific Women's Association. Its principal historian, Fiona

Paisley, identifies the Pan-Pacific Women's Association as 'one of the leading international women's social movements of the twentieth century'.[34] Formed out of the Pan-Pacific Women's Conference that was held in Honolulu in August 1928, the Pan-Pacific Women's Association (which was renamed the Pan-Pacific and South East Asia Women's Association in 1955) sought to unite women across the countries of the Pacific rim and to promote peace through understanding and friendship.[35] The organization was driven primarily by the efforts of a core group of white women from the United States, Australia and New Zealand, many of whom were already active in international women's organizations based in Europe.[36] After World War II, some Association members became conscious of the implied racism of the patronizing practice of white women representing indigenous women. Resistance to the white settler dominance of the organization was illustrated at the 1952 meeting, when a Maori delegate, Victoria Bennett, queried the absence of Australian Aboriginal women and rejected as inadequate a white Australian delegate's promise that modern Australians were forging 'a new-world civilization drawing on non-western cultures for its vibrancy'.[37] Samoan and Maori women called for national indigenous representation separate from white women.

It was no accident that a representative from the Maori Women's Welfare League was welcomed into the Association at this time. Mira Szaszy attended the Association's conferences as a New Zealand delegate in 1952 and 1955 when she was working closely alongside Cooper for the League, facilitating Cooper's connection with international women's organizations.[38] Cooper was instrumental in extending her advocacy for Maori women beyond the shores of New Zealand and into this prominent Pacific network, while sustaining its independent voice internally. In her final presidential report to the Maori Women's Welfare League at its sixth annual conference April 1957, Cooper carefully positioned the League as entrenched in Maori concerns that were not determined from the outside: 'Let us remember as a voluntary body we spring from the hearts, minds and needs of the Maori people as well as Maori women today,' she said. 'Our existence is not dictated to by any outside organization. We exist because of a need among our people, because they need such an organization as ours.' Yet she also stressed that the League was part of a wider women's movement that transcended national borders to extend into the Pacific region: 'We are part of the wider movement of the National Council of Women. We are also part of the Pan-Pacific Movement of Women. We have a standing in the world no other Maori organization has ever achieved.' Cooper's experience in the Pan-Pacific Association had given her insight into the greater efficacy Maori could gain by working with non-Maori reformers. She concluded: 'Should we not try to establish our real independence, linking ourselves more closely with the women's organizations as an autonomous body among our Pakeha sisters?'[39]

The Pacific historian, Patricia O'Brien, commented that Whina Cooper's activism 'was not aimed at rights for Maori women over that of Maori men, but rather for justice along racial lines between Indigenous Maori and the Pakeha [European] majority'. Many anticolonial women activists around the region 'did not perceive the main barrier to social equity to be oppression of all women by men, but the oppression of racial minorities'.[40] We suggest, however, that the position of Cooper was somewhat more complex. She was well aware that Maori women needed to find ways to assert their right to be heard within a male-dominated Maori context, while avoiding outright conflict with Maori conservatives. On the other hand, while working cooperatively with white women's organizations, she was mindful that Maori women needed to resist their domination for fear the issue of Pakeha discrimination against Maori people might become buried.

From 1958 onward, Cooper remained an active League member around the Auckland district. Having been appointed a Member of the Order of the British Empire for services to the Maori people in the 1953 Coronation Honours,[41] Cooper's contributions to Maori welfare and culture were again recognized in 1974 during the Queen's Birthday Honours with the award of Commander of The Order of the British Empire.[42] With the 1975 land march that brought the almost 80-year-old Cooper wide national recognition, she acted perhaps for the first time as a leader of both Maori and Pakeha. Her participation stemmed from the invitation of radical Maori activists to lead a campaign against further alienation of Maori land. Cooper proposed the symbolic march to Wellington to highlight their cause, at the conclusion of which some 5,000 marchers presented a petition from 60,000 people to the Prime Minister, Bill Rowling. Cooper's biographer, Michael King, stated that the march 'created and released a flood of Pakeha goodwill towards Maori causes'.[43] Despite her race and gender, Cooper demonstrated the capacity to lead and to unite diverse sections of the population of New Zealand – Indigenous and Pakeha – while applying her conception of collaboration and collective action that marked her approach to women's activism.

Called 'Mother of the Nation' in her later years, Cooper's death in March 1994 at the age of 98 elicited an outpouring of tributes; an estimated 30,000 people attended her three-day *tangihanga* (process of mourning).[44] Cooper's experiences in the global women's movement had endowed her with added authority and influence in her homeland. Interestingly, the trajectory of Molisa's very different career as an activist, to which we now turn, would ultimately point in the same direction.

Grace Molisa and a new regional solidarity

Grace Mera Molisa's participation in the Fiji Women's Conference in 1975, where she heard Cooper praised for her leadership of the Maori land march, marked the beginning of her advocacy for women in Vanuatu and the islands and for Pacific Island women's participation in international women's forums. Molisa emerged as an activist not only during a time of intense anticolonial sentiment within the New Hebrides but also on the global stage, as a new wave of feminists moved from the relatively cautious engagements of immediate postwar reformers to highlight gender issues in a more forceful style. Given her family background and experiences of education, work and networking, Molisa was poised in 1975 to lead collective action in her home islands and with other indigenous women from across the Pacific region. Molisa was exceptional in her capacity to enter into networks of women beyond the local into the region and beyond, to participate in international forums. Molisa's activist engagements in anticolonialism, her organization of women locally and regionally and her promotion of Pacific women into the international arena followed swiftly upon each other.

At the University in Suva in the 1970s Molisa met a notable Fijian anticolonial activist, Vanessa Griffen, with whom she began advocating for women's equality and equal political rights and for a nuclear-free, independent and environmentally sustainable Pacific. This initial personal encounter is highly symbolic of the ways in which Molisa's standing as an educated Vanuatu woman of respected status enabled her to promote local and regional issues beyond national borders. Molisa, Griffen and their fellow activists instigated a number of regional forums to unify Pacific Island women and prepare them for future international participation. Their work began with the indigenous-led First Regional Pacific Women's Conference in Suva. The United Nation's declaration of 1975 as International Women's Year offered an excellent opportunity for such a convention.[45] Indigenous representatives from Papua New Guinea, New Zealand, Australia, Vanuatu and elsewhere in the region engaged with an agenda intentionally broadened beyond 'women's issues', to enable delegates to bring to the platform the particular concerns of their island nations and of the region.[46] Though a vastly more expanded opportunity for outreach than Cooper herself had enjoyed, the Pacific Islanders continued Cooper's particular emphasis on collective strength. According to Griffen, this Suva gathering was the first in which Pacific women came together specifically 'to talk about *themselves* and look at the institutions which defined women: the family and traditional culture, religion, education, the media, the law, and politics'.[47] She noted that the conference, and the individual women who attended, coalesced around 'what is emerging as a Pacific women's consciousness and participation in the women's movement'.[48] This conference initiated a unified, regional women's movement driven by local Pacific women themselves, unlike the white middle-class leadership in the Pan-Pacific Women's Association. Molisa's position at the forefront of the movement foreshadowed the vision and ambition she amply demonstrated in the next decades.

Once Griffen, Molisa and other Pacific Island leaders appreciated that individual voices from island groups were inadequate, they sought to unify delegates specifically around two key issues that were uniquely important to the Pacific: French nuclear testing and independence for territories. Molisa noted of the 1975 conference that it presented an opportunity for women from the French Territories to meet, saying, 'This is the first time that I am able to hear anything from a Tahitian.'[49] She stressed, however, that Pacific Island women did not yet have a united voice because those 'who understand us are so few, and our people who are the masses are so much for us to cope with that the information has not been channeled back into the grass-roots effectively'.[50] In contrast to Cooper's emphasis on land rights in the context of white settler dominance, a key focus in the meeting was self-governance, a result of the different stages and forms of colonialism that each group confronted: Fiji itself won its independence from Britain the year of this meeting. Molisa noted the particular repression of ni-Vanuatu, still in 1975 living under colonial rule, and the resultant lack of educational opportunities for indigenous people.

Pacific Island women were aware in the mid-1970s, according to Griffen, that 'something related to women was going on in the world, but *what* it was, was hazy or misconceived'.[51] Some Pacific women's sense that it was a Western movement created tension between them and the international women's movement. Notwithstanding, Molisa and her colleagues seized the opportunity to engage with women across the globe by hurriedly finding a way to attend the first UN-sponsored World Conference on Women held that year in Mexico City, an event that proved to be inspirational for the Pacific delegates as for high numbers of the Third World women in attendance.[52] She attended the Non-Government Organization Forum that ran parallel to the Mexico conference and spoke at the Women's Tribune Meeting. She also participated in the Nuclear Free Pacific team alongside other prominent independence and indigenous rights activists, such as Déwé Gorodé from New Caledonia, Tea Hirshon from Tahiti and Hilda Halkyard-Harawira from New Zealand.[53]

While the new Pacific leaders promoted ordinary women to collaborate on common issues, uniting women on awareness of gender discrimination was not their key aim. Dividing women's interests from those of men would have been a barrier to the involvement of many village women. When she spoke at the first conference of Vanuatuan women on the island of Efate in 1978, when the anticolonial movement was at its height, Molisa declared firmly that activist women did not aim to pit themselves against Pacific men. She distanced herself explicitly from the radical wing of the new Western women's movement, calling it a 'European disease'. 'Hundreds of our women slave everyday for white women. They cook, clean, sweep, and wash shit everyday for crumbs from European women.' European women wanted to be liberated to go out to work like men, whereas women of Vanuatu already had more than enough to do. Moreover, their own key concerns, which were brought about by the destructive impacts of colonization, affected men also. 'Our societies are people oriented so we care for one another,' she said.[54]

To press the women's agenda forward at home, in May 1980 Molisa and Hilda Lini, wife of the inaugural Prime Minister of Vanuatu, founded the Vanuatu National Council of Women at the First National Conference of Native Women. The organization aimed to provide a network for women's groups, especially for those from the rural areas.[55] Here, consistent with her earlier stated goal of a 'total liberation' rather than 'women's liberation', Molisa insisted that the National Council was *not* a feminist organization. Rather, she argued, it was a 'gathering of ni-Vanuatu women actively concerned about the exploitation, oppression, suppression, disadvantages, low status, lack of welfare and lack of well-being of the ni-Vanuatu woman and those in her charge'.[56] As a founding member of the Vanuatu Association of Women Graduates, Molisa was later praised because she 'encouraged members to work together with other women's organizations in Vanuatu', highlighting her sense of the importance of unity amongst women in a place as diverse as the Vanuatu nation.[57]

Alongside the urgent need to set up organizations at home, Molisa continued her energetic efforts to connect Vanuatuan women's organizations with Pacific-wide networks. Nor did she cease her advocacy for Pacific women's entry into the international public arena, drawing on the emphasis within the UN conferences on increasing women's empowerment and their representation in political decision-making processes. Through the 1980s and 1990s, Molisa's formidable national and international activism continued unabated. Because of the success of the 1975 conference in Mexico, the UN General Assembly went on to declare 1976 to 1985 the 'UN Decade for Women: Equality, Development and Gender' and organized another three World Conferences on Women: in Copenhagen in 1980, in Nairobi in 1985 and in Beijing in 1995. Molisa participated in Pacific Island women's plans and preparations for all of these conferences: within Pacific forums, her participation and influence continued to be strong.

There can be no doubt that while Molisa's contact with other Pacific and international women's activists prompted a fledgling feminist consciousness, the process was hastened by experiences of gender discrimination in Vanuatu itself. Scholars such as Lissant Bolton, curator of the Pacific and Australian collections at the British Museum, have expressed the belief that Molisa was exposed to Western feminism when she studied in Fiji.[58] Molisa herself claimed that it was her practical experiences in Port Vila from independence onward that shaped her eventual stance on gender inequality. 'Before then, as far as I was concerned, people were people and in every community and every family men and women worked together,' she later wrote.[59] In 1980, Molisa aligned herself with the new Vanuatuan male leaders – her former compatriots in the independence movement – when she accepted the position of political advisor and secretary to the Prime Minister, the socialist Anglican priest, Father Walter Lini. Lini was head of the Vanua'aku Pati that he had formed during the independence struggle.[60] Molisa was disappointed at the outset when the party's women's auxiliary, the Vanua'aku Pati Women, endorsed the election of an all-male assembly. In 1984 she was still pleading: 'Women and men were united in the bid for independence,' and as a result, women along with men 'had equal right to exercise the power of their vote to determine Vanuatu's government system'.[61] When the government published a book on the new nation, Molisa challenged the male leaders to revise their gendered cultural expectations. Women in traditional society carried the world on their shoulders, she declared, while disunity amongst Vanuatuan women resulted from their continuing social, economic and political oppression: 'All women bear the same basic burdens, but when one differs from the rule, succeeds more easily, no opportunity is missed to pull her back into line; every possible fault is found to cut her down to size and any support for her may only begin to appear when all these attempts have failed.'[62]

Unlike the case of Cooper, Molisa became explicit about her emerging identification of Vanuatuan men's reluctance to treat women as equals, as Margaret Jolly has traced through Molisa's creative writing, including her poetry.[63] According to Molisa's husband, the Honourable Sela Molisa, she 'would wake up in the early hours of the morning to write and was always encouraging others to write'.[64] Molisa produced much of her poetry in the first decade after independence, becoming the first Vanuatuan woman to publish a book, with the appearance in 1980 of *Black Stone*, a collection of poetry.[65] In it, she voiced serious misgivings about the absence of genuine power sharing, pointing in particular to the gendered implications of Lini's call for the 'The Melanesian Way'. This doctrine was based on the ideas of Bernard Narokobi, the Papua New Guinean politician and jurist, who promoted pan-Melanesian identity and solidarity.[66] Lini and his male colleagues emphasized the notion of *kastom*, or traditional practices to the disadvantage of women, Molisa maintained, a charge she had earlier directed at white colonists. Her poems highlighted the disjuncture between an inherently masculinist national project and the traditional social, cultural and political systems of Melanesia, drawing a strong connection between the racism of colonialism and the enduring sexism implicit within postindependent Vanuatu society. In a poignant poem, Molisa named the oppression still experienced by ni-Vanuatu women: 'Vanuatu Womenfolk/half the population/ remain colonized/by the Free men/of Vanuatu.'[67] In 1990 Molisa found herself dismissed from her position as a political secretary because, some argued, she refused to pander to Lini's style of leadership.[68] In 1997 she founded the pressure group, Vanuatu Women in Politics, to train women to participate effectively in political parties, believing that without effective mentoring, women's entry into political office would continue to be problematic. She continued her work up until the time of her final illness and death in January 2002, just before her 56th birthday.

However many battles Molisa waged, her admirers were legion. The Prime Minister, Edward Natapei, referred to her as 'Amazing Grace': she was 'one of those rare and exceptional warriors that are hard to find', and her deeds would 'surely be remembered by Pacific generations and generations to come', he said.[69] Hundreds of women from Pacific and international women's organizations paid warm tributes to her work and vital presence. Fanaura Kingstone, the second woman elected to the Cook Islands parliament, wrote that Pacific women would miss 'the ever smiling and laughing Grace'.[70] Molisa had moved at the end from recognition within her own community to respect and affection from a wider network of indigenous and non-indigenous women activists. As with Cooper, Molisa's entanglements with women of many other countries and backgrounds had in turn become part of a local acceptance and, eventually, the celebration of her achievements.

Conclusion: forging new alliances

Dame Whina Cooper and Grace Mera Molisa forged new alliances in the Pacific by organizing their countrywomen into pressure groups and aligning them internationally in search of improved life chances for women, their families and their communities. Responding to de Haan's regret about the neglect in histories of the global women's movement of those activists whose agendas were multi-faceted, we have suggested a vital place for two women's rights advocates whose reform agendas included wider pressing concerns of their peoples. Cooper and Molisa, the former in the context of the relatively cautious style of feminism of the international

176 Patricia Grimshaw and Hannah Loney

women's movement in the 1950s and 1960s, and the latter, the more forceful and energetic feminism of the 1970s, 1980s and 1990s, contributed constructively to the international women's movement through their rhetoric, example and legacy. Born into chiefly families and educated beyond most of their peers, Cooper and Molisa were cognizant of the multiple disadvantages of indigenous communities of their region. They entered international spheres of influence on their own terms, distinct from those of most Western feminists whose preoccupations centred specifically on so-called women's issues. A study of the two women's careers enriches our understanding of the specificities of structural injustice in their home countries and of the diverse strategies that they, like other indigenous Pacific women, devised to overturn it.

Fully aware of gender disadvantages within their own communities, Cooper and Molisa nevertheless shifted their speaking positions on the internal politics of gender according to the pressures of other issues and of particular audiences. At times they defended indigenous men as similarly oppressed by colonialism, while at other times they made clear by deed or word their rejection of the men's assumption of dominance. Cooper in the 1950s sought to convince Maori men of the complementarity of women's social and political contributions and involve the men in the struggle to better conditions for Maori women and children. Twenty years later, during the independence struggle, Molisa fiercely defended the common interests of Vanuatuan women and men, yet became a critic of men's dominance once the fight was won and when she herself experienced the force of gendered antagonism. By the 1990s, while still fighting the legacy of colonial impositions, she adopted a vocabulary from international feminism through which to name gender oppression and to find strategies to empower women politically.

Cooper and Molisa's entry into networks of women within local sites, and beyond into Pacific and international women's organizations, enhanced their influence abroad and their legitimacy back home. What they brought to the international movement were the wider concerns of impoverished and previously subjected communities. The absence of such activists as Cooper and Molisa from accounts of women's international activism illustrates not these women's irrelevance but rather the fortunate social position from which many white First World feminists speak. Cooper and Molisa, like so many other activists of the Pacific region, pursued broad and generous agendas that should render them notable within histories of the global women's movement.

Notes

1 This chapter was a component of a paper delivered at the IFRWH conference in Sheffield in August 2013. We thank the audience for their comments, and we also thank the anonymous referees and the editors of this volume for their suggestions for revision. The research of Hannah Loney was funded by the Australian Research Council Linkage Grant, 'Minutes of Evidence'.
2 Hana Jackson, 'New Zealand', in Vanessa Griffen, ed., *Women Speak Out: A Report of the Pacific Women's Conference,* 27 October–2 November, Suva, Fiji: Fiji Times, 1976, p. 80.

For details of the conference in Fiji, see: Nicole George, *Situating Women: Gender Politics and Circumstances in Fiji,* Canberra, ANU e-Press, 2012, Chapter 2.

3 Nellie Wong, 'Socialist Feminism: Our Bridge to Freedom', in Chandra Talpade Mohanty, Ann Russo and Lourdes Torres, eds., *Third World Women and the Politics of Feminism,* Bloomington: Indiana University Press, 1991, p. 288.

4 Leila J. Rupp, *Worlds of Women: The Making of an International Women's Movement,* Princeton: Princeton University Press, 1997. See also Francisca de Haan, Margaret Allen, June Purvis and Krassimira Daskalova, eds., *Women's Activism: Global Perspectives from the 1890s to the Present,* London: Routledge, 2012.

5 Chandra Talpade Mohanty, 'Introduction: Cartographies of Struggle. Third World Women and the Politics of Feminism', in C. T. Mohanty, A. Russo and L. Torres, eds., *Third World Women and the Politics of Feminism,* Bloomington: Indiana University Press, 1991, p. 11.

6 Kumari Jayawardena, *Feminism and Nationalism in the Third World,* London: Zed Press, 1986; Chandra Talpade Mohanty, 'Under Western Eyes', in Mohanty, Russo and Torres, eds.,, *Third World Women and the Politics of Feminism,* 51–80; Antoinette Burton, *Burdens of History: British Feminists, Indian Women, and Imperial Culture, 1865–1915,* Chapel Hill: University of North Carolina Press, 1994; Clare Midgley, *Feminism and Empire: Women Activists in Imperial Britain, 1790–1865,* London: Routledge, 2007. See also M. E. Hawkesworth, *Globalization and Feminist Activism,* Lanham: Rowman and Littlefield, 2006; Amrita Basu, *The Challenge of Local Feminisms: Women's Movements in Global Perspective,* Boulder: Westview Press, 1995; Peggy Antrobus, *The Global Women's Movement: Origins, Issues and Strategies,* London: Zed Books, 2004; Bonnie Smith, *Global Feminisms Since 1945,* London and New York: Routledge, 2000; and Kimberly Jensen and Erika A. Kuhlman, eds., *Women and Transnational Activism in Historical Perspective,* Dordrecht: Republic of Letters, 2010.

7 Sylvanna M. Falcón and Jennifer C. Nash, 'Shifting analytics and linking theories: A conversation about the "Meaning-Making" of intersectionality and transnational feminism', *Women's Studies International Forum,* 50, 2015, 9.

8 Francisca de Haan, 'Eugénie Cotton, Pak Chong-Ae, and Claudia Jones: Rethinking transnational feminism and international politics', *Journal of Women's History,* 25:4, 2013, 182.

9 Margaret Jolly, 'The Politics of Difference: Feminism, Colonialism and Decolonisation in Vanuatu', in Gillian Bottomley, Marie de Lepervanche and Jeannie Martin, eds., *Intersexions: Gender/Class/Culture/Ethnicity,* Sydney: Allen and Unwin, 1991, pp. 52–74; Margaret Jolly and Martha Macintyre, eds., *Family and Gender in the Pacific: Domestic Contradictions and the Colonial Impact,* Cambridge: Cambridge University Press, 1989.

10 Caroline Ralston, 'The study of women in the pacific', *The Contemporary Pacific,* 4:1, Spring 1992, 165.

11 Fiona Paisley, *Glamour in the Pacific: Cultural Internationalism and Race Politics in the Women's Pan-Pacific,* Honolulu: University of Hawai'i Press, 2009; Angela Woollacott, 'Inventing Commonwealth and Pan-Pacific Feminisms: Australian Women's Internationalist Activism in the 1920s-30s', in Mrinalini Sinha, Donna Guy and Angela Woollacott, eds., *Feminisms and Internationalism,* Oxford: Blackwell Publishers Ltd, 1999, pp. 81–104; Marilyn Lake, *Getting Equal: The History of Australian Feminism,* St Leonards, NSW: Allen and Unwin, 1999.

12 De Haan, 'Eugénie Cotton', 183.

13 For biographical studies see: Michael King, *Whina: A Biography of Whina* Cooper, Auckland: Penguin Books, 1983; Selina Tusitala Marsh, 'Black Stone Poetry: Vanuatu's Grace Mera Molisa', *Cordite Scholarly: Cordite Poetry Review,* 45, February 2014.

14 See Patricia Grimshaw, 'Maori Agriculturalists and Aboriginal Hunter Gatherers: Women and Colonial Displacement in Nineteenth Century Southeastern Australia and Aotearoa/New Zealand', in R. R. Pierson and N. Chaudhuri, eds., *Nation, Empire, Colony: Historicizing Gender and Race,* Bloomington, IN: University of Indiana Press, 1998, pp. 21–40.

15 See James Belich, *Making Peoples: A History of White New Zealanders: From Polynesian Settlement to the End of the Nineteenth Century*, Auckland: Penguin Press, 1996. For a comparative study of colonial New Zealand, Australia and South Africa, see Julie Evans, Patricia Grimshaw, David Philips and Shurlee Swain, *Equal Subjects, Unequal Rights: Indigenous Peoples in British Settler Societies*, Manchester: Manchester University Press, 2003.

16 See Jeremy MacClancy, *To Kill a Bird with Two Stones: A Short History of Vanuatu*, Vila: Vanuatu Cultural Centre Publication 1, 2002.

17 Tony Ballantyne, *Entanglements of Empire: Missionaries, Maori, and the Question of the Body*, Durham: Duke University Press, 2014.

18 King, *Whina*, pp. 14, 21.

19 Ibid., pp. 11–17.

20 Grace Mera Molisa, 'Author, Poet, Publisher, Educator: "I have been a groundbreaker for my island, women and Vanuatu"', in Shirley Randell, ed., *Ni-Vanuatu Role Models*, Port Vila: Blackstone, 2002, p. 39.

21 Ibid.

22 Molisa, 'Author, Poet, Publisher, Educator', in S. Randell, ed., *Ni-Vanuatu Role Models*, Vanuatu: Blackstone Publishing, 2002, pp. 38–39.

23 Aroha Harris and Mary Jane Logan McCallum, '"Assaulting the Ears of Government": The Indian Homemakers' Claims and the Maori Women's Welfare League in Their Formative Years', in Carol Williams, ed., *Indigenous Women and Work: From Labor to Activism*, Urbana, Chicago and Springfield: University of Illinois Press, 2012, p. 225.

24 See Barbara Brookes and Patricia Grimshaw, 'Maori and Aboriginal Women's Activism in a Decade of Assimilation: New Zealand and Victoria, Australia, in the 1950s', in Margaret Allen and R. K. Dhawan, eds., *Intersections: Gender, Race and Ethnicity in Australasian Studies*, New Delhi: Prestige Books, 2007, pp. 10–22.

25 Te Puea Herangi CBE, First Patroness, '"Ko te puawaitanga o nga moemoea, me whakamahi. Dreams become reality, when we take action"', *Te Ropu Wahine Maori Toko I te Ora. Maori Women's Welfare League*. Online: www.mwwl.org.nz/maori-womens-welfare-league-history/

26 Whina Cooper, interviewed by Areta Koopu in Panguru on 29 June 1993, 'Te tīmatanga tātau, Te Rōpū Wāhine Māori Toko i te Ora', in Anna Rogers and Mīria Simpson, eds., *Early Stories from Founding Members of the Maori Welfare League as told to Dame Mira Szaszy*, Wellington: The League: Bridget Williams Books, 1993, p. 18.

27 King, *Whina*, pp. 170–171.

28 See Brookes and Grimshaw, 'Maori and Aboriginal Women's Activism in a Decade of Assimilation', in Allen and Dhawan, eds., *Intersections*.

29 King, *Whina*, p. 185.

30 Merimeri Penfold, in Deborah Shepard, ed., *Her Life's Work: Conversations with Five New Zealand Women*, Auckland: Auckland University Press, 2013, p. 108.

31 Mira Szaszy, interviewed in Maori by Anne Delamere and in English by Areta Koopu at the Maori Women's Welfare League headquarters in Wellington on 9 July 1991, in Roger and Simpson, eds., *Early Stories*, p. 222.

32 Te Arahori Potaka, interviewed in Whanganui on 30 July 1991, in Roger and Simpson, eds., *Early Stories*, p. 145.

33 J. C. Sturm, 'The maori women's welfare league', *Te Ao Hou: The New World Spring*, 9, Spring 1954, 8.

34 Fiona Paisley, 'A Geneva in the Pacific: Reflecting on the First Three Decades of the Pan-Pacific and South East Asia Women's Association (PPSEAWA)', *Women and Social Movements, International: 1840 to Present*. Online: http://wasi.alexanderstreet.com/help/view/a_geneva_in_the_pacific_reflecting_on_the_first_three_decades_of_the_panpacific_and_south_east_asia_womens_association_ppseawa

35 Pan-Pacific Union, *Women of the Pacific: Being a Record of the Proceedings of the First Pan-Pacific Women's Conference*, Honolulu: Pan-Pacific Union, 1928.

36 Paisley, *Glamour in the Pacific*.

37 Fiona Paisley, 'Glamour in the Pacific: Cultural internationalism and maori politics at pan-pacific women's conferences in the 1950s', *Pacific Studies* 29, ½, 2007, 72–73.

Women's organizing in the Pacific region 179

38 King, *Whina,* pp. 183–184.

39 Ibid., pp. 269–270.

40 Patricia O'Brien, 'Gender', in David Armitage and Alison Bashford, eds., *Pacific Histories: Ocean, Land, People,* New York: Palgrave Macmillan, 2014, p. 292.

41 *The London Gazette,* supplement no. 39866, 26 May 1953, p. 3005

42 *The London Gazette,* supplement no. 46312, 7 June 1974, p. 6830.

43 King, *Whina,* p. 228.

44 H. Ayrton, 'Dame Whina Names Her Heir', *New Zealand Herald,* 3 March 1994, section 1, p. 1.

45 Claire Slatter, 'Foreword', in Griffen, ed., *Women Speak Out,* p. iii.

46 Ibid., p. iv.

47 Vanessa Griffen, 'All It Requires Is Ourselves', in Robin Morgan, ed., *Sisterhood Is Global. The International Women's Movement Anthology,* Harmondsworth: Penguin Books, 1985, p. 522.

48 Ibid.

49 Grace Mera, 'New Hebrides', in V. Griffen, ed., *Women Speak Out: A Report of the Pacific Women's Conference, October 27–November 2,* Suva, Fiji: Fiji Times, 1976, p. 22.

50 Ibid., p. 23.

51 Griffen, 'All It Requires is Ourselves', p. 521.

52 Marilyn Lake, Katie Holmes and Patricia Grimshaw, 'Introduction', in Patricia Grimshaw, Katie Holmes and Marilyn Lake, eds., *Women's Rights and Human Rights: International Historical Perspectives,* Hampshire and New York: Palgrave, 2001, p. xix.

53 George, *Situating Women,* p. 58.

54 Grace Mera Molisa, 'The Status of Women in Traditional Society in Church and in Politics'. Paper presented at the First National Conference of Vanuaaku Women, Malarua Centre, North Efate, New Hebrides, 28 May–3 June 1978.

55 Molisa, 'The Status of Women in Traditional Society in Church and in Politics'.

56 Grace Mera Molisa, 'The Vanuatu National Council of Women', in UNICEF, ed., *A Situation Analysis of Children and Women in Vanuatu,* Port Vila: UNICEF: Vanuatu Government, 1991, p. 68.

57 Jeanette Bolenger, President, VAWG, Vanuatu, 'Grace Mera Molisa, Foundation Member of VAWG', in Shirley Randell, ed., *Pacific Creative Writing in Memory of Grace Mera Molisa,* Port Vila, Vanuatu: Blackstone Publishing, 2002, p. 39.

58 Lissant Bolton, *Unfolding the Moon: Enacting Women's Kastom in Vanuatu,* Honolulu: University of Hawai'i Press, 2003, p. 58.

59 Molisa, 'Author, Poet, Publisher, Educator', in *Ni-Vanuatu Role Models,* p. 39.

60 MacClancy, *To Kill a Bird with Two Stones.*

61 Grace Molisa, 'Vanuatu Women's Development Since Independence', in *Women in Development in the South Pacific, Barriers and Opportunities. Papers presented at a conference held in Vanuatu from 11 to 14 August 1984,* Canberra: Development Studies Centre, The Australian National University, 1985, p. 215.

62 Grace Mera Molisa, 'Women' in *Vanuatu: Twenti wan tingting long team blong independens,* Suva: Institute of Pacific Studies, 1980, p. 257.

63 See Jolly, 'The Politics of Difference: Feminism, Colonialism and Decolonisation in Vanuatu'.

64 Sela Molisa, 'Foreword', in *Pacific Creative Writing,* p. iv.

65 Grace Mera Molisa, *Black Stone: Poems,* Suva, Fiji: Mana Publications, 1983.

66 Bernard Narokobi, *The Melanesian Way,* ed. Henry Olela, Port Moresby: Institute of Papua New Guinea Studies, 1980.

67 Grace Mera Molisa, 'Colonised People', in Robert Borofsky, ed., *Remembrance of Pacific Pasts: An Invitation to Remake History,* Honolulu: University of Hawai'i Press, 2000, p. 333.

68 Norman Shackley, British Friends of Vanuatu Newsletter, *Tributes to Grace Mera Molisa.* Online: http://dlib.vanuatu.usp.ac.fj/library/Online/Vanuatu/Tributes.htm

69 Preface in Randell, ed., *Pacific Creative Writing,* p. xi.

70 Fanaura Kingstone, 'An Advocate for Women's Rights', in Randell, ed., *Pacific Creative Writing,* p. 30.

9

WOMEN AT THE INTERSECTION OF THE LOCAL AND THE GLOBAL IN SCHOOLS AND COMMUNITY HISTORY IN BRITAIN SINCE THE 1980s

Alison Twells

This final chapter moves beyond academic history to explore the relationship between women's history and the intersecting histories of the 'local' and the 'global' through the lens of schools and community history. Its focus is the 2007 bicentenary commemorations of the abolition of the transatlantic slave trade in the context of debates since the 1980s about the history that should be taught in British schools. The chapter argues that the practice of history in schools and community contexts continues to provide a fertile ground for the development of transnational perspectives in history. In addition, extra-academic history enables the exploration of what Pierre-Yves Saunier termed 'problem-oriented' history, which engages explicitly with issues of social inclusion, personal and political postimperial identities and the purpose of history.[1]

The interconnection between local and global history has been a neglected dimension in the scholarship concerning the debates over the school history curriculum in Britain since the 1980s, which has focused instead on the status of global in relation to national history. On the one hand, scholars have explored the resistance of successive Conservative governments to global history. The Thatcher governments of the 1980s, responsible for the centralising Education Reform Act (1988) which brought in the national curriculum for England and Wales, were especially antagonistic to the focus on peoples' and world history topics in the 'New History', the curricula developed by the Schools History Project to address the problem of the declining popularity of history in schools in the postwar years. Historians have discussed Prime Minister Margaret Thatcher's opposition to what she described as the 'shop steward syllabus' of the New History and the related argument of Education Secretary Keith Joseph that understanding of, and pride in, 'the development of the shared values which are a distinctive feature of British society and culture' could not, 'however expert the teaching, be conveyed through Roman history or American history or Caribbean history'.[2] They have also critiqued the claims of the more recent Conservative Education Secretary Michael Gove that history teaching is too influenced by 'post-colonial guilt' and his argument that a traditional chronological run through key landmarks in British political and constitutional history is essential to instil national identity and pride.[3] Robert Phillips's argument that the 'history debates' of the 1980s and 1990s were part of a 'hegemonic struggle over cultural transmission and heritage' forms the bedrock of such historical analyses, which interpret the Conservative agenda as symptomatic of anxiety about perceived challenges to a common British culture and identity wrought by globalisation, immigration and diversity.[4]

At the same time, historians of education have explored the scope for teachers to resist an overly British curriculum. Despite the focus on the nation, the revision of the national curriculum in 1994 to enable greater flexibility in the programmes of study led to 'unintended opportunities',[5] while more inclusive and multicultural agendas followed the Macpherson (1999) and Ajegbo (2007) reports and concerns about citizenship and social cohesion following the London bombings in July 2007.[6] As Nicola Sheldon argued, the first decade of the twenty-first century saw a discernible shift in school history away from the development of democracy and political rights in the context of the nation-state toward a focus on cultural diversity and the development of civil rights in a global context.[7]

However, the focus of historians on debates about the national-global relationships in school history has tended to obscure endeavours by teachers to link subnational local histories to global history, often through a focus on race and inclusion. In the 1980s and early 1990s, teachers and academic historians, many of whom were associated with History Workshop, countered the Conservative narrative with a proposal to engage critically with the history and legacies of British imperialism. Raphael Samuel, noting that '[m]uch of the animus directed against the "New" history seems to have more to do with its multi-culturalism than with the pedagogic issues ostensibly at stake,' argued for the reconstitution of British history not as inward looking but as connected to the world.[8] In the words of Shula Marks, '[w]ays have to be found of unifying "history from above" with "history from below," structure with process and individual agency, empire with "nation". . . . It is not that we need to jettison the small and the local – but that we do need to see connections between things.'"[9] A focus on cultural diversity and its local and global roots and manifestations was posed less as a threat to national identity than a means of remaking it. It was necessary, as Rozina Visram argued in 1990, not 'because the "ethnic minorities" want to learn about Black heroes and Black heroines and so gain self esteem, or because in a culturally diverse society we want to teach tolerance and respect for minority cultures', but 'because it is part of British history'.[10] School history, then, was an early component of the imperial and transnational 'turns' in British historiography in the 1980s and 1990s, which sought to explore the ways in which the local, national and global were mutually constitutive.

There has been little discussion of gender and women's history in relation to this debate on the local and the global. This is curious, not least because feminist historians were at the forefront of challenges to a traditional model of elite British history,

182 Alison Twells

and their explorations of complex relationships of gender, nation, race and ethnicity were central to the development of the new imperial history.[11] This neglect mirrors the long-standing absence of women's and gender history both in discussions of the curriculum by historians and in the history curriculum as a whole. As Hilary Bourdillon argued, even in the context of progressive initiatives such as the innovative focus of the Schools Council History 13–16 Project on 'approaches to knowledge' rather than 'bodies of knowledge', which provided scope for teachers to raise questions about the invisibility of women in the historical record, there was little development of women's history. Beyond the introduction of a learning resource on suffragette Emily Wilding Davison's death under the king's racehorse at the 1913 Epsom Derby, the women who appeared in the syllabus were mainly the wives and mistresses who also featured in traditional political and constitutional history.[12] This situation continued into the 1990s, despite the publication of new women's history resources for schools inspired by official recognition of women's history by the schools inspectorate and the Final Report of the History Curriculum Working Group and the possibilities opened up by the focus of attainment targets on the nature of history and historical interpretation.[13] And indeed in the years that followed, despite some interesting work – see, for example, Christine Counsell's work on 'historical significance'[14]– women all but disappeared. 'Where are we?' asked Joanne Pearson in a 2012 study which revealed that women featured in the curriculum as the wives and daughters of Henry VIII and as suffragettes. As Pearson writes, while 'communities of history teachers across the UK have given considerable thought to the representation of race and ethnicity through our curricula, it is almost as if the debates surrounding gender in academic history departments over the past 40 years have never taken place'.[15]

This chapter adopts a case study approach to explore some of the opportunities for, and challenges involved in, integrating gender and women's history into the interlinked histories of the local and the global in school history. It takes as its starting point *Olaudah Equiano in Sheffield*,[16] an educational resource I cowrote in 2007 for the Development Education Centre (South Yorkshire) in collaboration with Burngreave Voices, a community history project in inner-city Sheffield in the north of England. Aimed at children in Key Stages 2 (7–11 years) and 3 (11–14 years), this resource was initially conceived as an accompaniment to a play written and performed in primary schools by Dead Earnest, a touring company which presents theatre with a social conscience. Both resource and play focused on the 1790 visit to Sheffield of the famous former slave and abolitionist Olaudah Equiano. *Olaudah Equiano in Sheffield* explored how benefits from transatlantic slavery extended beyond port towns to non-coastal areas, uncovering what Geoff Cubitt has termed the 'footprint of slavery' in an inland industrial locality.[17] It also contributed to the widespread critiques of the way in which official commemorations of the bicentenary of the abolition of the slave trade were over-focused on eminent white men, especially the Member of Parliament William Wilberforce.[18] Its focus, therefore, was firmly on local-global interconnections; as we shall see, it was also on the agency of local actors in shaping global developments.

While the 'global' encompasses more than the history of European empires and colonial slavery, the transnational flows of goods, capital, people and ideas central to the history of the transatlantic slave trade, plantation slavery and the abolition movement make these appropriate foci for a discussion of local-global interconnections. The slave trade was central to the process by which Britain became a global power in the seventeenth and eighteenth centuries. In economic terms, the trade included not just the goods and human cargo that followed the triangular journey but the general wealth creation through associated trade, customs revenue, the development of the navy and imperial wars and the general development of trade with the Americas. The transnational crossing of borders and boundaries also happened at the social and cultural levels in, for example, the emergence of new consumer goods in European markets, the transformation of the Caribbean, the Americas and West Africa through forced migration, the development of slave cultures and the connections, interactions and networking involved in the Abolition Movement.[19]

This chapter opens with a discussion of the different tributaries in schools and community history that gave rise to the focus on local-global connections in *Olaudah Equiano in Sheffield*. It then moves on to discuss the individual women who feature in the resource: local Sheffield abolitionist and philanthropist Mary Anne Rawson, former slave and autobiographer Mary Prince and Jamaican religious and political leader, Nanny of the Maroons. It highlights the value of biographical approaches as a 'useful tool for attracting and holding interest in large, complex historical processes',[20] as highlighted in the first chapter in this book. As Carla Freeman argued, the exploration of personal experiences of globalisation are 'a way of bringing home the lived realities of these mammoth forces'.[21] They also draw attention to human agency in terms of everyday choices, albeit within certain confines and sometimes very coercive structures.[22] Biographies further allow consideration of the emotional and the intimate, including what Burton and Ballantyne refer to as the 'intimacies of global imperial violence'.[23] A focus on biographies thus emphasises the limits of macrostructural accounts, enabling in some cases an undermining of what Freeman critiques as 'masculinist grand theories of globalisation that ignore gender as an analytical lens and local empirical studies of globalisation in which gender takes center stage'.[24] A focus on women's lives, as is shown here, also has the potential to disrupt any simplistic dichotomy between the local and the global. However, as is discussed, there are significant challenges involved in developing such a focus in schools and community history contexts, ranging from difficulties of piecing together women's lives from fragmentary traces within the colonial archive to issues of purpose, audience and the negotiation of public perceptions.

The second part of the chapter turns to explore the crossing of disciplinary boundaries that Merry Wiesner-Hanks argued is also part of the 'trans' project.[25] My focus here, however, is less about drawing on methodologies used outside the academic discipline of history than in acknowledging the differences in approach and aims between academic history and school and community history. School and community history are explicitly concerned with the potentially transformative

184 Alison Twells

impact of history, evident in the use of history in capacity building and wider community cohesion in a community regeneration context and in the understanding of history in schools as a means of ethical and moral education, of 'creating tolerant, empathetic, responsible and questioning citizens'.[26] Addressing Tim Hitchcock's recent argument that there is in Britain 'a "crisis" in the humanities' which 'lies in how we have our public debates, rather than in their content',[27] I argue that we need to do more than launch our work into the public domain. Following Clare Anderson's proposal for 'destabilising' our focus on official archives 'as the only starting point for writing history' and engaging instead with 'the alternative knowledges and cultural practices of families and communities',[28] I argue that academic historians of the transnational might learn from this focus on wider questions about identity, inclusion and the purpose of history.

Inclusive and inter-connected histories: the myth of the local?

Olaudah Equiano in Sheffield was produced through collaboration with two Sheffield-based organisations, both of which place(d) a strong emphasis on the relationship of the local to the global. First, the Development Education Centre (South Yorkshire) is part of a network of national and international organisations which focuses on the development of a global curriculum in schools. Development Education promotes an approach to teaching and learning which combines an exploration of the unequal yet interdependent economic and cultural relationships between the Global North and South with a Freire-inspired pedagogy in which student-centred, enquiry-based active learning is central to the development of active citizenship.[29]

Since its emergence in the 1960s and 1970s, Development Education has seen changing fortunes in relation to school history in Britain. In the 1970s and 1980s, the network of Development Education Centres (DECs) in Britain joined with local authorities in the development and promotion of antiracist teaching materials. The emphasis was on the development of skills through which to handle information critically alongside a focus on 'histories' rather than a Great Tradition.[30] In the late 1980s and 1990s, practitioners found themselves in profound contestation with supporters of the new national curriculum in terms of approach and content, emphasising the value of experiential learning and empathy and arguing that British history could not be understood apart from global developments. This is made explicit in the title of *The Empire in South Yorkshire*, the 1992 publication by the DEC in Sheffield which explored the industrial revolution in global context and was a forerunner of *Olaudah Equiano in Sheffield*.[31] During the 1990s and 2000s, as both global education and active learning became more mainstream, the DEC in South Yorkshire worked with schools across the region to integrate global themes into the curriculum and to support the development of inclusive histories which recognise the diverse heritage of children.[32] *Olaudah Equiano in Sheffield* addressed the above issues while also attempting to build the confidence of teachers in dealing with difficult and emotive subjects such as the slave trade and abolition.[33]

The second organisation which gave rise to the resource is Burngreave Voices (2004–2007), a community history project in a deprived inner city area of north Sheffield. Community history emerged in Britain in the years surrounding the millennium to become a hugely popular form of public history. Projects involve members of a community, geographical or otherwise, usually untrained as historians, in producing history.[34] The movement has been hugely enabled by funding streams such as the Heritage Lottery Fund and UK and European regeneration initiatives which identified community history groups as a means of building capacity for wider regeneration initiatives.[35] In effect, such funding has extended the practice of local history beyond the largely middle-class Local History Society into many working-class postindustrial neighbourhoods. Minority ethnic groups are under-represented but by no means absent.

Burngreave Voices, funded jointly by New Deal for Communities, a regeneration programme introduced by the Labour government in 1998, and Museums Sheffield developed a number of initiatives to involve members of Burngreave's large immigrant population. While local history talks proved unsuccessful, Treasure Days, to which residents brought artefacts which represented an aspect of their life story, were much more popular. A short film about the corner shop – a minor institution in working-class neighbourhoods since the Industrial Revolution and a key component of Indian and Pakistani life in Britain since the 1970s – was created for a new display at Weston Park Museum in Sheffield. Oral history interviews were recorded and presented on the project website, which aimed to 'celebrate the history of the area and bring to life the stories of people living here'.[36]

The Development Education and community history contexts for the production of *Olaudah Equiano in Sheffield* complemented the imperative to provide school students with a means of understanding the contested nature of the abolition commemorations of 2007. We aimed to counter the 'abolition discourse' which represented the transatlantic slave trade as part of a very distant and disconnected past, even as 'other' to a Britain which placed abolition as central to its identity.[37] We explored the presence of slave traders and former slaves in the region through a focus on the papers of Benjamin Spencer, a merchant from Cannon Hall near Barnsley who was involved in the triangular trade in the mid-eighteenth century, and a painted portrait of the Earl of Chesterfield, his wife and children and an unnamed 'Nubian slave boy'. We brought together opponents of slavery from the Caribbean with national and local figures. James Montgomery, a Sheffield evangelical journalist and poet, left copious documentary evidence concerning his abolitionist and wider missionary activities. Joseph Mather, a filesmith and a street entertainer whose songs express his empathy for enslaved Africans alongside the exploited working people in early industrial Britain,[38] represented the Sheffield metalworkers who petitioned Parliament against the slave trade in 1789 and the working men who founded the Sheffield Society for Constitutional Information (a forerunner of the more famous London Corresponding Society, of which Equiano himself was a member).[39] Mary Anne Rawson was a celebrated abolitionist, a founding member of both the Sheffield Female Antislavery Society (1825) and the

Sheffield Society for the Universal Abolition of Slavery (1837), and she was memorialised in Benjamin Hayden's painting of the 1840 World Antislavery Convention. Rawson was one of three women in the resource, included alongside former slave and autobiographer, Mary Prince and Nanny, spiritual and political leader of the Jamaican Maroons. Their (brief) inclusion highlighted various challenges concerning the availability of sources and the interpretation and presentation of women's histories to a wider audience, as I now explore.

Mary Anne Rawson and female abolitionism

Mary Anne Rawson was at the centre of antislavery activity in Sheffield from the 1820s to the 1840s. With her mother Elizabeth Read, she was a founding member of the Sheffield Female Antislavery Society (1825) which emerged as part of the new campaign against plantation slavery from 1823. She was involved in the range of activities – fundraising, writing, the sugar boycott and later petitioning – that saw the creation of antislavery as a popular movement by the early 1830s.[40] After the Abolition of Slavery Act (1833) had ushered in the apprenticeship system whereby former slaves were required to work for their former owners for four more years, the movement was revived. Rawson raised funds for the Thompson Normal School in Jamaica and corresponded with Joseph Sturge and his sister Sophia during Sturge's investigation of the conditions of apprenticeship.[41] In 1837, she founded the Sheffield Ladies Association for the Universal Abolition of Slavery.

Abolition was part of Rawson's wider missionary–philanthropic activities, which included support for local Sunday schools and Bible and auxiliary missionary societies and later, the promotion of teetotalism and education of the poor. Philanthropic women have enjoyed a long visibility in history, academic and otherwise. Alongside queens, consorts and other female 'firsts', they were members of the original group of 'women worthies' who found their way into history books before the first wave of women's history writing in the 1980s. Such women were readily celebrated in the public domain, although it is their caring roles that are predominant over their campaigning and activism. See, for example, the image on the British five pound note of Elizabeth Fry reading the Bible to women and children, warders and other visitors in Newgate Gaol in 1816[42] and statues of Florence Nightingale as the 'Lady with the Lamp', which continue to adorn hospital grounds around the country. In school history, philanthropic ladies continued to be present in new women's history textbooks that emerged in the 1990s, where the celebratory narrative had progressed to address the issue of women's gradual movement into the public sphere.[43] They are also the most prominent women in early educational resources which sought to connect local and global history.[44] In the context of the decline of women's history in schools in the 2000s and 2010s, they are among the few women who are still reliably included in the history curriculum alongside the wives of Henry VIII and a handful of suffragettes.

In terms of academic history, a focus on local–global interconnections has informed a significant shift from understanding philanthropic women as do-gooders with free time due to servants and wealth,[45] to activists who lived 'lives of active engagement with what we would term politics and philanthropy'.[46] Historians have unpacked philanthropic women's position at the nexus of cultural webs to explore complexities of class, gender and empire. For example, Davidoff and Hall discussed the importance of philanthropy to the gender roles which gave shape to the new middle class, while Eileen Yeo explored the place of philanthropic practice in the creation of both middle-class women's public space and class identity, as working-class women were represented as in need of their civilising care.[47] The first sustained exploration of lady philanthropists as abolitionists came with Clare Midgley's *Women Against Slavery: the British Campaigns, 1780–1870*, which made visible hitherto hidden women as members of local ladies antislavery societies and placed them at the centre of the popular campaign of the 1820s and 1830s that saw the shift in focus from gradual to immediate emancipation.[48] Over subsequent years, in the context of the New Imperial History, historians examined the links between domestic philanthropy and missionary activity overseas. Antoinette Burton and Susan Thorne, for example, explored women's missionary philanthropic activities through the lens of 'imperial feminism' and 'missionary imperialism'.[49] My own monograph, *The Civilising Mission and the English Middle Class, 1792–1850*, focused on Sheffield to explore the significance of local (philanthropic) and global (missionary) reform agendas and practice in the making of the middle class. Mary Anne Rawson's family, the Reads of Wincobank Hall, were central to this new culture: nonconformist supporters of the radical Christian reform movement which aimed at domestic and global transformation.[50]

In the bicentenary year of 2007, women abolitionists occasionally featured in public history via local history booklets and BBC articles and websites.[51] For our resource, Rawson was an important inclusion – and an easy one given extensive source materials, including poems, pamphlets, abstention cards (to promote the boycott of slave-grown sugar) and letters to and from family members concerning their antislavery commitments. Her activities demonstrate that antislavery politics were never an all-male affair, centred only on Parliament and petitions. Indeed, we could have gone further in showing antislavery as promoted in kitchens (the boycott of sugar) and drawing rooms (antislavery tea services, sewing groups)[52] and as part of a pedagogy whereby evangelical mothers encouraged their children to write antislavery poems, to emphasise the place of abolitionism and other global concerns in the very fabric of women's daily lives.[53]

However, along with other antislavery women from her class and philanthropic background, Rawson nonetheless presents difficulties in terms of presentation to a wider audience. One issue concerns her imbrication in the kind of abolitionist standpoint that academics and the more radical commemorations in 2007 were keen to deconstruct. Brave, principled, energetic, pioneering and outspoken as they were, philanthropic women were also interfering, condescending and culturally imperialist in their desire to remake both slave and working-class cultures in a Christian middle-class image.[54] Even when recast less as individual Lady Bountifuls and more as members of a social and political movement, their abolitionism – as

188 Alison Twells

that of white middle-class men – was not straightforwardly about 'freedom'. Indeed, while a focus on women as principled campaigners and activists, battling against the conservativism of the male antislavery leadership, offers one way forward, their activities often worked against or at least compromised the agency of black and working-class abolitionists.[55] On reflection, this may have been an opportunity for us to link antislavery to contemporary practices, such as well-meaning Western volunteering in the 'Third World'.

Related to this are the attitudes that students bring to the school classroom, which have been shown to exert 'profound influences on their starting points . . . and on the version of the past . . . which [they] find most useable in understanding and explaining the present'.[56] Unlike the adventure in Equiano's account, the films featuring Wilberforce, the evidence of Mather's song writing and drunken performances and Nanny the freedom fighter, there is no equivalent popular cultural heroic narrative to attach to lady abolitionists, especially in a non-academic context where recovery and celebration are at least as important as critical evaluation. There may even be resistance to a focus on women and gender.[57] As Katherine Prior argued in relation to museums, academic and public historians often occupy 'two mutually incomprehending worlds' whereby the former understand little about the negotiation with public perceptions that are central to public history.[58] This raises important issues concerning audience and strategies for interpretation in the context of contemporary cultural attitudes that academic historians rarely negotiate.

The slave autobiographer and the Maroon leader

Neither Mary Prince nor Nanny of the Maroons had any Sheffield connection, but as we wanted to place our home-grown abolitionists – Montgomery, Rawson and Mather – in the context of the wider movement, we included Wilberforce to represent the national picture as well as the two women from the Caribbean to represent black peoples' resistance to slavery. They appear only fleetingly. The issue of extant sources (and confidence in using them) is pertinent here. While the twenty-five years since the publication of Barbara Bush's groundbreaking *Slave Women in Caribbean Society* has seen women's resistance to and survival and accommodation of slavery well documented by historians,[59] there remains little primary evidence relating to individual women's lives. As Clare Anderson wrote in relation to subaltern history in the Indian Ocean, 'Their foot*prints* are usually easy to see, but their foot*steps* are extraordinarily difficult to trace.'[60]

In terms of academic history, both *The History of Mary Prince* and the story of Nanny of the Maroons are hugely complex. Apart from the fact that no evidence remains of Prince's life after 1833, the year of the passage of the Abolition of Slavery Act, the narrative limits of her 1829 autobiography pose significant problems for historians and literary scholars. Prince related her story to an amanuensis and her text was variously shaped by the requirements of the abolitionist campaign, by Victorian ideals of respectable femininity and by conventions prohibiting the open discussion of female sexual choices and sexual abuse.[61] Similar points can be made about Nanny of the Maroons. While she appears in records of the first Maroon Wars against the British from 1733 to 1739, Nanny exists mainly in oral form, brought to life in stories that circulated after Jamaican independence in 1962. As Nicholas J. Saunders argued, in the case of Nanny, 'history and legend [are] hopelessly intertwined.'[62]

In terms of school history, however, Prince's story can be told in a straightforward way. Whether we call her Mary Prince, Molly Wood or Mary James, she was born in Bermuda and worked as a household slave on that island and in Antigua. She came to England in 1828 with her then owners, the Woods, with the hope that she could buy her manumission. This was denied her by Mr and Mrs Wood, who continued to maltreat her and force her to work, despite her arthritic joints and other disabilities, until she escaped to the office of Thomas Pringle, Secretary to the Anti-Slavery Society. There, abolitionist Susanna Strickland wrote down her story, making her patois accessible to a British audience. In our resource, we used Prince's own words, her statement at the end of the text that slaves want freedom.[63] In this context, Mary Prince gives a voice to enslaved women. Her journey to London shows, moreover, that transnational boundary crossings were not a male preserve. Like Freeman's Barbadian higglers, Prince resists the local/feminine, global/masculine dynamic while demonstrating how 'global processes enact themselves on local ground [and] local processes and small-scale actors might be seen as the very fabric of globalization'.[64]

Recent scholarship in transnational history suggests how much more we could have done with Prince's story. We might have included her heart-rending description of her mother dressing her children for market and witnessing them all sold away from her, for example. With older pupils, we might have discussed Prince's muffled references to the abuse she suffered, sexual and otherwise, and some of the sexual compromises she made along the way, to explore the limits placed by culture on what can be said and the double standard which saw sexual slurs cast on her character during the libel case.[65] These raise issues about choice in coercive cultures and make clear the gendered dimensions of enslavement as part of the 'intimacies of global imperial violence'.[66] Similar points might be made about Nanny of the Maroons. We might have raised questions about the limits of the colonial archive and explored why accounts of her life and her role in Jamaican history cannot be evidence based. As Jenny Sharpe argued, 'To consider Nanny as a historical agent . . . is to test the limits of that we traditionally consider to be history.'[67] We might have explored fictional representations of her life to ask why Nanny has become such a powerful icon of Jamaican national identity,[68] looking at her place in the realm of popular memory and 'intangible heritage' that is a current focus of research in public history.[69]

Indeed, research on race and heritage suggests the importance of such stories to black and ethnic minority peoples' lives in Britain today. Laurajane Smith recently argued that British Caribbean visitors approached museum displays in 2007 with a focus on gauging the public status of interpretations of their history which ran counter to what she termed the 'Authorised Heritage Discourse', elite and white-washed public history.[70] In a schools context, the importance of wider narratives

190 Alison Twells

about transnational and migration histories has been emphasised in a study of secondary school pupils at multi-ethnic schools in Britain and the Netherlands. Grever et al. found that pupils from immigrant backgrounds saw greater relevance in history that focused on transnational topics such as slavery, migration, non-European perspectives on European history and colonial wars; girls from immigrant backgrounds especially valued a curriculum that included religion and history concerning 'connection with my family'. The authors argued that to 'enable young people to construct continuity between past and present, and to enhance their understanding of their place in the world, it is imperative to connect local and national history to world history and the history of globalisation so that they can see "the bigger picture" of the world they are growing up in'.[71]

While research into museum audiences suggests the significance of the personal and the local in terms of individual engagement with public history,[72] historical figures such as Mary Prince and Nanny of the Maroons raise the further possibility that the personal may not always map onto the local, if the local is defined in a parochial way. For the many people in Britain who are members of diasporic communities, the global is part of their intimate daily lives, their local story. This is apparent in the stories on the Burngreave Voices website and in the Treasure Days, when artefacts from a migration story – a chillum pipe, a British passport, a ring belonging to a grandfather in Pakistan – took their place alongside a coronation teaspoon from 1902, a child's valentine card for his mum from 1946 and a 1980s Campaign for Nuclear Disarmament (CND) banner. Similarly, recordings of a small number of oral histories – see, for example, 'Growing up in Sanaa, Yemen', 'Home life in Burao, Somalia', 'Life on my grandfather's farm in Pakistan' and 'School days in Jamaica in the 1930s' – form an integral part of the project website.[73] Such a focus on artefacts and the migration journey brings women into the picture, both as migrants and settlers and as keepers of family and other archives.[74] In this sense, then, Mazlish's argument that the local is a 'myth' that needs discarding, that '[t]he reality is "glocalization", of a most complex sort', rings true.[75] Like Equiano, many Britons are also 'citizen[s] of the world'.[76]

Border crossings: academic, schools and community history

The above discussion of Mary Anne Rawson, Mary Prince and Nanny of the Maroons is suggestive of some of the differences between academic and other historical practices including, for example, the importance in schools and community history of strategies for interpretation in the context of contemporary cultural attitudes. While the fact of this difference is sometimes acknowledged by academic historians,[77] it is rarely explored. In this final section of the chapter, I argue that a focus on these wider questions of representation enables reflection on both the academic method and the purpose of history.

The difficult relationship between academic and extra-academic histories can be seen in a variety of contexts, including longstanding accusations by academic historians that museums and heritage sites are contributing to the 'dumbing down' of history and criticisms of school history teaching for 'spoon-feeding' and insufficiently preparing pupils for their undergraduate studies. It can also be seen in the approach to public engagement which focuses exclusively on correcting errors in the public narrative, a relationship conceived as a one-way process, rather like the old imperial history emphasis on the flow from metropolis to empire. This is perhaps most stark in Margaret Macmillan's anxiety-ridden suggestion that we – academics – have surrendered our territory to amateurs and need to claw it back.[78] This is not to suggest that our insistence on the value of academic history in allowing the exploration of complexities is anything but valuable and necessary – see, for example, Nicholas Draper's discussion of the role of media in distorting research findings of the Legacies of British Slavery Project at University College London (UCL).[79] But our practice should involve more than becoming gatekeepers of nuance and complexity in endeavours to counter 'bad' history.

For all of our current emphasis on 'impact', academic historians remain nervous and defensive about responses to our research in the public domain. This is very different from the preoccupation with audience and the importance of communication in schools and community history. In successful school history lessons, teachers seek to engage pupils of all ages and abilities through a range of sources – including visual evidence, film, narratives, including historical fiction – and investigative, imaginative and empathic activities, to foster pupils' intellectual and personal development.[80] The same is true in community history, where the focus on inclusion and integration, on bringing communities together to enable greater mutual understanding and the construction and consolidation of identities in the present, places less emphasis on evidence-based arguments and more on learning through the senses, inspiring empathy, engaging with popular discourses and political debates. Phillips sees such methods as free from the '"strait-jacket" of academic history'.[81] Husbands goes further to question whether 'an academic discipline called "history", a school subject called "history" and a widespread popular interest called "history" have the same meaning, despite their shared label'. Others have argued (albeit in an American context) that teachers have a greater kinship with public historians than with academics.[82] As Chris Culpin stated in his 2007 call to academics to join teachers in updating syllabuses and helping to write better resources, any relationship must be 'based on a realistic understanding of what history in the school curriculum is, and is striving to be'.[83]

This is our loss. While I am not suggesting that academic historians abandon our commitment to rigour and evidence, it is my belief that we have lost our way, despite the radical and democratic aims of 'history from below', women's history and the 'imperial turn' in the 1980s and 1990s, all of which were led by historians who linked their academic work with political agendas for social transformation. Antoinette Burton expressed the concern that a side effect of the imperial turn may well have been to leave 'the sanctity of the nation intact'. Transnational history, she claimed, can enable us to 'resist the seduction of national narratives and make sense of the violences they enact under the guise of patriotism, imperial and

192 Alison Twells

otherwise', if we 'convince students that this is a valuable project, connected to the development of civic participation and responsibility in the twenty-first century in transformative and enduring ways'.[84] To do that, however, we need a different style of communication. Helen Rogers's recent argument in relation to 'history from below', that at some point in the 1980s an obfuscating theory took hold which saw people and their agency left behind,[85] can also be made in relation to women's history. While feminist historians have long explored complex relationships,[86] recent years have seen a severing of links between feminist activism, adult education in women's history and academic research, and women's history has become a more inward-looking academic field, preoccupied with internal debates rather than wider interactions.[87] There is nothing to suggest that the current interest in intersectionality or in the deconstruction of the nation will be any different.[88] While I agree with Hitchcock that there is in Britain 'a "crisis" in the humanities' which 'lies in how we have our public debates',[89] we need to do more than launch our work into the public domain. Clare Anderson's argument for the 'opening up of the discipline of history' through an ethnographic exploration of contemporary understandings – in her research, of imperialism and its impact on society – is both radical and urgent. A closer relationship with schools and community history is one way of enabling this departure.

Such developments can be seen in recent collaborations which bring together women's history and the history of local-global connections in a public history context. 'Local Roots, Global Routes: Legacies of African Enslavement in Hackney', a film and museum resource produced as part of Legacies of British Slavery, aims to show amongst other things the role of the compensation of slave owners after abolition in British social, economic and cultural development during the nineteenth century. While women are absent from the early sections, both as historical subjects and expert historians, Mary Wollstonecraft and Anna-Laetitia Barbauld appear in a section entitled 'Hackney and Abolition'. The two late-eighteenth century writers, both of whom were members of the congregation of the Newington Green unitarian chapel, are represented as changemakers. They provide evidence that Wilberforce *et al.* are only one part of the story and women's choices via the abstention movement made antislavery a domestic and local campaign.[90] My own article on the South Yorkshire Through Time website takes a similarly biographical approach, contextualising Mary Anne Rawson both in terms of what she and other women add to our understanding of the national antislavery movement and in the context of a range of Christian approaches to poverty and slavery, but taking as a starting point the desire to commemorate in the community which has since grown up in the area of Sheffield in which she lived.[91]

Other projects reveal a creative approach to history, often combined with an explicit sense of purpose. The 'Women on the Platform' initiative, which emerged from a project funded by the Heritage Lottery Fund entitled Women in Stone, created by the Edinburgh Adult Education group Damned Rebel Bitches, celebrates Scottish women abolitionists as part of a campaign for more public commemorations of historical women. This work has included the production of a school teaching pack, an exhibition at the Museum of Edinburgh and a creative project of sculpted heads made by schoolgirls and unveiled at the Scottish Parliament. 'It is on the ground', group members wrote, 'at a local level and through the galvanising of ordinary citizens, that we will achieve real change'.[92] Moving away from philanthropists, a range of black history projects place a similar emphasis on inspiration.[93] Creative projects, such as 'An Interview with Mary Prince', which imagines Prince's own words which were omitted from her autobiography, make connections with the fictional representations of enslaved women for whom scant sources exist but which represent a profound need to see our ancestors represented in history.[94]

Such projects place communication at the heart of their practice, extending the postmodern critique which emphasises that history is not a value-free enterprise – a critique that we fully accept in academic work – to restore a sense of purpose to history. Collaborations which bring together academic research and community projects – see, for example, the explorations by Pakistani women in Rotherham of their life histories and heritage that are a key strand of the Imagine Project[95] and sponsorship of community history by the Women's History Network[96] – might enable a critical community of historians to create a new transnational history of women that spans universities, schools and public history.

Conclusion

Academics with expertise in transnational history are well placed to argue for the centrality of local-global connections to understanding national histories and to education for citizenship in the globalised world of the twenty-first century. In its focus on interaction, connection, entanglement, networks, movement, intersection, hybridity and crossing, transnational history 'bridges the national, the sub-national (local, regional), and the global by exploring actors, movements, and forces that cross boundaries and penetrate the fabric of nations'.[97] As Peter Mandler argued, it is in 'bringing to the table' the 'wider horizons' of their research that academic historians have something to contribute to schools and other history.[98]

In turn, schools and community history can bring things to our table as academics. They invite us to consider the ways in which a focus on the relationships among the local, the national and the global are linked to issues of inclusion and social cohesion; the relevance of contemporary concerns with identities and the importance of negotiating received ideas;[99] the significance of individual life stories, narratives and storytelling in the development of historical understanding and personal development;[100] and the importance of communication and all that implies in terms of priorities of engagement and audience. They challenge us to extend the postmodern insistence that history is not a value-free activity by adopting a less suspicious attitude toward the explicitly positioned and purposeful histories promoted by many teachers and public historians. In the words of a Head of History at one London school at the time of Conservative Education Secretary Michael Gove's reforms: 'I won't be adopting the curriculum. It is my duty to meet the learning and

194 Alison Twells

cultural needs of the community I serve.'[101] Such stances can inspire us to restore a sense of purpose to history and to develop a practice that is aware of our positionality and transparent about the nature of our bias and has humanity in mind in its aim of creating citizens.[102]

As I discussed in this chapter, scant sources and public perceptions can mitigate against the easy inclusion of women's history as central to the study of local-global connections. Indeed, it is hard to resist the conclusion, with Rob Phillips, that the local and global find a place in schools and, to a lesser extent, public history in Britain, precisely because they are part of a 'hegemonic struggle over cultural transmission and heritage',[103] because issues of national identity remain so alive.[104] It might be that we will only begin to have an equivalent discussion about women's history if academics engage more closely with public debates – for example, concerning sexual violence, the use of the figure of the woman in justifications of war, or antagonism to women in social media, or in exploring the 'treasures' and their associated stories which find representation in community history projects, public history representations of the slave trade and its legacies or in topics of religion and migration identified by the girls in the study by Grever et al.[105] Might that enable us to develop a critical community of historians to create a new transnational history of women that spans universities, schools and public history sites?

Notes

The author would like to thank Julie Carlier, Peter D'Sena, Clare Midgley and Helen Rogers for their helpful critical feedback on this chapter.

1 P.-Y. Saunier, *Transnational History*, Basingstoke: Palgrave, 2013, p. 32.
2 See K. Crawford, 'A History of the Right: the Battle for Control of National Curriculum History 1989–1994', *British Journal of Educational Studies*, 43, December 1995, 433–456; J. Slater, *The Politics of History Teaching, a Humanity Dehumanised?* London: University of London Institute of Education, 1989; N. Sheldon, 'Politicians and history: The national curriculum, national identity and the revival of the national narrative', *History*, 97:326, April 2012, 256–271. Joseph quoted in D. Cannadine, J. Keating, and N. Sheldon, *The Right Kind of History: Teaching the Past in Twentieth-Century England*, Basingstoke: Palgrave, 2011, p. 192.
3 T. Haydn, 'How and what should we teach about the British Empire in English schools?', published in *Handbook of the International Society of History Didactics*, Schwalbach: Wochenschau Verlag, 2014, 23–40. Online: https://ueaeprints.uea.ac.uk/51026/ p. 3; R. J. Evans, 'Michael Gove's history curriculum is a pub quiz not an education. The rote sets in', *New Statesman*, 21/3/2013.
4 R. Phillips, *History Teaching, Nationhood and the State: A Study in Educational Politics*, London: Cassell, 1998, p. 2. See also: A. Osler, 'Patriotism, multiculturalism and belonging: political discourse and the teaching of history', *Educational Review*, 61:1, 2009, 85–100; T. Haydn, 'History in schools and the problem of "the nation"', *Educational Sciences*, 2:1, 2012, 1–15; T. Haydn, 'Longing for the past: Politicians and the history curriculum in English schools, 1988–2010', *Journal of Education, Media, Memory and Society*, 4:1, 2012, 7–25; A. Waldman, 'The politics of history teaching in England and France during the 1980s', *History Workshop Journal*, 68:1, 2009, 199–221; N. Sheldon, 'Politicians and History'.
5 K. Jenkins and P. Brinkley, 'Always Historicise: Unintended opportunities in national curriculum history', *Teaching History*, 62, 1991, 8–14; J. Pankhania, *Liberating the National History Curriculum*, London: Falmer Press, 1994.

6 Sheldon, 'Politicians and History'; A. Kitson, C. Husbands with S. Steward, *Teaching and Learning History 11–18: Understanding the Past,* Maidenhead: Open University Press, 2011, pp. 118–133; Haydn, 'History in schools and the problem of "the nation"', p. 279.

7 Sheldon, 'Politicians and History', p. 270.

8 See R. Samuel, 'Grand narratives', *History Workshop Journal,* 29:1, 1990, 120–133. See also: R. Samuel, 'A Case for National History', Additional Paper Presented at 'History, the Nation and the schools Conference, Oxford, 1990. Online: http://centres.exeter.ac.uk/historyresource/journal5/Samuel.rtf

9 S. Marks, 'History, the nation and empire: Sniping from the periphery', *History Workshop Journal,* 29:1, 1990, 111–119, pp. 16–17.

10 R. Visram, *Ayahs, Lascars and Princes: Indians in 1700–1947,* London, Pluto, 1990, p. 170. See also R. Visram, 'British History: Whose History? Black Perspectives on British History', in H. Bourdillon, ed., *Teaching History,* London and New York, 1994, 53–61.

11 J. de Groot, *Empire and History Writing in Britain, c. 1750–2012,* Manchester: Manchester University Press, 2013, 214–258, pp. 241–242.

12 Bourdillon, *Teaching History,* p. 67; C. Adams, 'Off the record: women's omission from classroom historical evidence', *Teaching History,* 36, 1983, 3–6.

13 See Bourdillon, ed., *Teaching History,* pp. 69–70; A. Osler, 'Still hidden from history? The representation of women in recently published history textbooks', *Oxford Review of Education,* 20:2, 1994, 219–235.

14 C. Counsell, 'Looking through a Joseph-Butler-shaped window: focusing pupils' thinking on historical significance', *Teaching History,* 114, 2004, 30–33.

15 J. Pearson, 'Where are we? The place of women in history curricula', *Teaching History,* 147, 2012, 47–52. See also: F. Wilson, 'Warrior Queens, regal trade unionists and warring nurses: how my interest in what I don't teach has informed my teaching and enriched my students' learning', *Teaching History,* 146, 2012, 52–56; S. Johnson, 'Where are the women in school history?', Herstoria: history that puts woman in her place. Online: http://herstoria.com/?p=821; B. Lockyer, 'Complicating women's history: Reflections on the Final Workshop'. Online: http://teachingwomenshistory.com/moving-beyond-boundaries-project-blog/. For the lack of focus on gender, see P. Bracey, A. Gove-Humphries and D. Jackson, 'Teaching Diversity in the Classroom', in I. Davies, ed., *Debates in History Teaching,* London: Routledge, 2011, 172–185.

16 A. Twells and R. Unwin, *Olaudah Equiano in Sheffield,* Sheffield: Development Education Centre (South Yorkshire), 1992.

17 G. Cubitt, 'Bringing it Home: Making Local Meaning in 2007 Bicentenary Exhibitions', *Slavery and Abolition,* 2:30, June 2009, 259–275.

18 See: D. Paton, 'Interpreting the bicentenary in Britain', *Slavery & Abolition,* 30:2, 2009, 277–289; J. Oldfield, 'Repairing historical wrongs: Public history and transatlantic slavery', *Social and Legal Studies,* 21, 2012, 155–169; C. Hall, 'Afterword: Britain 2007, Problematising Histories', in J. Oldfield and C. Caplan, eds., *Imagining Transatlantic Slavery,* Basingstoke: Palgrave, 2010, 191–201; E. Waterton and R. Wilson, 'Talking the Talk: Policy, popular and media responses to the bicentenary of the abolition of the slave trade using the abolition discourse', *Discourse and Society,* 20:3, 2009, 381–399. See also: M. Dresser, 'Remembering slavery and abolition in Bristol', *Slavery and Abolition,* 30:2, 2009, 223–246; J. Oldfield, *Chords of Freedom: Commemoration, Ritual and British Transatlantic Slavery,* Manchester: Manchester University Press, 2008; E. Kowaleski Wallace, *The British Slave Trade and Public Memory,* New York: Columbia University Press, 2006; M. Sherwood, *After Abolition: Britain and the Slave Trade since 1807,* London: IB Tauris, 2007.

19 M. Ogborn, *Global Lives. Britain and the World 1550–1800,* Cambridge: Cambridge University Press, 2008, pp. 116–119; M. Berg, *Writing the History of the Global: Challenges for the 21st Century,* Oxford: Oxford University Press, 2013.

20 C. Anderson, *Subaltern Lives. Biographies of Colonialism in the Indian Ocean World, 1790–1920,* Cambridge: Cambridge University Press, 2012, p. 13.

21 C. Freeman, 'Is local : Global as feminine : Masculine? Rethinking the gender of globalization', *Signs: Journal of Women in Culture and Society,* 26:4, Summer 2001, 1007–1047,

p. 1010. See also E. Rothschild, *The Inner Life of Empires: An Eighteenth-Century History,* New Jersey: Princeton University Press, 2011.

22 Anderson, *Subaltern Lives.* See also D. Deacon, P. Russell and A. Woollacott, eds., *Transnational Lives: Biographies of Global Modernity, 1700-present,* Basingstoke: Palgrave Macmillan, 2010; L. Colley, *The Ordeal of Elizabeth Marsh: A Woman in World History,* London: Harper Collins, 2007.

23 T. Ballantyne and A. Burton, eds., *Moving Subjects. Gender, Mobility and Intimacy in an Age of Global Empire,* Urbana: University of Illinois Press, 2009, p. 25.

24 Freeman, 'Is local: Global as feminine: masculine?' p. 1008.

25 M. E. Wiesner-Hanks, 'Crossing borders in transnational gender history', *Journal of Global History,* 6:3, 2011, 357–379.

26 C. Husbands, A. Kitson and A. Pendry, *Understanding History Teaching: Teaching and Learning about the Past in Secondary Schools,* Maidenhead: Open University Press, 2003, pp. 118, 123. See also P. Seixas, 'The purpose of teaching Canadian history', *Canadian Social Studies,* 36:2, 2002, pp. Online: www2.education.ualberta.ca/css/Css_36_2/ARpurposes_teaching_canadian_history.htm; C. Culpin, 'What kind of history should school history be?' *Historian,* 95, Autumn 2007, 6–14, p. 11; T. Haydn, A. Stephen, J. Arthur and M. Hunt, *Learning to Teach History in the Secondary School: A Companion to School Experience,* London: Routledge, 2015, pp. 2, 30.

27 T. Hitchcock, 'Doing it in public; Impact, blogging, social media and the academy', *Historyonics,* 15 July 2014. Online: http://historyonics.blogspot.co.uk/2014/07/doing-iy-in-public-impact-blogging-html

28 Anderson, 'Subaltern lives: History, memory and identity in the Indian Ocean World', *History Compass,* 11:7, 2013, 503–507, p. 506.

29 A. Osler, 'Education for Development: Redefining Citizenship in a Pluralist Society', in A. Osler, ed., *Development Education: Global Perspectives in the Curriculum,* London: Cassell, 1994, pp. 32–49.

30 See for example: I. Law and J. Hendry, *A History of Race Relations in Liverpool 1660–1950,* Liverpool: Merseyside Community Relations Council, 1981; I. Grosvenor and R. Chapman, *West Africa, West Indies, West Midlands,* Oldbury: Sandwell Education Department, 1982; S. Collicott, *Connections: Haringey Local-National-World Links,* London: Haringey Community Information Service in association with the Multi-Cultural Support Group, 1986; I. Grosvenor and R. Chapman, *Britain and India: an Uncommon Journey,* Oldbury: Sandwell Education Department, 1988; A. Twells and R. Unwin, *Colonialism, Slavery and the Industrial Revolution: The Empire in South Yorkshire,* Sheffield: Development Education Centre (South Yorkshire), 1992. See also: J. Bush, *Moving on: Northamptonshire and the Wider World,* Northampton: Nene Publications, 1989.

31 Twells and Unwin, *Colonialism, Slavery and the Industrial Revolution.* See: S. Collicott, 'What history should we teach in primary schools?' *History Workshop Journal,* 29:1, 1990, 107–110, p. 110; J. Bush, 'Moving on – and looking back', History Workshop Journal, 36:1, 1993, 183–194; C. Hall, 'Race-ing Imperial Histories', History Workshop Journal, 41:1, 1996, 183–194; I. Grosvenor, 'History for the Nation: Multiculturalism and the Teaching of History', in J. Arthur and R. Phillips, eds., *Issues in History Teaching,* London: Routledge, 2000, 148–158; K. Myers and I. Grosvenor, 'Birmingham stories: Local histories of migration and settlement and the practice of history,' *Midland History,* 36:2, Autumn 2011, 149–162.

32 See www.decsy.org.uk/projects

33 See D. Lyndon, 'Integrating Black British History into the National Curriculum', *Teaching History,* 122, March 2006, pp. 37–43; C. Abel, P. Bracey and J. Siblon, eds., 'Black is also British: An investigation into the needs and opportunities for developing Black British history within the schools' curriculum in Northamptonshire', A report commissioned by Northamptonshire Black History Project and University College Northampton, Northampton: Northamptonshire Black History Project, University College Northampton, 2005. Online: www.northants-black-history.org.uk/images/reasearch_schools.pdf; Traille, K. '"You should be proud about your history. They made me feel ashamed." Teaching history that hurts', *Teaching History,* 127, 2007, 31–7; Historical Association, *T.E.A.C.H, Teaching Emotive and Controversial History,* London, 2007.

34 A. Twells, 'Community History'. Online: www.history.ac.uk/makinghistory/resources/articles/community_history.html
35 Burngreave Voices was jointly funded by Museums Sheffield and New Deal for Communities.
36 See www.museums-sheffield.org.uk/project-archive/burngreave-voices/about.html
37 See Paton, 'Interpreting the Bicentenary in Britain'; Oldfield, 'Repairing historical wrongs'; Waterton and Wilson, 'Talking the Talk'.
38 *The Songs of Joseph Mather, to which are added a memoir of Mather, and miscellaneous songs relating to Sheffield, with an introduction and notes by John Wilson,* Sheffield: Pawson and Brailsford, 1862.
39 P. Linebaugh and M. Rediker, *The Many-Headed Hydra: Sailors, Slaves, Commoners, and the Hidden History of the Revolutionary Atlantic,* Boston: Beacon Press, 2000, pp. 273–274.
40 C. Midgley, *Women Against Slavery: the British Campaigns, 1780–1870,* London: Routledge, 1992.
41 A. Twells, *The Civilising Mission and the English Middle Class, 1792–1850: The Heathen at Home and Overseas,* Basingstoke: Palgrave, 2009.
42 Fry is to be removed in 2016.
43 For women's history textbooks in the 1990s, see: C. Adams, P. Bartley and C. Loxton, Cambridge University Women in History series (1983–1994); F. MacDonald, *Working for Equality: Women History Makers,* London: Hampstead Press, 1988; *In Her Own Time,* Hamish Hamilton, 1989.
44 See for example Collicott, *Connections,* pp. 54, 78, 85.
45 F. K. Prochaska, *Women and Philanthropy in Nineteenth-century England,* Oxford: Clarendon Press, 1980.
46 S. Richardson, *The Political Worlds of Women: Gender and Political Culture in Nineteenth-Century Britain,* London: Routledge, 2013, pp. 64, 80.
47 L. Davidoff and C. Hall, *Family Fortunes: Men and Women of the English Middle Class, 1780–1850,* London: Hutchinson, 1987; E. Yeo, *The Contest for Social Science: Relations and Representations of Gender and Class,* London: Rivers Oram, 1996.
48 Midgley, *Women Against Slavery.*
49 A. Burton, *Burdens of History: British Feminists, Indian Women, and. Imperial Culture, 1865–1915,* Chapel Hill and London: University of North Carolina Press, 1994; S. Thorne, *Congregational Missions and the Making of an Imperial Culture in Nineteenth-Century England,* Stanford: Stanford University Press, 1999.
50 Twells, *The Civilising Mission.*
51 See for example: 'Elizabeth Heyrick'. Online: www.bbc.co.uk/leicester/content/articles/2007/03/20/abolition_elizabeth_heyrick_feature.shtml
52 C. Midgley, *Feminism and Empire: Women Activists in Imperial Britain, 1790–1865,* London: Routledge, 2007, 41–64.
53 Twells, *The Civilising Mission.*
54 C. Hall, *Civilising Subjects: Metropole and Colony in the English Imagination, 1830–1867,* Cambridge: Polity, 2002; Twells, *The Civilising Mission.*
55 See G. Whitlock, *The Intimate Empire: Reading Women's Autobiography,* New York: Cassell, 2000.
56 Kitson et al., *Teaching and Learning History 11–18,* p. 122. For the role of existing assumptions and affective dimension, see C. Husbands and A. Pendry, '"Thinking and feeling": pupils' preconceptions about the past and historical understanding', in Arthur and Phillips, eds., *Issues in History Teaching,* 125–134; A. McCully and N. Pilgrim, 'They took Ireland away from us . . .', cited in Kitson et al., *Teaching and Learning History 11–18,* p. 147.
57 See the interesting work on resistance to gender and feminist analyses on the part of students and trainee teachers in the US. K. M. Dalton and E. A. Rotundo, 'Teaching gender history to secondary school students', *The Journal of American History,* 86:4, 2000, 1715–1720; D. Langan and D. Davidson, 'Critical pedagogy and personal struggles: Feminist scholarship outside women's studies', *Feminist Teacher,* 15:2, Winter 2005, 132–158; T. Jordan, 'Engaging student resistance to feminism: 'How is this stuff going to make us better teachers?', *Gender and Education,* 12:1, March 2000, 21–37; B. Winslow, 'Clio

198 Alison Twells

in the curriculum: The state of women and women's history in the middle and high school curriculum . . . and perhaps a way forward', *Journal of Women's History*, 25:4 2013, 319–332.

58 K. Prior, 'Commemorating Slavery 2007: A personal view from inside the museums', *History Workshop Journal,* 64:1, 2007, 200–209.

59 See B. Bush, *Slave Women in Caribbean Society, 1650–1832,* London: James Currey, 1990; B. Bush-Slimani, 'Hard labour: Women, childbirth and resistance in British Caribbean slave societies', *History Workshop Journal*, 36:1, 1993, 86–99; H. McD Beckles, *Natural Rebels: A Social History of Enslaved Black Women in Barbados,* New Jersey: Rutgers University Press, 1989; J. Morgan, *Laboring Women: Reproduction and Gender in New World Slavery,* Philadelphia: University of Pennsylvania Press, 2004.

60 Anderson, 'Subaltern Lives', p. 503.

61 Whitlock, *The Intimate Empire*; J. Sharpe, *Ghosts of Slavery: A Literary Archaeology of Black Women's Lives,* Minneapolis: University of Minnesota Press, 2003; S. Salih, '*The History of Mary Prince,* the Black Subject and the Black Canon', in B. Carey, M. Ellis and S. Salih, eds., *Discourses of Slavery and Abolition: Britain and its Colonies, 1760–1838,* Basingstoke: Palgrave, 2004, 123–138.

62 N.J. Saunders, *Peoples of the Caribbean: An Encyclopaedia of Archaeology and Traditional Culture,* ABC-CLIO, 2005, p. 176.

63 M. Ferguson, ed., *History of Mary Prince, A West Indian Slave, Related by Herself,* Ann Arbor: University of Michigan Press, 1997.

64 Freeman, 'Is local: Global as feminine: masculine?', p. 1009.

65 Whitlock, *The Intimate Empire.*

66 Ballantyne and Burton, *Moving Subjects*, p. 25.

67 J. Sharpe, *Ghosts of Slavery*, p. 1.

68 See for example: K. Gottlieb, *The Mother of Us All: A History of Queen Nanny, Leader of Windward Jamaican Maroons,* Tenton, NJ: Africa World Press, 2000, p. 23.

69 L. Smith, *Uses of Heritage,* London: Routledge, 2006.

70 L. Smith, 'Affect and Registers of Engagement: Navigating Emotional Responses to Dissonant Heritages', in L. Smith, G. Cubitt, R. Wilson and K. Fouseki, eds., *Representing Enslavement and Abolition in Museums: Ambiguous Engagements,* London: Routledge, 2011, 260–303. See also K. Fouseki, 'Community voices, curatorial choices': Community consultation for the 1807 exhibitions', *Museum and Society,* 8.3, November 2010, 180–192. Online: www2.le.ac.uk/departments/museumstudies/museumsociety/documents/vol umes/fousecki.pdf. For the wider context of discussion of race and heritage, see R. Naidoo and J. Littler, eds., *The Politics of Heritage, The Legacies of 'Race',* London: Routledge, 2005.

71 M. Grever, B. Pelzer and T. Haydn, 'High school students views on history', *Journal of Curriculum Studies*, 43:2, 2011, 207–229, p. 208. See also K. Ribbens, 'A Narrative that Encompasses our History: Historical Culture and History Teaching', in M. Grever and S. Stuurman, eds., *Beyond the Canon: History for the Twenty-first Century,* Basingstoke: Palgrave, 2007, 63–76.

72 See for example, N. Merriman, *Beyond the Glass Case: The Past, the Heritage and the Public in Britain,* Leicester: Leicester University Press, 1991.

73 Online: www.museums-sheffield.org.uk/project-archive/burngreave-voices/stories Memories.html

74 See for example Northamptonshire Black History Association. Online: www.northantsblack-history.org.uk/index.aspx; and 'Home away from Home' at Birmingham Museum and Art Gallery. Online: www.gwacic.com/?page_id=2811http://www.thehistorypress. co.uk/womens-history-network-2014; also Runnymede Trust. Online: www.runnyme detrust.org/uploads/publications/pdfs/MakingBritishHistories-2012.pdf. For gendering the diaspora, see for example, C. Alexander, 'Marriage, migration, multiculturalism: Gendering "the Bengal diaspora"', *Journal of Ethnic and Migration Studies* 39:3, 2013, 333–351.

75 B. Mazlish, *The New Global History,* New York: Routledge, 2006, pp. 76–79

76 V. Caretta, ed., *Equiano, the African: Biography of a Self-Made Man*, Athens: University of Georgia Press, 2005, p. viii.

77 See for example Paton, 'Interpreting the Bicentenary in Britain', p. 278.

78 M. Macmillan, *The Uses and Abuses of History*, London: Profile, 2011, p. 35.

79 N.Draper,'Slave ownership,reparations and restitution:history and historians in Britain and Europe', 2013. Online: www.history.ac.uk/podcasts/franco-british-history-external/slave-ownership-reparations-and-restitution-history-and

80 Husbands et al., *Understanding History Teaching*, pp. 123, 116–137.

81 Philips, *History Teaching, Nationhood and the State*, p. 17; C. Husbands, *What is History Teaching? Language, Ideas and Meaning in Learning about the Past*, Buckingham: Open University Press, 1996, p. 5.

82 K. Barton, 'The Denial of Desire: How to Make History Education Meaningless', in L. Symcox and A. Wilschut (eds.), *National History Standards: The Problem of the Canon and the Future of Teaching History*, Charlotte, NC: IAP, 2009, pp. 265–282.

83 Culpin, 'What kind of history should school history be?'

84 A. Burton, ed., *After the Imperial Turn: Thinking with and through the Nation*, Durham: Duke University Press, 2003, pp. 2, 4, 13.

85 H. Rogers, 'The Revival of History from Below in Victorian Studies', May 2015. Online: www.youtube.com/watch?v=rToJag5WgWI

86 de Groot, *Empire and History Writing in Britain*, pp. 241–242.

87 See S. Morgan, 'Theorising feminist history: A thirty-year retrospective', *Women's History Review*, 18:3, 2009, 381–407.

88 See A. Curthoys, 'We've Just Started Making National Histories, and You Want Us to Stop Already?', in Burton, *After the Imperial Turn*, 70–89. For intersectionality, see S. Cho, K. Williams Crenshaw and L. McCall, 'Toward a field of intersectionality studies: theory, applications, and praxis', *Signs, Intersectionality: Theorizing Power, Empowering Theory*, 38:4, Summer 2013, 785–810.

89 Hitchcock, 'Doing it in public'.

90 'Local Roots, Global Routes: Legacies of African Enslavement in Hackney'. Online: https://vimeo.com/116435239

91 Online: www.southyorkshirethroughtime.org.uk/content/category/themes

92 'The "Women on the Platform" Project: Pushing for greater visibility of women in Edinburgh's history', *History Scotland*, 14:1, Jan/Feb 2014, p. 39; Online: www.theedin burghreporter.co.uk/wp-content/uploads/2014/01/DRB-Exhibition-Booklet.pdf

93 Online: www.northants-black-history.org.uk/events.aspx?itemTag=past_events&select Year=2013. See also: Glasgow Women's Library BME Women's Project; Online: http://womenslibrary.org.uk/about-us/our-projects/bme-womens-project, Oral Histories of the Black Women's Movement in Britain, part of British Library Sisterhood and After project. Online: www.bl.uk/sisterhood/about-the-project; Black Cultural Archives. Online: http://bcaheritage.org.uk/staying-power-photographs-of-black-british-expe rience-1950s-1990s; https://rememberolivemorris.wordpress.com/

94 Online: www.culture24.org.uk/history-and-heritage/art41922

95 Online: www.imaginecommunity.org.uk/projects/the-cultural-context/#10; www.gwacic.com/?page_id=2811

96 Online: www.thehistorypress.co.uk/womens-history-network-2014

97 M. Middell and K. Naumann, 'Global history and the spatial turn: from the impact of area studies to the study of critical junctures of globalisation', *Journal of Global History*, 5:1, 2010, 149–170, p. 160.

98 P. Mandler, 'History, National Life and the New Curriculum', keynote address at the SHP conference, 2012. Online: www.schoolshistoryproject.org.uk/ResurceBase/downloads/MandlerKeynote2013.pdf, pp. 20–21.

99 T. Haydn, 'What sort of school history do we need for the twenty-first century?', *History Education and Modernity: 2014 East Asia-Europe History Education International Conference, 2014*, unpublished paper. Online: https://ueaeprints.uea.ac.uk/51023/

100 See C. Hake and T. Haydn, 'Stories or sources?' *Teaching History*, 78, 1995, 20–22.

200   Alison Twells

101 'Back to the past for the school history curriculum?' Online: www.historyandpolicy.
org/opinion-articles/articles/back-to-the-past-for-the-school-history-curriculum
102 B. Southgate, *Why Bother with History?* Harlow: Pearson Education, 2000.
103 Phillips, *History Teaching, Nationhood and the State*, p. 2.
104 See G. Oostindie, 'Public memories of the Atlantic slave trade and slavery in contemporary Europe', *European Review*, 17:3–4, 2009, 611–626; Oldfield, *Chords of Freedom*.
105 See Grever et al., 'High school students views on history', p. 208.

INDEX

abolition 186–9, 192
Abolition of Slavery Act 186, 188
Africa: Italian Empire and 118, 120–1, 123–7; representations of 126–7
America: feminism and 27; imperialism 56, 61, 64, 77–8, 90; ties with India 23–4, 27
American women *see* women, American
Amfiteatrov, A. 101, 112
Anagol, Padma 14
Anderson, Clare 184, 188, 192
Anglicanism 18–20
Anthony, Susan B. 24
anti-semitism 101, 112
Aotearoa/New Zealand: indigenous rights 163, 166; Maori women 163, 165–6, 168–71; Pacific women 167
Arya Mahila Samaj 17–18, 21, 24
Association of Lithuanian Women 109
athletic uniforms 88

Balbo, Italo 128
Ballantyne, Tony 165
Barbauld, Anna-Laetitia 192
Bargagli Petrucci, Onorina 125
Barranco, Vicente 88
Bartholomew, Clyde 91–2
Baudouin de Courtenay, Romualde 107
Bauman, Zygmunt 62
Beknazar-Uzbasheva, E. 112
Bennett, Victoria 170
Bhabha, Homi 90
black history 193
Blaubaum, R. 106
Bobrikov, Nikolai 105

Bodley, Rachel 21
Bojanowska, Jozefa 107
Bolton, Lissant 174
Bourdillon, Hilary 182
Brahmoism: Christianity and 19; religious collaboration 16, 18–19, 21, 23, 27; revival of 17; social reform 14–15, 17, 26; women and 22–4, 27
Brahmo Samaj 14–23, 26–7
Britain: antislavery 185–8, 192; black market food 154; eating habits 150–1, 153–8; food trade 147–53, 156–7; Greenham Common 54–6, 61–9; history curriculum 180–94; national curriculum 180–1, 184; racism 63–4, 68; rationing 151, 153–4, 156; slave trade 182–6; wartime food shortages 153–8; women in wartime 148–9, 153
British Independent Labour Party (ILP) 42
British women *see* women, British
British Women's Patriotic League 150
Brookes, Barbara 168
Brown, Wilmette 68
Bundy, Walter 77
Burdett, Charles 119
Burngreave Voices 182, 185, 190
Burton, Antoinette 164, 187, 191
Bush, Barbara 188
Byelorussia (Belarus): oppression of 108–9; women's movement in 109

care work 35, 40–3, 47, 49
Carpenter, Mary 15, 17–18, 22
Carroll, James 166

202 Index

Carry Greenham Home (film) 61
caste 22, 25–6
Catholic Church: Aotearoa/New Zealand 166; France 110; Lithuania 110; Poland 108, 110; views on women 110, 113
Catholic Lithuanian Women's Union 110, 113
Cavan, Emilia 91–*2*
Chen, Xiangming 66
Choi, Hyeaweol 81
Christianity: Brahmoism and 19; Hinduism and 19; religious collaboration 14–15, 17; women and 24
Christian missionaries: athletics 88; colonized women and 80–1; dress and 80–1, 83–9, 91–2, 94; India 15, 20, 24, 26; nursing education 86–7; Philippines 77–9, 83–5; photography and 79, 81–2, 90
citizenship education 181, 184, 193–4
civilizing mission: dress and 82–3; photography and 81–2
Club of Muslim women 111
Cobbe, Frances Power 19
Collet, Sophia Dobson 19
colonialism 13–14; Aotearoa/New Zealand 165; dress and 80–1; women and 80, 164–5
colonial settlement 122–4
colonial training: camps for 117, 127–36; Italian girls 121, 127–8; Italian women 117–27; Nazi organizations and 121
Committee of Experts on Native Labour 45–6
community history 191, 193
Congress of Polish Women 108
contact zone 55–6, 67, 69
contract labour 43–4
Cooper, Whina 163, 165–6, 168–72, 175–6
Counsell, Christine 182
Cubitt, Geoff 182
Culpin, Chris 191
cultural identity 100
cultural otherness 61–3

Daba, Pio 77
Dall, Caroline Healey 23
Dall, Charles 17, 23
Department of Women's Suffrage 102
Development Education Centre (South Yorkshire) 184
Dock, Lavinia 87
Draper, Nicholas 191

dress: American women 79, 81, 83; athletic uniforms 88; class and 87, 91; colonization and 80–1; Filipina 83–5, 88–9; indigenous 82–5, 91; politics of 77–81, 84–7, 90–2, 94; resistance and 79, 87; *terno* 78, 83, 87, 90–1; uniforms 86–7

Edmonson, Linda 101
Education Reform Act 180
Empire Marketing Board 150, 157
England *see* Britain
Equal Rights International (ERI) 37
Equiano, Olaudah 182–5, 188
Ethiopia, Italian occupation of 120
evangelization 82–3

Falcón, Sylvanna 164
family allowance policy 39–43, 47
family policies 35, 47–8
Fasci Femminili 121, 123, 125–6
Fascist Colonial Girls 121
Fascist Colonial Institute 120, 136
fascist colonial propaganda: colonial training camps 127–33; creation of 133–4, 137; female organizations 117–18, 120, 133; handbooks 126–7; Italian 117–39
Fascist Institute for Italian Africa 121
Fascist National Party 118, 124
feminism: activism 192; antiracism in 68; Eurocentric 163–4; India 13–14, 28; liberal religious networks and 27; peace activism and 54; Russian women's rejection of 101; transnational 164
Fiji Women's Conference 171
Filipina women *see* women, Filipina
Finland: autonomy in 100, 105; Russification policies 105; women's suffrage 98, 105–6, 113
First All-Russian Women's Congress 112
First Congress of the Russian Union for Women's Equality 104
First National Conference of Native Women 173
food shortages 153–7
food trade: British women and 147–51; globalized 149–53, 157–8; wartime reductions 147, 151, 153–7
forced labour 43–6, 48
Fox, Evelyn *93*
Fox, Florence 85–6, 92–*3*
Fox, Isabel 85, 88, 91–3
free labour 34–5, 38
Freeman, Carla 183
Fry, Elizabeth 186

Index **203**

Gasprinskiy, İsmail Mustafa oğlu 112
Gaudenzi, Bianca 128
General Council of Trade Unions of Japan (*Sōhyō*) 59
Georgian Union for Women's Equality 104
globalization: British culture and 181; narratives of 1, 6, 8, 183, 190; reconceptualization of 4–5, 7; women's agency in 9
Global North: global curriculum 184; labour standards 34, 40, 42–3, 48; wage labour 34, 43; women's unpaid labour 40, 42
Global South: global curriculum 184; labour standards 34, 39, 43, 45–6, 48; subsistence policies 46; unfree labour 34, 39, 43, 45; women's labour 50
Gonong, Maxine 77–8
Gorodé, Déwé 173
Gove, Michael 181, 193
The Grassroots Network 64–9
Greenham Common Women's Peace Camp 54; Japanese women and 55–6, 61–9
Griffen, Vanessa 172–3
Guerra, Angela Maria 135–7

Haan, Francesca de 164, 175
Hale, Edward Everett 23
Halkyard- Harawira, Hilda 173
Hall, Catherine 148, 158
Harrison, Tom 148
Hayden, Benjamin 186
Hibbard, Laura 85
Hinduism: Christianity and 19; oppression of women 21–2; religious collaboration 14–15, 17; widows 22–3
Hirsch, Marianne 119
Hirshon, Tea 173
history: academic 190–2; black 193; communication and 191–3; community 191, 193; criticism of school teaching 191; extra-academic 190–1; feminist 192; local 181–5, 187, 190, 192, 194; migration 190; oral 185, 190; popular memory and 189; problem-oriented 180; public 185, 187–90, 192, 194; school curriculum 180–94; transnational perspectives 180–4, 186–94; women and gender 33, 181–3, 185–8, 192, 194
History Workshop 181
Hitchcock, Tim 184, 192
Hobsbawn, Eric 82
Hoganson, Kristin 84

home missionaries 85
Husbands, C. 191

identity: class and 187; dress and 78–9, 94; gendered 59, 92, 109, 113, 117, 119, 138, 187; Pacific women 168, 175; shared 62; transnational history and 67; whiteness and 135, 137; *see also* national identity
imperialism: American 56, 61, 64, 77–8, 82, 90; evangelization and 82; Italian Empire 119–20; Japan and 56, 64; politics of dress and 77, 90, 94; women's movements and 164
India: nationalism 23–6; ties with America 23–4, 27; women's suffrage 24
Indian National Congress 23–5, 27
Indian women *see* women, Indian
indigenous rights: Aotearoa/New Zealand 163, 166; gender discrimination and 164
International Advisory Committee of Women (IACW) 42
International Council of Women 24, 45
International Federation of Trade Unions (IFTU) Women's Committee 41–2
International Labour Organization (ILO): development of 33–4; family allowance policy 39–43, 49; maternity policies 35–8, 49; native workers 43–7; subsistence policies 43–8; unfree labour 45–7; unpaid labour 38–9, 48
International Women's Suffrage Alliance 106
Italian Colonial Institute-IFAI 125–6, 132, 133
Italian Empire: colonial settlement 122–4; emigrants 119–20, 123; Eurocentrism and 138; fascism 118–20; fascist colonial propaganda 117–39; feminine models in 120; imperialism 119–20; national identities 118; tourist campaigns 128–9
Italian women *see* women, Italian

Jackson, Hana 163
James, Selma 68
Jansen, Elizabeth White 84
Japan: boundaries and 66–7; cultural otherness 61–3; ethnic nation of 56–7, 60; peace activism 58–60, 64; political protests 56; Westernization 57–8; women's movement in 56–8
Japanese Communist Party (JCP) 59
Japanese women *see* women, Japanese
Japan Socialist Party (JSP) 59
Jayawardena, Kumari 164

204 Index

Jewish equality, Russian women and 101
Johnson, Anna V. 92
Johnson, Rebecca 59, 61
Jolly, Margaret 164, 174
Joseph, Keith 180
Joshi, Anandibai 21, 23

Kalaw, Pura Villanueva 90
King, Michael 171
Kingstone, Fanaura 175
Kondō, Kazuko 60–1, 64
Kosambi, Meera 21
Kothari, Uma 157
Kuczalska-Reinschmit, Paulina 107

labour history: international policies 33–5;
    unpaid labour 33–5; women and 33–4
labour law: equality in 36–8; international
    policies 34; unpaid labour 39
labour standards: free labour 34–5; Global
    North 34, 40, 42–3; Global South 34, 39,
    43, 45–6, 50; maternity policies 35–8;
    native workers 43–5; sex-specific 36–7;
    subsistence policies 43–6; unfree labour
    34–5, 43, 45–6
Lake, Marilyn 164
Lamson, Kate 81
land rights, Maori 163, 166, 172
Last, Nella 148, 157
Laubach, Effa 84
Laubach, Frank 81
League of Nations 33, 40–1
League of Women's Equality 102–3, 114
Lessona, Alessandro 123–4
Liaison Group of Women Opposed to
    War 64
Libya: colonial tourist industry in 128–9,
    131; colonial training camps in 117,
    129–35; Italian occupation of 120, 122–3
Lini, Hilda 173
Lini, Walter 174–5
Lithuania: autonomy in 100; oppression of
    108; women's movement in 109–10
Lithuanian Women's Union 113
Local Roots, Global Routes resource 192

Maandig, Isabel 92–3
Macintyre, Martha 164
Macmillan, Margaret 191
Madge, Charles 148
Mandler, Peter 193
Manning, Elizabeth Adelaide 19
Maori: land rights 163, 166, 172;
    marginalization of 165
Maori women see women, Maori

Maori Women's Welfare League 163,
    168–71
Marks, Shula 181
Martineau, Harriet 24
Mass Observation Archive 147–50, 153–5,
    157, 159
maternity policies: incapacitation and
    37–8, 49; labour standards 35–9; for paid
    labour 36
Maternity Protection Convention 36–8
Mather, Joseph 185, 188
men: forced labour 44–6; peace activism
    59–60; wages 41–2
Mendoza-Guazon, María Paz 90
Mera, Basil 167
Midgley, Clare 164, 187
Mirovitch, Zinaida 105
Mitchison, Naomi 154
Moghadam, Valentine 68–9
Mohanty, Chandra Talpade 164
Molisa, Grace Mera 163, 165–8, 171–6
Molisa, Sera 167, 174
Montgomery, James 185
motherhood insurance 39
Mukti Mission 14
Müller, F. Max 19
Muslim women, suffrage 111–12
Muzumdar, Chunder 23

Nanny of the Maroons 183, 186, 188–90
Narokobi, Bernard 175
Nash, Jennifer 164
Natapei, Edward 175
national autonomy: Finland 105; Russian
    Empire 104
national curriculum 180–1, 184
national identity: British food habits
    148; cultural identity and 100; history
    curriculum 181, 184–5, 194; Italian
    belonging 118, 135–7; popular
    memory and 189; suffrage and 105–6;
    transnational history and 6, 8, 55; women
    and 108–9
National Indian Association 21
native workers: forced labour 43–6; labour
    standards 44–5, 49; resettlement of 44–6;
    unpaid labour 34–5, 43; women 46–7
Nazi organizations: colonial settlement 122;
    colonial training and 121
Nedzialovsky, Karl 110
Nelson, Knute 77
Netherlands, history curriculum 190
The Network Connecting Grassroots
    Voices for Peace 61
New Zealand see Aotearoa/New Zealand

Ngata, Apirana 166
Nightingale, Florence 186
nursing education 86–7
nursing uniforms 79, 86–7, 94

O'Brien, Patricia 170
Olaudah Equiano in Sheffield 182–5
Open Door Council 37
Open Door International (ODI) 37–8, 42
oral history 185, 190
Orzeszkowa, Eliza 108

Pacific women *see* women, Pacific
Paisley, Fiona 164, 170
Pan-Pacific Women's Association 163–4,
    170, 172
peace activism: antiracism in 68; Greenham
    Common 54–6, 61–9; Japanese women
    and 58–60, 64–6, 69; male domination
    of 59–60
Pearson, Joanne 182
Penfold, Merimeri 169
Petrazhitsky, L. 103
Philippines: assimilation 78–80, 83–5;
    independence of 78; indigenous dress
    83; nursing education 86–7; Protestant
    missionaries 77–8, 83
Phillips, Robert 181, 191, 194
photography: civilizing mission and
    81–2; dress in 79; expression through
    90; missionaries and 79, 81, 90; native
    women and 82
physical education 88
Poland: autonomy in 100–1, 106–7;
    influence of 108–9; national identity and
    108, 113; women's suffrage movement
    106–8, 113
Polish Partition 106
Polish Women's Rights Association 108
Porter, Bernard 148, 158
Potaka, Te Arahori 169
Prarthana Samaj 14, 16–18, 24–6
Pratt, Mary Louise 55
Presbyterian Foreign Mission Society 87
Prince, Mary 183, 186, 188–90, 193
Pringle, Thomas 189
Prior, Katherine 188
Protestant missionaries 77–9
public history 185, 187–90, 192, 194

racism 63–4, 68
Ralston, Caroline 164
Ramabai, Pandita 13–14; agency 18, 20–1;
    Brahmoism and 17, 20–1; education 16;
    Indian women and 17–18, 20–8; medical

training 18; public platform 21–3;
    religious beliefs 15–20, 24–6; school for
    widows 25–6
Ramabai Association 23, 25–6
Ramabai Circles 23
Ranade, M. G. 24–5
rationing 151, 153–4, 156
Rawson, Mary Anne 183, 185–7, 190, 192
Read, Elizabeth 186
religious collaboration 14–15
religious liberals: American 14–15, 21,
    23; British 14–15, 19; feminism and
    27; social reform 15–16; trans-Indian
    network 14; transnational networks
    14–15, 17, 26–8
Rendall, Jane 55
Rogers, Helen 192
Rohrbaugh, Olive 84
Rose, Sonya 148, 158
Rossi, Orsola 133–4
Rowling, Bill 171
Roy, Rammohun 16–17, 19–20
Russian borderlands: national autonomy
    112; women's suffrage movement 98–9,
    108–13
Russian Empire: national autonomy 104;
    national movements in 100; religion 100;
    structure of 99–100; subnational level
    108; universal suffrage 102; women's
    suffrage movement 98–104, 113–14
Russian Orthodox Church 111
Russian Revolution: Finnish nationalism
    105; national autonomy 112; women's
    suffrage movement 101–2, 113
Russian Social-Democratic Party 102
Russian Union for Women's Equality
    100–5, 107–8, 112–14
Russian women *see* women, Russian
Russian Women's Mutual Aid Society
    102–3, 112
Rutchild, Rachelle 105

Salim, Jadji 48
Samuel, Raphael 181
Sarkar, Tanika 27
Saunders, Nicholas J. 189
Saunier, Pierre-Yves 180
Schauman, Eugen 105
School of Rendsburg 121–2
Schools Council History 13–16; Project
    182
Schools History Project 180
Sen, Keshub Chunder 15, 17, 19, 22
Shakhmatova, N. 101
Sharada Sadan 25–6

206 Index

Sharpe, Jenny 189
Sheffield Female Antislavery Society 185–6
Sheffield Ladies Society for the Universal
  Abolition of Slavery 186
Sheldon, Nicola 181
Sibaud, Gianna 132
slave trade 182–9, 192
Smith, Laurajane 189
social reproduction 33–5
Societies of Muslim Women 111
Society for the Promotion of Education
  among Muslim Women 111–12
Society of Caucasian Women 112
Solonevicth, Lykian 109
Spencer, Benjamin 185
Spitzer, Leo 119
Spivak, Gayatri 13
Strickland, Susanna 189
Sturge, Joseph 186
Sturge, Sophia 186
subsistence policies 43–8
Suganuma, Katsuhiko 55, 67
Sulkunen, Irma 105
Sumpter, Hiro 55, 61–9
Swanson, Ruth 85
Szaszy, Mira 169–70

talking (*kataru*) 61
Te Puea Herangi, Princess 168
terno 78, 83, 87, 90–4
Te Waka, Heremia 166
Te Waka, Hohepine *see* Cooper, Whina
Thatcher, Margaret 180
Thomas, Albert 36–8
Thomas, Norma Waterbury 88
Thompson, Krista 82
Thorne, Susan 187
Tilak, B. G. 25–6
Tokyo Manifesto 58–9
trade unions: family allowance policy 41–2;
  male wages 41–2
Transcendentalism 14–17, 23
transnational history 1, 4; gendered 2–7;
  identity and 67; national identity and 6,
  8, 55; school curriculum 180–4, 186–94;
  sources 5–7

Ukraine, autonomy in 100
unfree labour 34–5, 43–7
uniforms 86–7
Union of Equal Rights for Polish Women
  (UERPW) 107–10, 113
Union of Lithuanian Women 110, 113
Union of Russian People 112

Union of Russian Women 112
Unitarians 19–20; activism 7; missionaries
  17; religious collaboration 14–18, 21, 23,
  27; religious tensions 25–6; support for
  Hindu widows' home 23; women and 27
unpaid labour: care work 35, 40–3, 47;
  family allowance policy 39–43, 49;
  family policies 35; international policies
  34–9, 48; maternity policies 35–9, 49;
  native workers 34–5, 43, 47; subsistence
  policies 49; women 33–41, 43, 50
UN World Conference on Women 68
Usubbəyova, Nəsib bəy 112
Usubbəyova, Shafiga 112

Vanuatu: colonial rule in 173; gender
  discrimination 174–5; independence of
  167; women in 165, 171–4
Vanuatu National Constitution Committee
  167
Vanuatu National Council of Women 173
Vanuatu Women in Politics 175
Visram, Rozina 181

Western clothing 79–81, 84, 87–8, 90
widows 22–3, 25–6
Wiesner-Hanks, Merry 55, 183
Wilberforce, William 182, 188, 192
Wildenthal, Lora 121
Wilson, Verity 80, 90
Wollstonecraft, Mary 192
Woman's Home Missionary Society 77–8
women: athletic uniforms 88; care work 35,
  40–3, 50; Christianity and 24; dress and
  79, 82; education 17–18; family allowance
  policy 39–43; free labour 38; labour
  history 33–4; low wages and 42; maternity
  policies 35–8, 49; missionaries and 78,
  80–1; native workers 47; peace activism
  54–5, 58, 64; physical education 88;
  religious collaboration 15; silencing of 6;
  unpaid labour 33–43, 45, 50; working 36
women, American: dress and 79, 81, 83–5,
  91–4; missionaries 78–80, 83–6, 88,
  91–4; modeling modern womanhood 88;
  terno wearing 92–4
women, British: food practices 149–51,
  153–4; household duties 155–6, 158;
  wartime food shortages 147–9, 151–8
women, Filipina: assimilation 84–5, 94;
  athletics 88; basketball and 88–9; class
  and 85, 87, 91; dress and 79, 83–94; as
  healers 87; modern womanhood and 88,
  94; suffragists 90; *terno* 78, 83, 87, 90–3

women, Indian: activism 13; agency 13–15, 18, 22, 27–8; Brahmoism and 22–4, 27; caste and 22, 25–6; colonial views of 13–14, 20, 22, 28; education 15, 17, 21, 23; Hinduism and 21–2; political participation 24; religious collaboration 15, 28; social reform 18; widows 22–3, 25–6
women, Italian: colonial settlement 123–4; colonial training camps 118–36; fascist ideals 120, 133, 137; identity formation 117; professional opportunities 123–5, 139; propagandists 133–7, 139
women, Japanese: activism 57–8, 67–8; community of 65–6; contrast with British women 62; Greenham Common activists and 55–6, 61–9; oppression of 66; peace activism 55, 58–61, 64–6, 69; talking (*kataru*) 61
women, Maori 163, 165–6, 168–71
women, Pacific: activism 163–76; class and 165–6; leadership 163, 166–8, 171–2, 175; religion and 165–6
women, Russian: civic activity 101; Jewish equality and 101; rejection of feminism 101; suffragists 100–4
women abolitionists 185–9, 192
Women on the Platform initiative 192
women's history: biography 183, 185–7; British curriculum 181–3, 185–9, 192, 194; transnational perspectives 2; unpaid labour 33; women abolitionists 185–9
Women's History Network 193
women's movements: biographical approach to 164–5; colonialism and 164; imperialism and 164; Pacific women 163–4; transnational 164
women's organizations: family policies 39, 41–2, 46, 49; indigenous women in 170–1; labour protection 45–6; labour standards 46–7; maternity policies 37–8, 49; native women workers 45–6; native workers 46–7; peace activism 55, 64–6; transnational networks 68–9
Women's Progressive Party 102–3, 112, 114
women's suffrage movement: Byelorussia 109; Finland 105–6, 113; Georgia 112; India 24; Lithuania 109–10; Muslim women 111–12; national autonomy advocacy 104–5; national ideals 100; Philippines 90; Poland 106–8, 113; religion and 110–11; revolutionary actions 103; Russian borderlands 98–9, 108–13; Russian Empire 98–104, 113–14; Swedish opposition to 105; transnational 104, 113–14
Wong, Nellie 163
Woollacott, Angela 164
Worcester, Dean C. 80, 82
World Antislavery Convention 186
World Conference against Atomic and Hydrogen Bombs 58–60
World Conference on Women 173–4
Wright, Anna Rodgers 83

Yeo, Eileen 187

Zimmerman, Susan 99
Zweiniger-Bargielowska, Ina 147, 156